LIBRARY, ST.PATRICK'S COLLEGE, DUBLIN 9
LEABHARLANN, COLÁISTE PHÁDRAIG, B.Á.C. 9

000187656

ĠAN

HAP

WITHDRAWN

WITHDRAWN

499 36ʳ

WITHDRAWN

WITHDRAWN

George Fitzmaurice: 'Wild in His Own Way'

Biography of an Abbey Playwright

George Fitzmaurice: 'Wild in His Own Way'

Biography of an Abbey Playwright

Fiona Brennan

Carysfort Press

A Carysfort Press Book

George Fitzmaurice: 'Wild in His Own Way'
Biography of an Abbey Playwright
by Fiona Brennan

First published in Ireland in 2005 as a paperback original by
Carysfort Press, 58 Woodfield, Scholarstown Road,
Dublin 16, Ireland
Revised edition February 2007
© 2005, 2007 Copyright remains with the author

Typeset by Carysfort Press
Cover design by Alan Bennis

Printed and bound by eprint limited
35 Coolmine Industrial Estate, Dublin 15

This book is published with the financial assistance of
The Arts Council (An Chomhairle Ealaíon), Dublin, Ireland

Leabharlann Coláiste

000187656

CLASS 822.912 FIT/BRE

DATE 23/10/07

PRICE

DROIM CONRACH

Caution: All rights reserved. No part of this book may be
printed or reproduced or utilized in any form or by any
electronic, mechanical, or other means, now known or
hereafter invented including photocopying and recording,
or in any information storage or retrieval system without
permission in writing from the publishers.

This paperback is sold subject to the conditions that it
shall not, by way of trade or otherwise, be lent, resold,
hired out, or otherwise circulated in any form of binding,
or cover other than that in which it is published and
without a similar condition, including this condition, being
imposed on the subsequent purchaser.

to my parents John and Kathleen
with heartfelt love for a home full of books

ST. PATRICK'S
COLLEGE
LIBRARY

Playwright

"I don't know why I've lived so long."
George Fitzmaurice

Hiding in the stage loft
he clings to lost pride;
Maunsel and Roberts, 1914.
The sparkle has faded from
red, brown and blue glasses
dulled by Irish critics.
Nearby, at Mount Jerome,
plot 29414 awaits.
Soon, he will leave his children
a faded photograph
and a topsoil barren of flowers.

Fiona Brennan

Contents

Chronology

1821	Reverend George Fitzmaurice born in Duagh House.
1842	Winifred O'Connor born in Duagh.
1861	Reverend Fitzmaurice marries Winifred O'Connor.
1877	28 January: George Fitzmaurice born Bedford House, Listowel.
1891	Reverend Fitzmaurice dies. Family moves to Kilcara Beg, Duagh.
1897	Irish Literary Theatre is formed in Dublin.
1900	George begins working in the Hibernian Bank, Cork.
	March: First short story appears.
1901	George assumes a temporary clerkship in Dublin.
1906	First play submitted and rejected by the Abbey:
	The Wonderful Wedding is co-written with John Guinan.
1907	The Playboy of the Western World met with riots.
	October: *The Country Dressmaker* staged at the Abbey.
1908	19 March: *The Pie Dish* receives poor reviews.
	Leave of absence from his Civil Service position.
1909	February: Abbey Tour to Manchester includes *The Pie Dish*.
	April: Fitzmaurice dismissed from his position in the Civil Service.
1910	*The Pie Dish* staged in Oxford.
1911	1 June: *The Pie Dish* staged in Cambridge.
	5-7 June: *The Pie Dish* billed alongside *The Playboy* in London.
1912	Abbey Theatre revives *The Country Dressmaker*.
	November: George sends *The Magic Glasses* and
	The Dandy Dolls to the Abbey.
1913	January: *The Country Dressmaker* is revived.
	George also travels to Dublin that month.
	April: *The Magic Glasses* premiered at the Abbey.
	June: The Magic Glasses and The Country Dressmaker staged in London.
	September: Letter to Lady Gregory regarding the rejection of *The Dandy Dolls*.
	December: Fitzmaurice reinstated to his Civil Service position.

1914 *Five Plays* published by Maunsel & Roberts.
   14 March: *The Country Dressmaker* plays in Chicago during
   Abbey Tour in the USA.
   George joins the British Army.
   The Country Dressmaker revived.
1915 *The Country Dressmaker* revived.
1916 The Easter Rising in Dublin.
   Ulysses Fitzmaurice dies in Kilcara Beg.
   The Country Dressmaker revived.
1917 American edition of *Five Plays* published by Little, Brown & Co.
   The Country Dressmaker revived.
1919 Winifred Fitzmaurice dies.
   George returns from the Front.
1921 *The Country Dressmaker* reissued, green paperback with textual
   changes.
1923 8 March:*Twixt the Giltinans and the Carmodys* at the Abbey.
   The Green Stone also submitted to the Abbey that year and rejected.
1924 *The Linnaun Shee* published in the Dublin Magazine.
1925 The Abbey Theatre becomes a state-subsidized theatre.
1926 The Green Stone published.
1928 The Gate Theatre opens.
1930 Maurice Fitzmaurice dies.
1932 Una Fitzmaurice dies.
1935 Two letters written by Fitzmaurice to the Abbey.
1939 World War Two begins.
   W.B. Yeats dies.
   Third letter written by Fitzmaurice to the Abbey.
1942 George retires from the Civil Service.
   The Country Dressmaker revived.
1943 *The Country Dressmaker* revived.
   Twixt the Giltinans and the Carmodys published.
1945 2 & 9 December: *The Dandy Dolls* premiered by
   the Lyric Theatre Company.
1946 Lyric Theatre's revival of *The Magic Glasses*.
1948 13 September: *The Moonlighter* premiered by Lyric Theatre Co.
   Ollie Fitzmaurice dies.
   There Are Tragedies and Tragedies published.
1949 15 May: *The Linnaun Shee* premiered by Lyric Theatre Co.
   The Magic Glasses performed by the Green Circle
   Theatre Club, London.
   One Evening Gleam published.
   The Country Dressmaker revived by the Abbey.
1950 Georgina Fitzmaurice dies. George buys burial plot at Mount
   Jerome Cemetery, Dublin.
   George moves to Rathmines.
1952 *One Evening Gleam* produced by the Fortune Society, Dublin.
1953 4 January: *There are Tragedies and Tragedies* premiered by
   St Mary's College Musical and Dramatic Society, Dublin.

1954   Listowel Players win All-Ireland One-Act Finals with
        The Magic Glasses.
1956   George moves to Harcourt St.
1957   *The Enchanted Land* published in Dublin Magazine.
1961   Lady Longford receives a letter from George.
1963   12 May: George Fitzmaurice dies at No. 3 Harcourt St, Dublin.
1964   Ivyside Players, Pennsylvania State University stage
        The Enchanted Land and *One Evening Gleam.*
1966   *The Moonlighter* and *The Waves of the Sea* staged at the
        Micheler Theatre, Pennsylvania.
1967   *The Toothache* published in *The Malahat Review.*
        15 September: *The King of the Barna Men* and
        The Magic Glasses staged at the Peacock Theatre.
        The Plays of George Fitzmaurice Volume One: *Dramatic
        Fantasies* published by Dolmen Press.
1968   *The Moonlighter* produced by the Listowel Players.
1969   *The Plays of George Fitzmaurice* Volume Two:
        Folk Plays, published.
        Abbey Theatre stages *The Dandy Dolls.*
        One Evening Gleam staged for Gaelic Arts Society, USA.
1970   *The Plays of George Fitzmaurice* Volume Three: *Realistic
        Plays* published. *The Dandy Dolls* staged by the Abbey Theatre
        at The Old Vic, London.
        The Country Dressmaker produced by the University of Akron.
1971   *The Crows of Mephistopheles and other Stories*, ed. Robert Hogan.
1972   George Fitzmaurice and His Enchanted Land published.
        Wicked Old Children of George Fitzmaurice aired on Radio One.
        Produced by Kieran Sheedy.
1973   June: *The Toothache* presented during Listowel Writers' Week.
        The Dandy Dolls : Produced for Radio One (repeat).
        For Him the Flowers Smile: Radio One Documentary
        produced by Tim Danaher.
1975   *George Fitzmaurice* by Arthur McGuinness published.
1976   *The Pie Dish* and *The Enchanted Land* staged at the Abbey.
        October: *One Evening Gleam* Broadcast Radio One.
1977   Listowel Writers' Week: Listowel Drama Group presents
        The Magic Glasses.
        15 June: Druid Theatre Company stages *There are
        Tragedies and Tragedies.*
1978   *The Wonderful Wedding* by George Fitzmaurice & John Guinan
        published.
        The Green Stone: Rathmore Drama Group runners up in the All-
        Ireland One-Act Finals.
1979   *George Fitzmaurice* by Carole Gelderman published in the U.S.A.
1982   *The Magic Glasses* repeated on Radio One.
1993   14 & 15 July: Druid Theatre Company stages *There are Tragedies and
        Tragedies* and *The Ointment Blue.*

1994   Headstone erected over Fitzmaurice's Grave, Mount
        Jerome Cemetery.
        Rivers of Words Documentary on life of George Fitzmaurice produced
2000   *Seanchaí* Kerry Literary and Cultural Centre, Listowel, opens.
2001   5 June: A Tribute Evening to George Fitzmaurice takes place in the
        Stephen's Green Hotel with special guest, Eamon Kelly.
2002   5-9 March: *The Dandy Dolls* is staged by TCD School of Drama,
        directed by Conall Morrison.
        5 September: *The George Fitzmaurice Society* officially launched by
        Prof. Howard Slaughter.
2003   January: *The Country Dressmaker* produced by Sliabh Luachra
        Drama Group, Scartaglin, Co. Kerry.
        May: 40th anniversary commemorations marking Fitzmaurice's death
        take place in Dublin.
        Bowman's Saturday, RTÉ Radio One, special broadcast on George
        Fitzmaurice.
        December: Marjorie Fitzmaurice dies.
        The George Fitzmaurice Society is granted legal copyright to
        Fitzmaurice's work.
2004   October: *The Dandy Dolls* is staged at the Peacock Theatre as part of
        the *Abbeyonehundred* celebrations.
        The Ennis Players win the All-Ireland One-Act Finals with *The Dandy
        Dolls.*
2005   Fitzmaurice receives international acclaim as the Ennis Players
        present *The Dandy Dolls* during the World Festival of Amateur
        Theatre (Mondial du Théâtre), Monte Carlo.

Illustrations

Front Cover: Scene from *The Dandy Dolls*, by George Fitzmaurice, directed by Conall Morrison at the Peacock Theatre, 2004. By kind permission of the Abbey Theatre. Photographer Kip Carroll.

1   Bedford House: an aerial view of Bedford House, where the playwright was born in 1877. (Date unknown).
     Courtesy of the Relihan Family, Bedford.   p.10

2   This photograph is believed to have been taken about 1930 and includes from left: Mr Creagh Hartnett (Abbeyfeale); Georgina Fitzmaurice (playwright's sister); George Fitzmaurice, playwright. Other individuals unknown.
     Author's own.   p.103

3   Georgina and Ollie Fitzmaurice outside their cottage in Kilcara Beg, with, it is believed, an American cousin home on holiday. (Date unknown).
     Courtesy of Bridie O'Connor, Finuge.   p.116

4   Marjorie Fitzmaurice with the author.
     Photographer: Margaret Carty.   p.140

5   A gathering outside St Stephen's Green Hotel, June 2001. The group includes from left: Jimmy Deenihan TD; Ann McAuliffe; Eamon and Maura Kelly (centre); Fiona Brennan (second from right); Greg Collins (first from right).
     Photographer: Mike O'Sullivan   p.151

Author's Preface

When I first came across a reference to George Fitzmaurice in Elizabeth Healy's book, *A Literary History of Ireland*, I became interested beyond what is usual for me. Later, having found his plays in Tralee Library, I looked for his burial place in Mount Jerome Cemetery, Dublin on a crisp frosty January morning in 1999. I was absolutely certain that by laying some fresh flowers on his frozen grave I would find myself at the end of a journey. Instead, I found myself at a beginning. According to an old Native American Indian saying, a story can stalk you. The story of George Fitzmaurice and his literary genius has stalked me since. Throughout the months of research I was overcome by the amount of kindness from total strangers when I approached them for help with my research. It has been a privilege to have encountered so much goodwill towards this project and I am forever grateful to those who helped to make this biography possible.

Sincere thanks must go to the following individuals: Ben Barnes; John Bowman; Eamonn Browne (Tralee Library); Kathleen Browne (County Librarian); Mary Rose Callaghan; Margaret Canty, Carrigaline, Cork; Kip Carroll; Dr Patricia Casey, Mater Hospital, Dublin; Greg Collins; Michael Costello (Tralee Library); Andy Crook; Jimmy Deenihan; Christopher Fitz-Simon; Dan Flynn; Brian Friel; Eileen and Dan Joe Galvin; Fianna Griffin; John Guinan (Offaly); Danny Hannon; Dr Maurice Harmon (UCD); Garry Hynes; Una Kealy; Dan Keane; Mary Keane; Paddy Keane; Prof. Nora Kelley (New York); Maura Kelly; Prof. Declan Kiberd UCD; Tom Kilroy; Dr Mark Leahy (College of Arts, Dartington, UK); the late Brian Looby, Tralee Library (who always smiled when I arrived in to the Local Studies Section, and knew me as the 'Fitzmaurice lady'); Janice MacAdam, Director of Public Affairs (Acting), Abbey Theatre; Owen MacMahon; Margaret McElligott; the late Sarah McGroary; Dr Pat McKeon, St Patrick's Hospital, Dublin; Ann McAuliffe; Val Moynihan; Paddy Murphy; Dr Chris Morash, NUI Maynooth; Brian O'Connor; Bridie O'Connor; Maurice O'Keeffe; Barney O'Reilly; John Stephen

O'Sullivan; Tadhg Pey (Offaly); Richard Pine; Tony Quinn; Tom Relihan and family, Bedford; Ann Russell; Prof. Howard Slaughter (University of Akron); Sr Labouré Sheehy; and Vincent Woods.

There were many hours given to trawling through archives and books. The National Library of Ireland, Dublin became a favourite Dublin haven of delight. My deepest thanks to the Staff there. Killarney and Tralee Libraries became my County Kerry havens. Thank you to all the Staff in both branches, and, in particular, to Mary Murray and the Staff at Killarney Library whose interest in and enthusiasm for this research is most appreciated. My thanks also go to: Mairead Delaney, Archivist, Abbey Theatre; National Archives, Dublin; General Register Office, Dublin; Valuation Records Office, Lwr. Abbey St, Dublin; Cara Trant, Manager, Seanchaí Literary and Cultural Centre, Listowel; Kieran Hoare, Lyric Theatre Archives NUI Galway; Administration Staff, Druid Theatre, Galway; Manuscripts Dept, Trinity College, Dublin; Ian Lee, Radio One Sound Archives; Cork City Library; Leslie Martin, Chicago Historical Society; Sharon Snow, Special Collections, Wake Forest University, USA (re Dolmen Press Collection); Sliabh Luachra Drama Group, Scartaglin, Co. Kerry for trusting in Fitzmaurice in 2003; Mary Butler, Assistant Librarian, Offaly County Library; Church of Ireland Library, Braemor Park, Dublin; San Francisco State University; Northwestern University, Louisiana; Dr Barbara Ní Fhloinn, Irish Folklore Commission; Public Records Office, Kew, Surrey, UK, (re World War One Archives); Poetry Ireland, Dublin (re Austin Clarke Library Collection); Imperial War Museum, London; Dublin Writers' Museum; John Bridges, Assistant Dean, The Theatre School, DePaul University, USA.

When I first met Fintan O'Toole, his generosity amazed me. Fintan gave of his time for a long interview in 2003 and again when asked to write the Preface to this biography. His belief in Fitzmaurice and this project will not be forgotten.

Conall Morrison, Associate Director, Abbey Theatre, also deserves special mention. Conall has always been willing to help in any way possible since we first met in 2003 and I thank him for endorsing this book and helping me to 'fight the good fight'.

I came to know Dr Ger FitzGibbon as an MA student of Drama and Theatre Studies in UCC within the 2005 class. I thank him for his time and valuable advice regarding my work on George Fitzmaurice.

I remember fondly the late Eamon Kelly who probably understood Fitzmaurice better than we ever will. That night we met at the Abbey Theatre for a chat about George is one I will never forget.

I also remember the late Marjorie Fitzmaurice whose words, 'We ought to have been proud of him' have echoed many times in my head and kept me going.

Sincere thanks to all at Carysfort Press: to Lilian Chambers; to Eamonn Jordan for believing in the possibilities of such a biography from the time I first sent him two draft chapters. Heartfelt thanks to Dan Farrelly who was always so patient and good humoured throughout the editing process.

Thank you to the George Fitzmaurice Society for permission to quote from Fitzmaurice's work and personal papers.

To Prof. Howard Slaughter: sincere thanks for access to his vital PhD thesis on Fitzmaurice's life and work.

To the late Robert Hogan: I just do not know if this biography would ever have seen the light of day if it were not for his painstaking work in editing the diaries of Joseph Holloway. His belief in George's work was incredible.

To Gabriel Fitzmaurice, who was the first person I approached about George Fitzmaurice. Gabriel's support throughout was second to none. To him, his wife Brenda and family, thank you for your friendship.

There are many others, too numerous to mention, who often asked me, 'How is the book going?' To all of you I say thank you. A special thanks to Stephen Dempster who once reminded me of the possibility of dreams.

Love and thanks to my parents, to whom I dedicate this book.

Finally, but not least, to my partner and best friend, Mike O'Sullivan, who has been beside me for every step and word along this journey. There are no words to explain my love and gratitude.

Fiona Brennan

Foreword

Fintan O'Toole

In 2004, when the Abbey Theatre staged Conall Morrison's superb production of *The Dandy Dolls* as part of its centenary celebrations, there was a scent of regret in the air. The play, arguably George Fitzmaurice's best, belonged to the history of the Abbey's first century only through its absence. It was rejected by W.B. Yeats and Lady Gregory in 1913, and Fitzmaurice was consigned to a purgatory of appalling neglect until his death, a full fifty years later. He became the great lost soul of twentieth century Irish theatre. *The Dandy Dolls* reminded us of the zest and tang of his language, the breadth of his imagination and his mastery of a concentrated theatrical form in which the verbal and the visual engage in a fandango of terror and delight. In doing so it made it all the harder to understand how Fitzmaurice, one of the first important Abbey playwrights, could have been so ruthlessly excluded from the official theatrical canon for so long.

How could such a gifted innovator have been left theatrically homeless after 1923, when the last of his new plays to be accepted by the Abbey was staged? When Fitzmaurice died in obscurity forty years later, he left behind the most heart-rending legacy in Irish literary history: a battered suitcase beside his bed containing copies of his published plays and unpublished manuscripts with a note in pencil:

> Author is prepared to sell outright all rights in 14 plays dealing intimately with life in the Irish countryside. Most have already been either printed or published. Suitable to which to build musicals, television etc. Pass to anyone interested.

As Fiona Brennan points out in this important and immensely welcome book, this note can be misleading in giving a false impression of a Fitzmaurice entirely unappreciated by younger writers and producers, but it remains a poignant testimony to the ultimate homelessness of a great talent.

The neglect of Fitzmaurice may have been perverse, but it was not entirely accidental. It was rooted in a fundamental difference between his attitude of mind and those of Yeats and Gregory. It is not just that he went to the music hall while they went to the theatre, that they campaigned against conscription while he joined up and served in the trenches, that they were Protestants in search of an accommodation with Catholic Ireland, while he was born, as the child of a Protestant parson and his Catholic bride, into precisely such an accommodation. These facts themselves point to a larger difference: Fitzmaurice accepted the world, while Yeats and Gregory set about inventing a world. He was at home in the twentieth century, while they felt themselves to be, to some degree, refugees from it. And these differences expressed themselves through opposite attitudes to a pivotal cultural nexus: the relationship between modernity and folklore.

The approach of the Irish Literary Revival to the folkloric world is summed up in the very word 'revival'. Folklore, to them, was vestigial. It had barely survived the onslaught of modernity. It was a relic of a full and more holistic civilization, which might now be brought back to life. And this, in turn, was part of a larger revival: the return to life of a half-dead nation. Recording and re-working folklore was at once an act of homage to an imagined past and an act of present-day political resurrection.

Yeats in particular saw Irish folk culture as a route by which the country might return to the Middle Ages. In his Nobel Prize acceptance speech in 1923, for example, he claimed that:

> Synge's work, the work of Lady Gregory, my own *Cathleen ni Houlihan*, and my *Hour Glass* in its prose form, are characteristic of our first ambition. They bring the imagination and speech of the country, all that poetical tradition descended from the middle ages, to the people of the town.

Fitzmaurice, on the other hand, regards folklore not as a survival from the distant past, but as part of modern life, not as an escape from the sordid material world of the twentieth century, but as a troublesome and inescapable part of it. He does not regard it as a symbol of paradise lost or of political romanticism. He simply does not see it as symbolic at all. In his great plays of the natural and the supernatural, what is immediately striking is his acceptance of the demons and spirits as part of the quotidian universe. He considers, as Ibsen does in Peer Gynt, the world of folk belief to be as real or as unreal as that of everyday material reality. His view of life is one in which the imagined is as powerfully present as the real. To Wittgenstein's famous aphorism that 'the world is everything that is the case', he adds, with Derek Mahon, 'but also everything that is the case imaginatively'.

Fitzmaurice's approach to folk material is at once more complex and more direct than that of Yeats and Gregory. They took from it its language and its awareness of the other-worldly. Fitzmaurice went to the core and took its form. And it is the form of folk art that connects it to the early twentieth-century avant-garde rather than to the Middle Ages. Concentration in time and place, emotional intensity, rapid action and minimal characterization are as crucial to folk stories and ballads or to mumming plays as they are to twentieth-century art and theatre. The Fitzmaurice of the short one-act plays usually called 'dramatic fantasies' found in folklore a form that placed him, not with the would-be revivers of an ancient culture, but with the avant-garde of European modernism. When this is recognized, his rejection by the Abbey is less strange than it seems, for alongside the subsequent rejections by Yeats and Gregory of Sean O'Casey's *The Silver Tassie* and Denis Johnston's *The Old Lady Says No!* it forms a pattern. Fitzmaurice was the first important victim of the Abbey's determination to keep its distance from the European expressionist movement, but he was not the last.

There is indeed an almost exact parallel between Yeats's attitude to Fitzmaurice and his view of O'Casey. Both were fine when they were producing socially realistic plays like *The Country Dressmaker* or *Juno and the Paycock* that Yeats did not much like but also did not feel threatened by. Both became intolerable when Yeats could not patronize them as box-office magnets of a lower artistic standing than the holy trinity of Yeats, Synge and Gregory. O'Casey's move into expressionism and Fitzmaurice's into the fantastical were uppity encroachments onto Yeats's own poetic territory. The trespassers had to be evicted.

Only the obsession with a national literature, with the idea of Irish writing as a revival continuous with the Irish past, could have prevented us from seeing the obvious connection between Fitzmaurice and the European avant-garde of his time. Fitzmaurice's approach to traditional Irish culture is of a piece with that of Kandinsky, Picasso or Chagall taking their inspiration from peasant painting or from African mask-makers. His journey as a dramatist is connected to Antonin Artaud's attempts to find in the traditional theatre of Bali a theatre not unlike Fitzmaurice's own: a theatre not built on the exploration of psychology and motivation through dialogue but rather unfolding through and in poetry and movement, wicked humour and startling violence, a theatre of delight and vague but profound terror. He is connected, too, to Brecht's scrutiny of Chinese theatre for strange, alienating forms with which to break the Aristotelian mould.

And naturally but most ironically, he is connected to Yeats himself, who came to want that kind of drama too but sought it in the suitably noble Japanese Noh tradition rather than in the demotic gutter of music halls, mummers and cottage firesides. Yeats might have learned a great deal from Fitzmaurice, but he seems instead to have written him off after the initial success of the relatively naturalistic *The Country Dressmaker* as one of those common crowd-pleasers that were good for box office but bad for the soul. In his diary in 1909, he coupled the latter play with the middle-class urban comedies of the now-forgotten W.F. Casey, noting 'how much I dislike plays like *The Man Who Missed the Tide* and *The Suburban Groove*, and of course works like *The Country Dressmaker.*' (*Memoirs*, p.168) Having dismissed Fitzmaurice as a vulgarian on the basis of his first play, he simply refused to engage with the radicalism of *The Pie Dish* and *The Dandy Dolls*.

That radicalism makes Fitzmaurice the dramatist whose non-existence the anthropologist Henry Glassie lamented in his marvellous study of Irish mummers, *All Silver and No Brass*: a playwright who could bring the mumming spirit onto the stage:

> The mummers play was perhaps too close. But it could have provided modern dramatists with guidance like that Kandinsky found in peasant painting, for it was spectacle of the kind they imagined: manneristic, poetic, strange. Captain Mummer tells us his play is not from the tradition of classical Western drama: 'The like of this was never acted on a stage ...' Mumming is not a theoretical symbolic art like a mediaeval morality, nor is it empirical descriptive art like a play by Ibsen. It rises between those poles of Western thought, falsifying their purity, uniting them in mysterious imagery.

This could be an exact description of Fitzmaurice's dramatic fantasies, making him, in spirit at least, the heir to the mummers. For Fitzmaurice not only rises between the opposing poles of Western thought, he undermines each in turn, clearing a space in which he can overturn all opposites. In his best plays, the symbolic world is undercut by placing it beside unheroic reality and reality is satirized through the exaggerations of folklore. The two worlds cancel each other out, leaving a vacuum that is the empty space in which the most daring theatre unfolds.

One of Fizmaurice's most thrilling confounding of opposites is the way he makes folklore Protestant. For the Protestant leaders of the revival, the folkloric world was the Other, an acceptable point of entry into a Catholic mental universe. Fitzmaurice gleefully turns this attitude on its head, making folklore an extension of the modern Protestant individualist mindset. In *The Linnaun Shee* or *The Dandy Dolls*, in *The Pie Dish* or *The Magic Glasses*, it is the man most in thrall to folkloric belief, to the world of magic and the supernatural – Jamesie Kennelly, Roger Carmody, Leum Donoghue, Jaymony Shanahan – who is most Protestant in his insistence on the rights of individual conscience, on the personal relationship with the supernatural which is the essence of the Protestant frame of mind. It is not accidental that such characters are so often set directly against the Catholic priest.

Contrary to the Yeatsian view of the folkloric as an aspect of a unified, holistic, neo-mediaeval world, Fitzmaurice's folkloric visionaries are creators of social disruption and division. This notion of the folkloric as a disrupter of distinctions, and unsettler of assumptions and a disturber of neat oppositions is underlined by Tzvetan Todorov's distinction, in his studies of folk tales, between the marvellous, the uncanny and the fantastic. The marvellous presents the supernatural but does try to explain it. The uncanny describes events that seem to be supernatural but turn out to be explicable by natural means. But the fantastic suspends itself between the natural and the supernatural, the rational and the irrational. As Todorov puts it:

> the limit between the physical and the mental, between matter and spirit, between word and thing, ceases to be impervious... The physical world and the spiritual world interpenetrate; their fundamental categories are modified as a result.

This kind of fantasy, Fitzmaurice's kind, 'uses words to recreate a vision of the world before it was divided up by words', which is to say the world of the very young child. Fitzmaurice's own description of his characters as wicked old children reminds us that we are dealing in his plays, not with the prelapsarian childhood innocence of Victorian and Edwardian literature, but with the dangerous, contradictory, perverse world of the old child in which the very categories by which we understand reality are put in play. He gives us the child's freshness of vision without the infantile sentimentality.

Fitzmaurice's world, in which reality is drenched with fantasies, images and inventions is even more recognizable now in the media-saturated twenty-first century. The magic glasses of consumerism fit even more snugly before our eyes than they did on the faces of our ancestors in the early twentieth century. This is why Fitzmaurice seems such a contemporary writer, why a play like *The Dandy Dolls*

could seem so startlingly alive on the Abbey stage in 2004. There is
even, for us, a kind of pay-off for the long years of neglect in that
actors and directors, as well as audiences, can approach Fitzmaurice
now almost as a new writer, a wild, mind-blowing punk of a young
genius who throws down exciting challenges of staging and
interpretation.

Fiona Brennan's meticulous gathering of what can be known about
Fitzmaurice's background, life and literary career will be a crucial map
for anyone wishing to venture into that untamed and largely
undiscovered country. It is delightfully appropriate that in telling
Fitzmaurice's story she has drawn not just on the written record but
also on the spoken memories and oral traditions that may be the most
telling vestiges of his odd, angular life. The man who most successfully
engaged with folklore has, in a sense, returned to it. He has become
one of the wonderful, poignant, contrary stories of Irish culture and in
telling it so generously and lucidly, Fiona Brennan has surely added to
the growing number who are prepared to listen.

1 | Life in Bedford

It is generally accepted that with the death of George Fitzmaurice, playwright, in 1963, an almost forgotten line of the Lords of Kerry, the Duagh Fitzmaurices,[1] came to an end in Kerry. Sadly, the fate of the playwright and his siblings does not quite read as one might have expected for descendants of this once powerful Anglo-Norman family. Whilst stories abound of flamboyant ancestors and family ghosts, a darker tale that relates to the playwright's immediate family can now be told.

An inherent weakness existed in the family, a weakness that involved the chasing of dreams to the point of obsession. That underlying genetic weakness for dreaming and obsessing tormented the playwright throughout his literary career. His father's great secret, which had a huge influence on George's later work, has lain hidden for well over a century. Its consequences resulted in the definite psychological harm of George and his siblings, while the truth reveals how George's father lived a life far from reality, much to the detriment of those closest to him. Now it is time to disclose it.

George Senior was born on 20 May 1821 at the ancestral home of Springmount, the third son of ten children (eight boys and two girls). The boys all received a university education at Trinity College Dublin and made very successful careers for themselves as doctors, bankers, farmers and one as a schoolmaster. George Senior became a Church of Ireland clergyman and became known locally as *The Parson*, or, *Parson Fitzmaurice*. Both of his sisters married well and the eldest, Elizabeth, though widowed quite young, married for a second time to the Reverend Rowland Bateman of Abbeyfeale. Rowland was the second son of Colthurst Bateman, formerly of Bedford House, Listowel. Paradoxically, this relationship would result indirectly in serious repercussions for the Parson, his family and the Batemans during the years that followed.

A fine classical scholar and fluent Irish speaker, the Parson entered Trinity on 12 October 1838 aged seventeen, graduating with a BA in 1844. Although it is not recorded, we can assume that he studied Irish as a Divinity School subject. This was common at the time, enabling Church of Ireland clergymen to converse in the native tongue of their potential converts. Following a year as curate in Killashee, County Kildare, he had a further preferment in Kilcornan, County Limerick, beginning in 1847.[2] In all, Parson George spent nine years or so ministering actively, but eventually, sometime during the 1850s, he decided to abandon ministering altogether. At that point, he was living in the Gate Lodge to Bedford House two miles outside Listowel on the road to Ballylongford. It is almost certain that Colthurst Bateman gifted the Lodge to the Parson, the Bateman family having built Bedford House during the 1770s.

The secretly ambitious Parson began to find life as a country clergyman rather boring and one that did not lend itself to his notions of life as a country squire. The Parson was, quite simply, a dreamer. The problem however, was that he chased his dreams to the point of obsession, completely disregarding the reality surrounding him. His ambitions grew on a daily basis, as did his envy of his siblings' more desirable lives. Every minute spent in the Gate Lodge was a further indictment of the fact that he was living off the charity of Colthurst Bateman. The very fact that this was common knowledge further fuelled a desire to amend his situation. He had a dream of life in a larger house where he could tend to prize-winning greyhounds and horses. Despite the fact that a regular income was imperative he selfishly decided to give up his position as a clergyman, a decision that annoyed and embarrassed his family, particularly his sister Elizabeth.

The Parson craved the prestige associated with living in a Georgian residence but resolutely refused any labour which would help to attain such an ambition.[3] He secretly looked towards Bedford House with its attractive potential, although Dr Samuel Raymond MD occupied it at the time.[4] His ambitions were further fuelled when he spied a young dairymaid by the name of Winifred O'Connor working at the Great House for Dr Raymond. She was not, as has been previously asserted, the Parson's 'servant girl'.[5] He fell for her instantly, and when Raymond died in 1859 the Parson knew his chance had arrived. Having already proved himself a charming and persuasive individual, he was about to prove so once again by successfully seeking Colthurst's permission to move into Bedford House. Little did the family realize that his occupation would span an acrimonious thirty-two years until his death in 1891. The Batemans would live to regret their father's kind nature. A close study of the substantial evidence, as illustrated in the

Valuation Records for Listowel, not only tells the real story regarding ownership of Bedford House, but also paints a darker portrait of the Parson himself.

The townland of Bedford seems to have taken its name from the house, as *Bedford* itself has no Gaelic connotations. *Atrohis* is the seventeenth century form of the townland name, while another variation *Ahatrohish* is found in a nineteenth century Bedford estate map held in the National Library of Ireland (NLI) in Dublin. The 1841 census records the name as *Áth an Trochais,* while Fr Gaughan in his book *Listowel and its Vicinity* alludes to two holy sites in the area – a well and an old burial ground. Another variation on the name is *Átha an Turais* or Ford of the Journey or Pilgrimage. This is probably the correct Gaelic name because there are three holy wells recorded in the vicinity: *Tobair Rí an Domhnaigh, Tobair Naomh Partalon,* and *St. Bartholemew's Well.*[6] The house itself, although in ruins today, was surrounded by rich, flat, arable land that was let to tenants. Many older locals still recall the large wood and orchard that once occupied a substantial part of the Bedford Estate. The avenue to the ruin still follows its original line, and the high walls that once surrounded the kitchen garden are clearly visible.

In 1861 the charming Parson caused an incredible sensation when he married his young nineteen-year-old, pregnant, Catholic sweetheart, Winifred. A local man, Paddy Murphy, recalls his father's reminiscences regarding the twice-married Parson, although it is unclear who the Parson's first wife might have been. The Parson's own father and eldest brother were certainly married twice and there is a possibility that some confusion may have arisen during the intervening years.[7] Sr Loreto Relihan is adamant that there is truth in this Bedford lore and that Winifred was his second wife. The fact that the Parson was thirty-nine years old when he married Winifred makes such a theory quite plausible. However, as this is not officially recorded, it remains unsubstantiated. There is no mention of this in *Burke's Irish Family Records* or in any other genealogical article available on this branch of the Fitzmaurice family. Interestingly, the couple's playwright son would later write a short story entitled *Cupid and Cornelius* about a rich widowed farmer with young children, who is wrestling with his conscience over his love for a servant girl working on his farm (see *The Crows of Mephistopheles* edited by Robert Hogan). Might this have been George's approval of his parents' socially unacceptable and unorthodox marriage?

The first Valuation Records available for Listowel date from 1859 to 1876. They record that Bedford House became unoccupied in 1859 upon the death of leaseholder Dr Samuel Raymond. Upon Raymond's death the Parson moved from the Gate Lodge into Bedford House. Such was the Parson's opportunistic nature that he led everyone to believe the house was rightfully his, thus assuming a vital position in the community as a country gentleman. Over the following years locals assumed that the Parson's continuing occupation of the house meant he held ownership of it. In fact, this was, for a short time, incorrectly recorded in the Valuation Records Volume I (1859-1876) for the Listowel district. As a result, academics studying the works of George Fitzmaurice, including his previous biographers, have recorded the Parson's ownership as de facto, although Marjorie Fitzmaurice rightly insisted that the Batemans owned the property.[8] The Valuation Records also record that the Parson subsequently leased the Gate Lodge to a Mr Edmund Costello. This was merely a deliberate attempt to dupe the locals into believing his new and farcical role as landlord. The Parson had preyed on his family's relationship with his sister's father-in-law, and on close inspection the actual facts of the matter reveal the Parson as nothing more than a squatter.

Critically, the Valuation Records clearly illustrate a necessary correction at this time as the Parson's name is crossed out as being the owner or lessor. Later, upon Colthurst Bateman's death, the Valuation Records Volume II record that a John Bateman assumes ownership of Bedford House. The records then illustrate a legal dispute between the Parson and John Bateman, who obviously had had enough of the Parson's deviousness. Through due legal process Bateman had hoped to succeed in putting an end to the nonsense that Colthurst had accepted so as to safeguard the family name, as well as for the sake of avoiding gossip. The Parson's delusions of grandeur were costing the Batemans revenue as he effectively paid only a pittance in rent. The Valuation Records illustrate that there was no increase in rent in all the time he lived there.

Until his death the Parson had arrogantly resisted the legal challenge instigated by John Bateman and, by doing so, had managed to deceive everyone into believing he owned Bedford House. It is highly possible that by this time he had even convinced himself that he was the rightful owner. The records are, however, unambiguous as to actual title. Whilst in possession of Bedford the Parson lived well above his natural station. According to Paddy Murphy, the Parson even managed to throw harvest festivals for the locals whom he regarded as his tenants. Thus a fascinating portrait is conjured up of a man who spent his life wheeling and dealing, living totally out of touch with reality as he repeatedly proved himself the black sheep of an otherwise very successful Fitzmaurice family. The Valuation Records prove beyond doubt – despite both Howard Slaughter's and Carole

Gelderman's assertions to the contrary – that Parson Fitzmaurice never owned Bedford House, or any substantial property, such as the five hundred acres as stated by them. Slaughter and Gelderman, being previous biographers of George Fitzmaurice, have recorded that the Parson sold off large tracts of the Bedford Estate when in fact all Parson George Fitzmaurice had ever owned at Bedford was the Gate Lodge.

Comparatively little is known of Winifred or the O'Connor family, but descendants insist today that the family members were all very intelligent and well read, having possessed a deep love of learning.[9] Winifred was the daughter of John O'Connor of Knockundervaul, Duagh, and the family were known locally as the *Tass Connors*.[10] She is remembered as being a very down-to-earth intelligent woman and her marriage to the wily Parson proves a certain strength of character and resolve. After all, she had managed to procure a marriage while pregnant to a man that was seen as a leading member of the community. His seemingly devil-may-care attitude may have been an important factor in his decision to marry Winifred as he would have undoubtedly delighted in his family's total abhorrence of this unacceptable marriage, as well as the extremely embarrassing situation regarding Bedford House. Although Slaughter records Parson Fitzmaurice's love for Winifred, citing the fact that he sent her to boarding school, one wonders whether he desired his peasant wife to learn the essentials of deportment and manners in order to fulfil the role of Lady of the Big House more easily. Winifred had to endure life in a boarding school for young ladies for some length of time, but it is doubtful the Parson was able to pay for this scheme in the long term and, more than likely, his family paid the tuition fees. Winifred's destiny was set: she was to spend her life with a man who was already showing signs of an evident personality disorder.

Though no substantial evidence remains of the Parson's relationship with his own family regarding his marriage to a servant girl, the late Fr Edmund Stack, a North Kerry priest, interviewed in the *Rivers of Words* television documentary, recalls hearing the story that the Parson was 'pelted out of Bedford' when news came through of this impending union. Marjorie Fitzmaurice recalls her aunt, Elise Chute, speaking of this marriage as a tragedy. Elise Chute also recalled that the Church of Ireland community would have been very close-knit and the congregation very small. Members would have been 'seldom out of their own classes and kind before the turn of the century, but it was fairly common that illegitimate children would have been known by their father's name and sometimes acknowledged'.[11]

Between 1861 and 1881 the couple had twelve children, all born in Bedford, with five of the seven daughters dying before adulthood. The couple's eldest child was Elizabeth (born 1861), while Margaret and Una were both born before 1864. The remaining four daughters were: Mary Georgina (born 1868), who was known as Georgina; Agnes Amelia (1871); Honoria, known as Hanora (1872); and Eleanor (1873). The exact dates are unrecorded. The boys were: Maurice Rowland (born 3 January 1866); Oliver (born 23 March 1867); and then George (born 28 January 1877). The two youngest boys were Henry (17 May 1879) and Ulysses (25 June 1881).[12] Although local belief has always maintained that the girls were brought up as Catholics and the boys as Protestants, this is an incorrect assumption. While Winifred remained a practising Catholic throughout her life the children were all brought up as Protestants, a fact that is verified by Marjorie Fitzmaurice in her correspondence with Carole Gelderman. Strangely, none of the Fitzmaurice children would show the slightest interest in practising the Protestant faith during their adult years.

Although previous biographers of George Fitzmaurice have dwelt on the relevance of the family's move to Duagh, they have neglected his formative years in Bedford. Winifred's short time at boarding school and her marriage to the Parson both reflect that she was expected to assume the correct etiquette for a gentleman farmer's wife, almost to the point of denying her own cultural upbringing. During her childhood in Duagh, Winifred would have attended the local hedge school, where the opportunity to learn from whatever source was almost universal. Her native language, lore and traditions were rooted in her Catholic Gaelic heritage and in this regard, her influence on George's future writing was unquestionably more significant than his father's. The rich colour that characterizes all of George's works was, primarily, maternal in influence, not, as others have suggested, a paternal legacy. The same can also be said of J.M. Synge who was influenced by his mother's West Cork heritage long before he went to the Aran Islands. It would be the Fitzmaurice family's later move to Duagh that would ultimately prove to be the springboard for the playwright George Fitzmaurice in capturing the dialect and life of a unique people.

Despite all this, young George grew up influenced by both Catholic and Protestant traditions, and was surrounded by acres in which to roam. His fertile imagination soaked up the spirit of rural life and the natural history that surrounded him: the orchard scents and sounds, the meandering Galey River, the wild flowers in the fields and hedgerows, and barn-owls screeching in the stables. Being naturally shy he became a great observer and listener, while Winifred, her education rooted in the hedge school tradition, fuelled his imagination further by encouraging him to learn whenever and wherever the opportunity arose. However, keeping in mind his father's unstable personality, one wonders about the way in which the Parson may have shared Walter Scott's classic tales as well as his own ideals and experiences with his vulnerable son. The Parson's influence is certainly inherent in the darkness that lurks in George's short stories and plays.

The Parson did introduce *Georgie,* as he affectionately called him, to writers such as Sir Walter Scott, who was to remain a lifelong favourite of George's. A couple of Scott's books were found among his scant possessions after his death. Undoubtedly, dismal attempts at breeding champion greyhounds and leading the life of the gentleman farmer, as well as disputing ownership of Bedford House, were the Parson's priorities. The rearing of the children was left to Winifred. Quite frankly, there is an obvious paternal influence on George, as his prolonged absences from work in later years mirrored his father's earlier decision to give up his salaried position. Not only that, but George's personality would reveal inordinate fears later in life. He would never own property and he would often move accommodation whilst living in Dublin, cherishing his anonymity. He would eventually become consumed by an irrational fear of spending any money at all. George would never forget the memories of early home life and the results of his father's illusions and schemes. A later short story of his features a scoundrel servant attempting to marry a servant girl by pretending to be Lord of the Big House (see the short story *Maeve's Grand Lover* in Fitzmaurice's collected stories *The Crows of Mephistopheles*). This now seems quite unsettling in light of the truth about the Parson as it is revealed in this biography for the first time. Parson Fitzmaurice had regarded his ministry and life in a Gate Lodge as handicaps to his life as a member of the gentry, just as George undoubtedly regarded his Civil Service job as an unwelcome intrusion into his dream of life as a full-time writer.

All of the children attended the Church of Ireland National School in Listowel. George and his brothers also attended St Michael's College in the town, where the eldest son Maurice achieved very well, winning a prize in the Intermediate Examination in 1881.[13] George however, would not continue his secondary schooling after his father's death, having to make do with learning from his older brothers, as well as spending hours upon hours by himself reading and writing. George's father, being a fluent Irish speaker, is likely to have conversed through Irish with his wife and neighbours. Two of their elder daughters, Maggie and Hanora, who died in their formative years, won prizes for their fluency in Irish. Strangely enough, it appears that young George never spoke in Irish, but the language and the transition from Irish to English in the late 1800s and early 1900s proved vital to his nurturing as a writer.

Death was a regular visitor to the Fitzmaurice household with the premature deaths of five daughters, probably all from TB. This undoubtedly took its toll on the family as a whole. Elizabeth, the eldest, and the sister who cared for George and his younger siblings, was the first to die, aged nineteen. Agnes and Amelia died in infancy or childhood, while Margaret and Hanora died during their teenage years. There can be no doubt that there were prolonged periods of gloom and sadness that hung over the house after each of these tragic deaths. Death would further strike the family in 1891 when they would lose their father to pneumonia. His death would ultimately reveal his cruel legacy to his poverty-stricken and homeless family as well as to the local community. Life would change utterly for George, his siblings and their fifty-one-year-old mother Winifred.

Parson Fitzmaurice died two days before George's fourteenth birthday. Even today, people living in the locality still believe that upon his death a local butcher, Michael McDonnell, had Winifred and her family thrown out of Bedford House on account of an unpaid bill of £60.[14] This story is still told locally and was related to me by Paddy Murphy. When McDonnell's young wife later died tragically, the local people regarded her death as an act of divine retribution for his treatment of the widow. Although the Parson died more than a century ago, this story of the widow's eviction leaves us with an unfair account of the realities that pertained at the time. It is time to set the record straight regarding the somewhat unfortunate Michael McDonnell and the devious Parson Fitzmaurice.

2 | The Move from Bedford

After Parson Fitzmaurice passed away, people should have begun to see the reality of the situation, and his deceptions should have finally been laid bare. Yes, he had left many unpaid debts including the butcher's bill, but what sense can really be made of a story that has McDonnell managing to gain, as collateral, a great house and an extensive estate for a debt of just £60? The fact is that the Parson's death revealed the true nature of his occupancy of Bedford House. The Fitzmaurice's secret was unfolding and cruelly the Parson was no longer around to share the utter despair and embarrassment he had bestowed on his wife and children.

The reality, as we now know, is that Parson Fitzmaurice never owned Bedford House. The only property available as collateral for the unpaid butcher's bill, was of course, the Gate Lodge. According to the Valuation Records, Volume II, McDonnell does indeed assume ownership of the Lodge in 1891, but *not* the house.[15] After 1891, the Valuation Records confirm that Bedford House stayed in the Bateman family for a number of years. The position regarding Michael McDonnell's occupancy of Bedford House is simple: according to the Records, he is credited with leasing Bedford House from about 1899 until the McDonnell family actually bought it thirteen years later. What makes this whole story so much stranger and tragic is that the meat purchased by the Parson from Michael McDonnell's butcher shop had been bought, not to feed the family, but to feed his greyhounds. This illogical sense of priorities and pretentious fancies certainly teaches us much about George's later psychological state.

Figure 1: Bedford House: An aerial view of Bedford House, where the
playwright was born in 1877. (Date unknown). Courtesy of the Relihan
Family, Bedford.

Following the Parson's death the family was now effectively homeless.
It was of paramount importance to Winifred that she locate a home for
herself and her children, a home that was nowhere near Bedford as the
truth about her husband was finally beginning to unfold. Being a
proud woman, Winifred could never again face her Bedford
neighbours whom she felt had been let down by her husband's
behaviour. Ironically, it was the Bateman family that came to their
rescue when the Parson's brother-in-law, Reverend Ronald Bateman,
allowed Winifred to move into a large farmhouse in Kilcara Beg, about
a mile outside Duagh Village. Paradoxically, the Parson had already
been leasing the farm, which again illustrates the lengths he had gone
to in order to assume the role of landlord. The move to Duagh was far
enough away from all that had previously happened, so the family
could try to pick up the pieces and make a new beginning.

The people of Duagh responded discreetly to the family's
embarrassment by always treating its members as an integral part of
the community. Their welcome for the widow and her family was
genuine and without compromise, and the whole community treated

them very humanely. Help was always at hand. They saw Winifred as one of their own: a local woman who had just lost her husband and her home. Local men helped out on the farm and the house became an open one, with neighbours passing in and out every day, as was the case throughout rural Ireland almost to the end of the twentieth century. With very few Protestant families in the area, Winifred was amongst her own class again, but her children remained quite reserved and, for the most part, would never fully adapt to their changed circumstances.

The present-day ruin of the Fitzmaurice house at Kilcara Beg is hidden below the road a couple of hundred metres from the main Listowel to Abbeyfeale carriageway. While it was originally built in two cottage wings with a thatched roof, a photograph reveals that the thatch was replaced at some point with a corrugated roof. It is nowadays utilized as a turf shed. Bridie O'Connor of Finuge, Lixnaw, and formerly of Creggane, Duagh, recalls the house in vivid detail.[16] It had the traditional half-door, which led into a mud-floored porch. To the front of the house, the door had a large imposing brass doorknob. It had a kitchen living area with a stone fireplace on one sidewall, while a large room lay off the entrance hallway. Marjorie Fitzmaurice recalled the story that a servant boy moved with them from Bedford.[17] This conjures up images of the unnamed servant boy who spent hours with the young W.B. Yeats, teaching him the 'pleasure of rhyme' as they searched the trout pools and roamed the countryside listening to the local folklore and ghost stories.[18] Yet the overriding difference between these Irish literary giants, whose paths would cross in the early 1900s, would be one of class. George, who could not even finish his secondary school education, would never rejoin the gentry.

As well as bearing the stigma of their parents' marriage, the family also had to bear the Parson's destructive legacy. Upon his death there was little if anything left for his wife and surviving children. The family's attempts at dealing with their plight remained evident throughout their lives, as they tried in part, to live a life not unlike that of the gentry. The move from Bedford had an incredibly embarrassing and psychologically damaging effect on several members of the family. The following years would still see Miss Una and Miss Georgina[19] continue a pretence of grandeur in Kilcara Beg, taking pride in the baby grand piano in the parlour and the silver that adorned its sideboard, as well as in the immaculate flower and vegetable gardens that surrounded the whitewashed cottage.

George Junior's psychological make-up reflected all that had happened around him. However, despite the negative impact that manifested itself in his personality during his adult years, the move from Bedford to Duagh was to have an overall positive effect on him. He continually responded to the special network of feelings and thinking that is characteristically Irish. He also responded positively to the mix of Catholic and Protestant cultures and the move to Duagh would further nurture his imagination and stimulate his creative mind.

George had access to a rich sociological and anthropological past as is generally captured in the North Kerry oral and literary traditions. His creative spirit benefited greatly from the indigenous customs, characters, language and dialect of the area. George was to spend a significant part of his life in Duagh and he would hold the place and its people in special affection. Living there offered him a unique insight into rural North Kerry life and, from his mid teens onwards, he spent hours strolling by the River Feale near his home, as well as wandering about the farm exploring every acre and listening to all who passed through or worked there. As a teenager he spent most of his time with visiting adults or his younger siblings, and images abound of George and his younger brothers playing hide and seek in the woods along the river valley.

The level of culture among the ordinary people was high and fine poetry was much appreciated and treasured. Irish people spoke 'a vivid and cultivated language'[20] and their memories were fully stocked with the native oral literature that had come down from their ancestors. Irish speakers used phrases of great beauty that introduced rhythm and alliteration to their speech, giving a certain harmony to the everyday conversations heard all around. A love of the countryside was something that was handed down orally from generation to generation, and this *seanchas* included local family history, traditions and placenames. The young Fitzmaurice began to tap into this rich heritage and, importantly, his Protestant background allowed him to view the community from the outside. This enabled him to provide a successful and honestly written commentary in his short stories and in his later plays on the North Kerry where he grew up.

Fitzmaurice's Norman ancestors fought alongside the Gaelic chieftains in the Desmond Rebellion and paid heavily for it by forfeiting their lands down through the subsequent years. They had also battled against the great McCarthy clan in a dispute that lasted four generations. Men from different cultures had sat down together around the campfire at night, exchanging those fantastic tales that make the Irish oral tradition so spectacular, an oral tradition that George kept returning to in his later writings. During his early years in Duagh, George fed off the community's rich bounty of stories, songs, pishogues[21] and folklore through the oral tradition. The men in the fields and on the farm, the women conversing with his mother, the storytellers in the rambling houses he visited, all contributed to his formation as a writer. George became a familiar sight waiting by the roadside in order to meet anyone passing by. Locals still remember his hunger for news and gossip, as well as his delight in observing people's reactions to events in their surroundings and day-to-day life. With time on his hands, imagination became George's best friend and he became a close observer of the personalities of those who worked the family farm, as well as of the neighbours who were regular callers to his home. During the 1890s Fitzmaurice observed a culture, dialect and way of life that he would capture forever in his plays.

He was an intelligent young man and even as a teenager he was well aware of the great upheaval suffered by the people who had made the recent language transition from Irish to English. His mother had grown up during the beginnings of the transitionary period between the use of English and Irish. The influence of Irish on the English language as it is still spoken in rural Ireland today is based on phonetics and pronunciation. Some letters in English, such as the 't' and 'd', sound different when used in the Irish language. The influence of Irish words in a sentence spoken in English is a common thread through Fitzmaurice's work, an idiom that is borrowed from the Irish language. Towards the end of the eighteenth century, Irish had begun to lose ground as the first language of the people. From the late 1880s onwards, Irish was in most cases no longer the language of young people and children were even examined for confirmation through English.[22] The Catholic Church did not encourage Irish as a first language and contemporary census reports confirm the decline of Irish in the Barony of Iraghticonnor, which includes Duagh.[23] As Irish people attempted to adapt to English they did so at a pace that left them fully articulate in neither language.

By the beginning of the twentieth century a unique Irish culture was still active in many respects. There is evidence of a growing interest in dancing, racing and other entertainments. People visited houses where storytelling and the exchange of news were to be had. The seanchaí, or storyteller, would entertain listeners with ghost stories, as a glance into the unknown and the supernatural was very popular with people at the time. With respect to the increased usage of the English language in rural Ireland, people in the Duagh area can still recall the many phrases that were unique to North Kerry. It was also common to hear un-translated Irish words being used in the course of a sentence. George realized that he was in the presence of a new and exciting phenomenon, a dialect resulting in the shift from Irish to English as a first spoken language. Eamon Kelly, the Seanchaí,

who graced the Abbey stage for many years, taught in Listowel before
turning to professional acting. Kelly, a master of the oral tradition, was
later to play the lead in several Fitzmaurice productions and had a
particular affinity with the playwright's work. He declared that what
made Fitzmaurice's plays special was that they were written in a
tongue that was ' ... his from the cradle'.[24] George Fitzmaurice took
that unique dialect and moulded its beautiful lyricism into the spoken
words of the characters in his plays. His early years in Kilcara Beg
were critical in his development as a writer, and night-time saw the
family sitting by the fireside as their mother recalled her childhood
lore.

Religion readily played its part as a result of the power assumed by
the Catholic Church from the early nineteenth century onwards, and
efforts had been made by a small number of Catholic clergy to root out
non-Christian practices. However, the pagan element was never
completely forgotten and survived in the Christian rites of passage.
The mythological cycles and early bardic poetry remained influential
on the Irish character. George's dual cultural upbringing allowed him
to consider the pagan and Christian elements of life in an unromantic
way. This is also true of the depictions in his plays of the customs of
rural Ireland, such as arranged monetary marriages and the hunger
for land. He saw absolutely nothing romantic in the reality of the
sometimes harsh lives of his neighbours, where their futures seemed
almost predestined.

Although people spoke in English, they were still thinking in Irish.
Throughout North Kerry during the eighteenth and nineteenth
centuries, hedge school standards were very high with some teachers
versed in the classics, sciences, mythology, Irish language and
literature. A love of learning is well documented in the North Kerry
area as having existed throughout the ages. Gabriel Fitzmaurice, in his
book of essays, *Kerry on my Mind,* records that in 1692, Sir William
Petty noted that, 'the French and Latin tongues ... were known ...
amongst the poorest Irish and chiefly in Kerry'.[25] He also recalls that
George Story, chaplain to the Williamite forces in Ireland, is recorded
as having commented that, 'every cow-boy amongst the Kerry people
could speak Latin to save them from the gallows'.[26] With a strong
classical tradition in the area, a command of fine words, poetry, song,
story and colourful language was the order of the day if the storyteller
was to hold the attention of his audience. Some areas had the
traditional seanchaí, but almost all adults and children would have
had constant access to poetry, songs, ghost stories, pishogues and local
history because neighbours rambled to each other's houses at night.
For centuries, Irish people were associated with the tradition and art

of the ancient *File*, or poet, who was held in high esteem. George's subconscious heritage would have stemmed from the local bardic schools in places such as nearby Lisselton. These schools had a lasting effect on the North Kerry community and cannot be ignored or disregarded. In Lisselton in the eighteenth century, Pádraig Liath Ó Conchubhair, a man of undoubted scholarly ability, with a great command of the classics, was leader of a great following of fellow schoolmasters, Irish being their first language. A 1959 issue of the *Shannonside Annual* records how the North Kerry bardic school was known as Cúirt na Súagh. Although very little remains in manuscript form, memories still hold a considerable grip on the North Kerry psyche. The fact that a legacy of literary tradition had already been created in North Kerry is of great importance to the literature of George Fitzmaurice.

Duagh also had its local poets and balladeers that maintained this strong literary tradition. The Irish Folklore Commission records two poets in the Duagh area whom George must have been familiar with: T. McGovern (1873-1928) and Patrick O'Donnell (1838-1903). He would almost definitely have come into personal contact with these poets and would certainly have listened to other people reciting from their work. The last Mayor of Duagh, Ulick Ó Keirín, claimed to be Duagh's major Irish poet. He and his father Donnacha had been travelling weavers who originally came from Castleisland.[27] George would have been familiar with this type of travelling workingman, or *spailpín* in Irish, and may have harboured a romantic image of them as they passed through the locality hawking their trade. These men claimed descent from the *File* and were admired for their way with words and welcomed for the news and stories they brought with them. Just as Synge had enjoyed such wandering tramps, George may have thought to follow their philosophy and lifestyle, wandering around Duagh in search of news and gossip and new themes for his stories. He walked the roads and travelled to Lyons's pub in Duagh or further afield to Abbeyfeale and Lyreacrompane to meet and chat with others. In some respects George Fitzmaurice was a wanderer with no secure position in society despite his ancestral name. This almost nomadic trait would be recognizable in his later life in particular. The oral tradition of the past was identified, ultimately, in the Celtic renaissance of the nineteenth century. The importance of folk tales and lore was recognized by collectors such as Crofton Croker and later still by the instigators of the Irish Literary Revival, such as W.B. Yeats and Lady Gregory. Indeed, Lady Gregory and Yeats looked to the Irish folklore and pagan elements as a new way forward, in which Irish literature and theatre would herald a Celtic Golden Age.

In his later years Fitzmaurice described the characters in his plays as *wicked old children,* which Austin Clarke refers to in his introduction of the first volume of Fitzmaurice's plays.[28] It can be assumed that he was also describing the characters from whom he had learned a great deal. The Duagh people constituted a unique community and are remembered to this day for their innate roguish characteristics and reticence in refusing to conform to what is expected. Such was the community into which the Fitzmaurices were absorbed and, memorably, despite dire warnings from Catholic priests regarding the entering of a Protestant church, locals waked each Fitzmaurice family member in turn in Kilcara Beg, as well as attending their Protestant funeral services.[29] George recognized this innate characteristic and would later illustrate this device of non-conformity in his plays, when the dreamers of his dramatic fantasies fail to conform to what society dictates, even though it results in total despair or even death.

Over the years, George had become familiar with every nook and cranny and every field and ditch in and around Duagh. Local lore tells of the trees and the bushes whispering to him and George was often overheard answering them back.[30] Despite opting for solitude from an early age while making up his stories and plays, he never came across as being an extraordinarily literary young man. As he grew older, it seemed that his talking to himself was merely an attempt to pass the time of day or night. Although George, a man of medium build, had a shy demeanour, he was witty and humorous and occasionally a local prankster. It never seemed obvious at the time though, that his imagination was so far reaching and wild as to conjure up the magical flights of folk fantasy, which he later put to paper.

Locals still correctly associate characters from George's plays with actual people who lived in Duagh. The attitudes established in an early twentieth century Irish community were brought to the fore in the wonderful rhythmic dialect of a George Fitzmaurice play. George's romantic notions, wanderings, stories and dreams were in opposition to his family's plans for him, but his family would eventually win through and secure employment for him outside of Duagh and North Kerry. If he were to make it as a writer, he would have many obstacles to overcome along the way.

3 | The Short Stories

Reading had always been an important factor in the Fitzmaurice children's upbringing. Their father, despite his failings, fostered in them a deep love of literature and books. During the siblings' early adult lives, a wide variety of books and newspapers occupied every shelf of the farmhouse at Kilcara Beg. The two spinster sisters, Miss Una and Miss Georgina, availed of the popular English fiction of the time as a means of temporary escape from the mundane. All at Kilcara Beg treasured the daily newspaper and it was the literary page that first made George aware of the possibility of seeing his own work in print. From a very young age, George had found solace in books. He spent hour upon hour reading in the loft, the high field, the orchard, and Dominic's Cave,[31] as well as in his own bedroom. Besides his fascination with the written word, we know that the spoken word of the locality also filled him with wonder. George's fascination with the Hiberno-English dialect was an important consideration in his early writing and it makes perfect sense that he would write in the dialect of the local people. However, particular authors and genres also had a strong influence on Fitzmaurice.

As mentioned earlier, Sir Walter Scott was among his favourite authors. Scott was influenced by the dark Scottish legends and balladry as well as European writers' themes of man's non-conformity in contemporary society. The Scottish writer possessed an immense knowledge of the stories and legends of the local people in the Borders and Highlands' countryside and was also a voracious reader of ballads and historical romances. His early imitations of Scottish and German ballads of terror and the supernatural enabled him to give 'a vivid reflection of how man thought and felt in earlier ages about the mysteries that lie behind the world of everyday experience'.[32] Although the influence of Scott's work on Fitzmaurice has never been explored, perhaps the similarities should not be ignored, as George's early years deserve more critical attention and study.[33]

Influences on Fitzmaurice that are found nearer home are in the works of Listowel writer and journalist D.C. Hennessy whose writings were probably part of the Fitzmaurice library.[34] Hennessy's story, *The Bashful Lover and His Friend*, tells the tale of Francis Sullivan who is in love with Miss O'Brien. The smitten Francis relies on the skill of Nolan, the matchmaker, who has, it turns out, been working all along towards getting the girl for himself, much to the detriment of the foolish Francis.[35] This story illustrates some similarities with Fitzmaurice's tales of the wily matchmaker. It seems also that he may not have been the first person in the wider family that had dreamt of a writing career. An ancestor, Henry Fitzmaurice, had a story *Original Tales* serialized and published in five issues of the *Kerry Magazine* in 1854. Vividly, Henry placed himself in these romantic and fantastical stories, which are set in far-flung places such as the Amazon and America.

Around the turn of the new century Fitzmaurice was, of course, only one of a multitude of young hopefuls like Padraig Colum and Seumas O'Sullivan, who was later the editor of the *Dublin Magazine*, seeking publication. Although his short stories tend to illustrate what Robert Hogan calls a 'style of narration and description of nineteenth century prissiness', the dialogue is flawless.[36] Fitzmaurice's early prose is laboriously stilted and his longwinded descriptions result in their being hastily overlooked. Although Augustine Martin, reviewing the volume of short stories for *The Irish Press*, may have been correct in stating that the stories 'would not merit republication if they were not by Fitzmaurice', it is unfair to make comparisons between his short stories and his later plays.[37] The prose requires some perseverance on the reader's behalf, but it still allows a critical insight into the development of his keen sense of North Kerry life and its people. When Fitzmaurice drops all narrative formality his excellent construction of dialogue is clear, while the plots and themes reveal his early development as a writer of dark humour and farce. In all, Fitzmaurice had ten short stories published, nine of which feature in *The Crows of Mephistopheles* edited by Professor Robert Hogan.[38] Between 1900 and 1907 his short stories were published in various newspapers and literary journals.

The publication chronology is as follows:

'Peter Fagan's Veiled Bride', *The Weekly Freeman*, March 1900;

'Maeve's Grand Lover', *The Irish Weekly Independent and Nation*, November 1900;
'The Plight of Lena's Wooers', *The Weekly Freeman*, December 1900;
'Peter Praisin'', *The Irish Weekly Independent*, June 1901;
'The Disappearance of Mrs Mulreany', *The Weekly Freeman*, November 1901;
'The Bashfulness of Philip Reilly', *The Weekly Freeman*, March 1904;
'Chasing The Ghoul', *The Irish Emerald*, May 1905;
'Cupid and Cornelius', *The Irish Weekly Independent*, May 1906;
'The Streel', *The Weekly Independent*, March 1907;
'The Crows of Mephistopheles', *The Shanachie*, Summer 1907.

Of these stories, at least two were published during his short time working in a bank in Cork. By the end of 1901 he had five stories published in all. He did not hoard materials and he had relatively few personal belongings at any stage in his life. The only short story found among his possessions at the time of his death was a typescript copy of *The Crows of Mephistopheles*. The likelihood is that it will never be known if he wrote more stories or threw away other drafts or rejected manuscripts. While deception and marriage are almost ever-present themes in these stories, the theme of true love features only in *The Bashfulness of Philip Reilly* and *Cupid and Cornelius*. This may suggest that Fitzmaurice was quite cynical when it came to the Irish tradition of marriage through matchmaking. Perhaps it also suggests that he did not believe in true love at all. One must wonder if his feelings might have resulted from his supposed failed romance in and around 1900, referred to by Fr Stack in the *Rivers of Words* documentary.[39]

His first publishing success came in March 1900 with *Peter Fagan's Veiled Bride*. This story deals with a deceptively cunning matchmaker who manages to fool the gullible Peter Fagan into marrying the less attractive of two sisters. It ends happily enough when Peter and his surprise bride decide to make the best of a bad situation.

The second story, *Maeve's Grand Lover* (November 1900), finds Fitzmaurice attempting to parody the popular fictional romantic image of love that Maeve finds in her novelettes. One wonders if it is merely incident or irony that this parody of love was published around the time of George's supposed failed romance. Although local man Jamesie is in love with her, Maeve falls in love with a man she thinks is Mr Shandrum Dandrum, lord of the big house, but who is really a wily servant. Fortunes turn and the results of one woman's fictional hopes and dreams illustrate the reality of a bitter and harsh world. In the cold light of day, an un-heroic and foolish Jamesie lies on his deathbed, all for love. When Maeve finally realizes what she has done, she repents by burning all her books. Darkly, Fitzmaurice surrounds her with the neighbours' sniggers and titters of laughter. Dying for love might have been an acceptable fictional notion, but for George it was nothing short of downright foolish and ugly. This story echoes Fitzmaurice's later play, *The Country Dressmaker*, as the same inherent dark tones survive in the play.

Another wily matchmaker, Lanty Mudoon, appears in *Peter Praisin'* (March 1901). Lanty joins forces with Peter who, by singing the praises of his 'angel' niece, leads poor Jaymony MacNamara to fall for a woman whose sharp tongue would otherwise have driven her uncle Peter to his grave. The story ends with Peter celebrating the fact that 'there's nothin' like praisin'; but all the praisin' in the world won't praise her away from Jaymony'.

The Streel (March 1907), is a story with an added twist when the cunning matchmaker is conned. Written in three parts, it tells the story of Sylvester Dansell, a fifty-year-old bachelor whose forty-three-year-old unattractive and lazy sister Maura is without a dowry and therefore unmarried. She and matchmaker Peter Halpin trick Sylvester into selling his farm by telling him how much better life could be if he sold it, while this would of course provide a dowry for her. Peter then tricks his cousin Martin Tobin into a match with Maura whom he coaches in the ways a lady ought to behave. When Sylvester changes his mind regarding the sale and arrives home unexpectedly with Martin, they find Maura as she always is; 'her clothes bedraggled and fixed on her anyhow, her unstockinged feet showing through her brother's broken, unlaced cast-off brogues'. Martin is totally disgusted and, much to Sylvester's delight, the marriage is called off and Maura and the wily matchmaker get their just desserts.

Mrs McGrath takes on the role of matchmaker in *The Plight of Lena's Wooers* (December 1900). A substantial farmer, she has £600 in the bank and is insistent that her only daughter, Lena, marries a well-off farmer. However, Lena is in love with the impecunious Martin Foley. Mrs McGrath tries arranging a number of prospective matches by inviting men to visit. Unknown to her, the two lovers have ambushed each of these men on their arrival and hidden them in the hay barn. Mystified by the fact that none of the men keep their appointments, Mrs McGrath eventually relents and allows her daughter to marry Martin. Returning home from the wedding ceremony, all is revealed when she finds the kidnapped suitors in the barn and learns that Lena has been deceiving her. Although she vows never to forgive her daughter, this is short-lived and eventually all is forgotten.

The first of Fitzmaurice's stories to demonstrate true love, *The Bashfulness of Philip Reilly* (March 1904), also introduces his first returned Yank. Local man Philip Reilly is in love with Katie Dolan and, shyly, has watched her during the rambling house dances. His awkwardness results in his missing an opportunity to dance with her and eventually rumour has it that she is to marry returned Yank, Martin Doolen. Locals believe the Yank should not waste his £400 on this match but instead buy himself a farm. Eventually, Philip musters up the courage to call to Katie's house to see her one last time. On his arrival Katie's mother berates him for trying to win her daughter, as he is poor. Yet when the Yank hears that Katie has Philip's name written on her bedroom wall, he ends the match and at long last Philip can confess his love to the long-suffering Katie.

The second story, *Cupid and Cornelius* (May 1906), is a tale of Cornelius, a widower farmer in love with his servant girl Mageen. He fears the neighbours' gossip and so avoids revealing his true feelings until he hears of Mageen's plans to emigrate. Eventually he proposes to her and all ends happily. One cannot help but wonder if the story's conclusion is George's personal commentary on the local reactions to his own parents' marriage:

> ... it is true that for a time the high relations vigorously protested, and they used every effort to dissuade the widower from his rash project. But the lofty determination of Cornelius soon frowned them out of contenance, and ridiculed their self-righteous asservations. One by one, they lapsed into silence, disconcerted, almost ashamed. What did the neighbours say? "Was there iver a man of since like Carnaylus"? No fortin, sez you? But what blessin' is eukul to a good woman in the house? Mageen is her own fortin', and Curnaylus knew his bargain.[40]

Only three stories dispense with the marriage theme: *The Disappearance of Mrs Mulreany*, *Chasing the Ghoul*, and *The Crows of Mephistopheles*. The first of these, *The Disappearance of Mrs Mulreany* (November 1901), tells the story of Donnacha O'Donoghue who visualizes himself as a poet. His imagination gets the better of him when Mrs Mulreany has not been seen in town for more than a week and this leads him to suspect her of infidelity. He concocts a wild story but once the truth is out, he meets with the wrath of his neighbours whom he tries to blame for spreading his initial rumours.

The first story with any hint of the supernatural was *Chasing the Ghoul* (1905).[41] Daniel Tobin, a shy man, is known to suffer greatly after once seeing something utterly terrifying. Since then he refuses to travel home on his own at night. In actual fact he is nothing more than an 'arrant coward' who has let his imagination get the better of him. When he misses a lift home on the night in question, he goes back to the pub for some Dutch courage in order to walk home alone. He eventually leaves the pub so drunk that he is convinced he hears something supernatural taunting him repeatedly with the words: 'Out late!' However, it turns out to be merely a corncrake and no real 'sperit' at all.

Most commentators agree that Fitzmaurice's last short story, *The Crows of Mephistopheles,* first published in *The Shanachie* in June 1907, is his best. This farcical and sinister tale introduces us to farmer, Michael Hennessy, 'a quiet, simple, honest, hardworking man'. Huge numbers of crows have bothered him on his farm for three years and the stress has changed him greatly. His very appearance is one of a person burdened, as his eyes are sunken and his cheeks leaden. He begins to believe the crows are in league with the devil and allows his farm to deteriorate. His hatred of the crows grows daily and even his nightmares reveal the crows as laughing at him. Neighbours begin questioning his wife Eileen, who, afraid that the family will be disgraced and their daughters' prospects ruined, pretends Michael is grand. However, her poor attempts to convince her neighbours make them doubt her even more. Eileen becomes a woman obsessed, so much so that the neighbours begin to believe both individuals are insane.

When scarecrows prove useless, Michael goes to the Big House to borrow a gun from the master in order to kill the crows. Much to the neighbours' delight, Michael, never having handled a gun before, simply lays it on the ground shouting 'bang bang!' whenever the crows perch on it. Wondering why His Honour would give him a gun that doesn't work, he goes back to the Big House to complain. Naturally, the master can hardly contain himself on hearing what Michael has done and kills several crows himself, telling Michael to hang them up in order to ward off the others. Weeping for joy, Ellen and Michael delight at the sight of their fallen persecutors as the crows lay there in a pile. Perhaps the moral of the tale, subtitled *A Study on Simplicity,* is that honesty and common sense would have been the better policy and would have saved the Hennessys so much grief. Importantly, Michael's nightmares allude to the darkness and demons, themes and characters of Fitzmaurice's later folk fantasies.

During the period when these stories were being written, the demise of the Irish language was an important factor in a resurgence of all things Irish. The Irish Literary Renaissance was already concentrating on the creation of a national literature in the English language. Its objective was to increase interest in Irish themes, encouraging enthusiasm for mythological and legendary tales. This resulted in the ordinary peasant being seen as a descendant of the heroic Irish legendary and mythological character. Thus, the Irish peasant began to be depicted as 'angels in red petticoats'[42] in the new national literature of the time. As his short stories reflect, Fitzmaurice observed that, in reality, the Irish character had not fully inherited the noble and legendary heroic Celtic spirit the revivalists sought and admired. As Synge records in *The People of the Glens*:

> ... it is possible to find many individuals who are far from admirable in temper or in morals. One would hardly stop to assert a fact so obvious if he had not become the fashion in Dublin, quite recently ... to exalt the Irish peasant into a type of almost absolute virtue ... [though] the Irish peasant has many beautiful virtues, it is idle to assert that he is totally unacquainted with the deadly signs, or with any minor rogueries. He has, however ... a fine sense of humour, and the greatest courtesy.[43]

Throughout his stories, George Fitzmaurice attempted to entertain the reader by utilizing both comic and satiric strands. The fearful power of the satire, once associated with the bardic school, was certainly not lost on Fitzmaurice, whose uniquely dark touch added a subtle but grotesque element to his early fiction. The inherent qualities he identified in the Irish were blaggardism, cunningness, greed and foolishness; qualities that were epitomized in his fictional characters. Therefore it is no surprise that Fitzmaurice reflected an obvious tarnish on the lofty aspirations of the Literary Revival. Never comfortable in either of the Catholic or Protestant worlds, he became a unique observer of everyday life and cunningly revealed the darker element of the Irish psyche. The reader catches a glimpse of the underbelly of Irish life as it really was: harsh and desperate, while sometimes violent in word and deed. These combinations would develop further in Fitzmaurice's dramatic theatre of farce and grotesquerie encompassed in that unique dark humour. Throughout the centuries, the Gaelic prose tradition had been a comic and satiric one and from early times inclined towards fantasy, the burlesque or phantasmagoria.[44] Developing his own interpretation of the truth, George never fell into the trap of romantically idealizing those people he knew and loved. Though Fitzmaurice never denied North Kerry people their rich past or present, he declined to hide from life's harshness behind any wall of pretence or romance. Life for Fitzmaurice's wicked old children as he had personally witnessed it was one of survival and was never a million miles away from life in a Fitzmaurice short story.

4 |An Introduction to Theatre

While Fitzmaurice had quietly celebrated his early publishing successes, he had been content to hide himself away with his books and stories. His vision may have been to become a full-time writer, but reality dictated that this was an option only when his means might permit it. During his late teens and early twenties his family had watched him and were worried about his future. By 1900, and now at almost twenty-four years of age he was still at home, never having held a job. No one could have blamed his family for questioning how realistic his dreams of literary success were. Eventually, and inevitably, the family gave him an ultimatum: it was time to make his own way in the world and to contribute to the well-being of the household that was already heavily dependent on regular contributions from Mossy and Ollie. The genetic link between father and son served only to heighten their fears as George was forever wandering about the place, talking to himself and indulging in the flights of fantasy which would become so evident in his later plays.⁴⁵

He was eventually forced to take up a position in one of the main banks in Cork City.⁴⁶ This position was secured by Mossy who himself had begun his career as a bank clerk. Mossy was obviously well suited to a career in finance, eventually becoming Manager of the Hibernian Bank in Tubercurry, Co. Sligo. Despite his efforts on behalf of George, Mossy was to be disappointed in his younger brother who lasted less than a year in Cork. However, this period in Cork was important to George as it was there he encountered an element of cultural life that made an urban existence tolerable for him; the popular commercial theatre.

For some literary historians, popular theatre productions were viewed as 'inartistic constructions of mere escapism and repetition'⁴⁷ and therefore little attention was focussed on their importance to Irish theatre history. The popular theatre had an indisputable influence on writers such as Joyce and O'Casey. Meanwhile Yeats, among others, believed that popular theatre was unintellectual and the Irish Literary Theatre manifesto of 1897 would reflect this thinking in its desire to disassociate itself from the popular theatre. The inherent belief was that popular theatre was far from literary because it catered for the masses, whereas the true literary theatre would cater for more lofty spiritual ideals. Stephen Watt argues that the remnants of such thinking have led to an 'oversimplification of pre-Abbey drama in Ireland'.[48] These unfair interpretations also seem to be contradicted by the increasing numbers of people from the middle and upper classes that attended the popular theatre at the end of the nineteenth century.

Popular commercial theatre had thrived in Dublin since the early nineteenth century and English touring companies had begun to visit other towns such as Belfast, Cork and Waterford. It made perfect sense for these companies to tour large centres of population as the novelty of their shows ensured profitability, thus enabling their very survival. Economic survival meant that popular theatre dramatists wrote for as inclusive an audience as possible, which was distasteful to some. George Moore claimed that 'all that is done for money is mediocre',[49] while Joseph Holloway championed the Queen's Royal Theatre by viewing popular theatre productions, for example, those by J.W. Whitbread, as 'breaking new ground towards the establishment of a modern Irish drama'.[50] By the end of the nineteenth century, Holloway's thinking was justified as other commentators agreed that the melodramas at the Queen's were a welcome move away from the distasteful stage Irishman image: that dramatic 'arrah-begorra' caricature.

As well as presenting political melodramas during the hotly charged political climate of the time, the theatregoer also had a wide choice of music hall entertainment, melodrama, farce, minstrel shows, and Shakespearian plays, as well as work by English playwrights. Irish theatres also staged plays by Richard Brinsley Sheridan and Oscar Wilde and welcomed the visiting London theatre companies performing contemporary plays of Henrik Ibsen and other international literary figures. Audiences were huge and the popular theatre gave Dublin some of its great mainstream theatre of the time, proving that melodrama and musical comedy were only part of these theatres' repertoires. This reality was ignored and popular theatre was branded as being simply cheap entertainment. Possibly the fact that melodrama offered audiences a form of escapism and emotionalism added to this reputation. However, Watt argues successfully that in ignoring the strong historical role of the commercial theatre at the time, this action disposes of a means of analysis for the pre-1897 Irish theatre. The popular theatre had a strong influence on the formation and development of George Fitzmaurice's playwriting genre. Indeed, Fitzmaurice was not the only aspiring playwright so influenced. Lennox Robinson travelled from his home outside Cork City to the Opera House to watch shows there, claiming this was his first serious introduction to theatre. The story was a similar one for future Abbey playwrights such as T.C. Murray and George Shiels.[51]

The unwarranted concentration on the stage Irishman and his associations with popular theatre did not help, but merely distorted the picture of Irish drama and popular culture of the time. With regard to Fitzmaurice's early playwriting career, the melodrama's reflection of Irish society, notably in the work of Dion Boucicault, deserves in-depth critical reflection. Boucicault's work was also of major importance to the future careers of Synge and others. When one looks at religion, patriotism and economic position as demonstrated in Boucicault's colourful, daring and popular melodramas, in particular the priest and rebel figures, noticeable similarities occur in Fitzmaurice's work. The priest becomes a pathetic and laughable character in the shorter plays, facilitating the author's attempts to make fun of the Church, while the radical is identified in Fitzmaurice's protagonists' rebellion against the ordinary and socially acceptable means of individual behaviour. Other elements of commercial theatre, such as the colourfulness, action, escapism and sheer vitality, are also characteristic of Fitzmaurice's later fantasies and folk plays. It seems as though he was daring to do the unthinkable: to combine what the Irish Literary Theatre considered 'low' theatre, with the 'literary'. Meanwhile, during his time in Cork, Fitzmaurice had a choice of entertainment at either the Opera House or the Palace. During his months there, entertainment included Sheridan's *School for Scandal* and Wilde's *Lady Windermere's Fan*. In these, his first theatrical excursions, George Fitzmaurice's North Kerry world collided with the theatrical world.

Taking into account the demise of the Irish language, writers now used English as a medium for moulding a new literature around the material left by their Gaelic ancestors. The rich Hiberno-English dialect was recognized as something special in itself. Douglas Hyde, in his 1892 address, *The Necessity for De-Anglicizing Ireland*,[52] argued the link between Ireland's language and culture. The following year saw the publication of *The Love Songs of Connacht*,[53] which was of paramount importance in recording the Hiberno-English dialect. Having witnessed the European cultural movement and a revival of European folklore, such as Wagner's operatic productions of mythology and folktales, W.B. Yeats was encouraged to believe that a similar movement could be created in Ireland. He advocated the revival of the romantic and idealistic ancient Celtic spirit.

A desire to foster native poetic drama accessible to all of the people heralded the founding of the Irish Literary Theatre (ILT) in 1897. This movement sought to produce plays that were hitherto not being staged by the commercial theatre. W.B. Yeats, Lady Gregory, Edward Martyn and George Moore co-signed a letter stating that Dublin would see 'certain Celtic and Irish plays which ... will be written with a high ambition, and so build up a Celtic and Irish school of dramatic literature'.[54] The objective was to illustrate an Ireland that was 'not the home of buffoonery and of easy sentiment, as it has been represented, but the home of an ancient idealism'.[55] By ignoring the popular theatre and the Irish theatre history that had preceded the foundation of the ILT, the mentors of the ILT managed to believe that it could imagine 'afresh its relationship to Irish history'. Its make-believe ideologies regarding Irish Theatre pre-1897 made it possible for them to envisage the training of an 'uncorrupted and imaginative audience' in how to listen 'by its passion for oratory'.[56] The ILT lasted for three years and ironically in that time, productions employed English companies with professional English actors.

Yeats's *The Countess Cathleen* was the first ILT production and caused much controversy. The action of the play, which takes place during the Famine, portrays a landlord willing to sell her soul to the devil to save her people. Such productions led Joseph Holloway to believe that Yeats and other members of the ILT were only 'pretend[ing] to know all about what stage work ought to be, and despise all real playgoers like myself'.[57] Edward Martyn's play, *The Heather Field*, concerning a landowner obsessed by a field, also formed part of the ILT's repertoire, while later plays included Martyn's *Maeve* as well as Alice Milligan's *The Last Feast of the Fianna* – plays that illustrated the ILT's firm mythological line during its initial seasons.

By late 1901 George had returned home to Kilcara Beg having given up his position in Cork because he did not like it. He made it clear to his mother and older brothers that he would not spend another minute in a job he despised. In so doing, he willingly sacrificed a regular week's wage. The parallel between father and son's behaviour was obvious and ominous. However, by November of that year a second position was secured for George in the Civil Service on the recommendation of a Mr J.H. Leahy, of Killarney. He was to commence his civil service duties in Ballyhaunis, County Mayo, but the supervisor there refused to take an inexperienced clerk onto his staff. Instead, and not for the last time, fate played a hand and

Fitzmaurice was sent to work in the Land Commission offices in Dublin, the centre of the literary revival and the fledgling dramatic movement.

Fitzmaurice's move to Dublin gave him further chances to see commercial theatre regularly, but it also offered him an opportunity to observe the formation of the new national theatre. It is probable that he was a member of the audience during the 1902 and 1903 seasons that saw productions such as Padraig Colum's *Broken Soil,* Yeats's *The Hour Glass* and Lady Gregory's *Twenty-five.* Fitzmaurice's own name begins to appear around 1906 in Joseph Holloway's diaries.[58] Holloway, who never missed an opening night between 1899 and 1940, kept remarkable journals and records Fitzmaurice's attendances at early Abbey Theatre productions as well as recording his earliest submissions to the Abbey. It seems that it was not difficult to turn to drama during those years in Dublin because many other writers were doing so at the time. As Lady Gregory records in her autobiography *Our Irish Theatre*:

> It is the existence of the Theatre that has created play-writing among us ... and Mr Fitzmaurice, Mr Ray, and Mr Murray – a National Schoolmaster – would certainly not have written but for that chance of having their work acted.[59]

However, with no extant diaries or letters belonging to Fitzmaurice, which might shed light on his first years in the capital, Holloway's entries regarding Fitzmaurice are of critical importance.

As he had no short story published between December 1901 and February 1904, we must rely on the strong suggestion that he quickly turned to writing plays on his arrival in Dublin. The dramatic movement captivated George's imagination to such a degree that he began to struggle with the short story form although he did not abandon it completely. Drama offered him a challenge through which he could express his creativity more easily and freely. Realistically, this new dream of having his work produced for stage appealed to him as being much more exciting than having another short story published. Whilst at home in County Kerry, George's sole means of entertainment had been the men and women about the farm who shared with him their parochial stories, poems and ballads. As George held this myriad of characters about the hinterlands of Duagh and Abbeyfeale in great affection, his fertile imagination was filled with his very own stage players. He was determined to develop further the linkage between his own creativity and the wealth of native culture which had surrounded him at home.

A significant move by the ILT during its third season in 1901 had
been the staging of Hyde's one-act play, *Casadh an tSúgáin*. Both
Moore and Martyn had by now resigned, having been unable to work
with Yeats.[60] The play was directed by a new associate member of the
ILT, W.G. (Willie) Fay. Willie and his brother Frank were well known
in amateur dramatic circles, and along with members from the
Ormonde Dramatic Society and Inginidhe na hÉireann, formed the
Irish National Dramatic Company and became associated with the
ILT. The brothers' involvement 'transformed what, up to now, had
been a predominantly literary movement into a living theatrical entity
with its distinct national flavour and stylistic form'.[61] By 1902 they
were ready to perform Yeats's *Cathleen Ni Houlihan*, which opened on
2 April alongside George Russell's play, *Deirdre*. Yeats's play, with the
revolutionary Maud Gonne in the leading role, incited fervent
nationalist reverie and would haunt Yeats for a long time afterwards.
The Fays, along with Yeats, Lady Gregory and Synge, believed that this
theatre's first objective was to achieve artistic excellence, a notion that
would later clash with that of Douglas Hyde and Maude Gonne who
saw theatre as an instrument for patriotic propaganda.

This changing shape of the theatre was reflected in its renaming as
the Irish Literary Theatre Society (ILTS), and Yeats's poetic theatre
was to be 'universal in outlook and idealistic in sentiment'.[62] Its first
season opened in a blaze of controversy with a new play by John
Millington Synge. Yeats and Lady Gregory believed Synge was a
playwright who epitomized the Irish Theatre's hopes and dreams.
However, *In the Shadow of the Glen*, first produced in October 1903,
incensed nationalists who believed that it was a complete slur on Irish
womanhood, as the main character, Nora Burke, decides to leave her
husband and her unhappy marriage behind, to travel the roads with a
tramp she has just met. Maude Gonne and Douglas Hyde vehemently
opposed the play and eventually withdrew completely from the
Society.

While attempting to turn to playwriting, Fitzmaurice had a chance
to observe all that was happening in the theatre. Although his earliest
work, in its themes and writing, would indicate that he had problems
with the lofty ideals of the literary revivalists, he recognized the
importance of Lady Gregory's and Synge's plays, which established the
Hiberno-English idiom as an important Irish dramatic medium. Lady
Gregory recorded the dialect from the Kiltartan district in County
Galway, while Synge moulded the dialects of County Wicklow, the
Aran Islands and the Great Blasket Island into a unique dramatic
language of his own. It is ironic to think that both Synge and
Fitzmaurice had spent hours roaming the countryside in their own

localities, absorbing all that had been going on about them. Now, as Synge attempted to force audiences to come to grips with a reality 'purged of sentiment, piety, morals, optimism, benevolence, idealism', he was reactivating 'the age-old tension between pagan and Christian in Irish life and culture'.[63]

Although Lady Gregory, Synge and Yeats had tried to tap into the Gaelic folkloric tradition, George recognized that they had ignored the popular theatre of the time as well as the prevalent theatrical folk tradition in many parts of Ireland: that of the mummers and the mumming plays. A major feature of Irish culture, mummers were companies of players who acted at popular gatherings, e.g., fairs, weddings and wakes. The mummers performed mischievous tricks, and all players were masked (until this became illegal), and their antics were often quite objectionable. Plays could be darkly offensive and grotesque, for instance, when the mummers played at a young woman's wedding to a much older man, whom she married for money, or at a wake where the dead person might not have been very popular. The plays followed the cycle of death and rebirth and the continuation of the natural cycle. Mummers operated according to a symbolic and cultural logic, but were seen as part of the Irish oral culture and not proper theatre.[64] It was the influence of such a tradition that Fitzmaurice would bring to bear on his drama, its rationale being the springboard he needed in order to begin focusing on his own dramatic ideals.

Stemming from the Irish literary revival, the Abbey Theatre would see the emergence of the peasant play, a development influenced by the Fay brothers. They trained Irish actors in a realistic style that would become known as the 'Abbey Method', thus encouraging new writers and a new audience, although this was a direct contradiction of the ILT's original attempts at developing a poetic theatre. It is ironic that in later years Yeats would have to look elsewhere to have his own plays produced. Meanwhile, George had tunnel vision regarding his destiny; he would see his work produced on stage. In order to achieve this he was prepared to observe these developments and eventually write in the confines of the peasant play.

When Synge's *In the Shadow of the Glen* and Yeats's *The King's Threshold* were performed as part of a tour of England, Annie Horniman was so impressed by what she saw that she offered to build a theatre in Dublin to house the company. A building was found and Joseph Holloway was hired as consultant architect. Willie Fay was hired to oversee the remodelling of the theatre attached to the Mechanics Institute. The Abbey Theatre opened its doors in December 1904 with performances of Yeats's *On Baile's Strand* and *Cathleen Ní*

Houlihan, Lady Gregory's *Spreading the News*, as well as Synge's *In the Shadow of the Glen*. However, attendances were low for the Abbey Theatre's first nights. Two nights after the opening performances, Holloway wondered:

> Is it possible that there is not an audience with a love for the beautiful in Dublin sufficient to fill the little theatre for more than one night at a time?[65]

Attendances got worse and the rifts between players were tense and would not disappear for the foreseeable future. Nationalists attacked yet another of Synge's plays, *The Well of the Saints*, during its February 1905 staging. It was only after two months that William Boyle's *The Building Fund* offered the theatre some financial solace and a full house during its run.

However, the theatre's problems were economic and, ultimately, short runs could not allow for the exploitation of popular plays such as Boyle's. Players were amateur and therefore dependent on fulltime jobs, so touring, which might have addressed the economic problems, was not a possibility during this time. By late 1906, discussions centred on the formation of a new theatre society so as to try and reverse the ongoing problems. The result was the registration of the National Theatre Society Limited. Players' salaries were guaranteed, which would enable players to turn professional. But control was now ultimately in the hands of Lady Gregory, Yeats and Synge, which split the Society, and most of the founding members resigned. Although the Fays were still involved at the time, neither Willie nor Frank was on the Board of Directors. In the interim, a new society, the Theatre of Ireland, whose membership was amateur, had been formed in opposition to the National Theatre by Edward Martyn.

Throughout all this turmoil in the new National Theatre, Fitzmaurice was writing and planning his playwriting career. After his initial 1907 success with the realistic cottage comedy *The Country Dressmaker*, he would begin a lifelong battle with those literary demons that would haunt him throughout his life. Should he continue to write within the confines of the Abbey peasant drama, or should he be true to himself and his own definition of drama? Critically, Fitzmaurice's purpose in life became clear. At this time he wanted success at the Abbey Theatre, despite his later move towards fantasy. Apart from the few references to Fitzmaurice in Joseph Holloway's journals, there is little evidence of what he was writing during those early years in Dublin. However, we know for certain that his motivation to write plays was further fuelled by his friendship with a Civil Service colleague and fellow writer, John Guinan. An understanding of Guinan's relationship with Fitzmaurice is critical in any attempt to analyse Fitzmaurice's early writing days in Dublin before his initial Abbey success. Meeting a like-minded person in the Civil Service helped him considerably in passing the long and tedious days at work. Just as Guinan aspired to a literary future, Fitzmaurice focussed on the possibility of proving his family wrong by achieving success.

5 | Life in Dublin: The Early Years

Guinan and Fitzmaurice were a couple of civil servants captivated by the literary capital of Ireland. Despite the fact that much of their relationship is lost to time, it is still possible to surmise and piece together some elements of their friendship from Joseph Holloway's journals. Guinan, who was born in Ballindown, County Offaly in 1874, also began his literary career by writing short stories. Although his stories remain uncollected, he was successful in having a number of them published.[66] Despite the fact that Guinan had been submitting plays to the Abbey before Fitzmaurice, his career proved more difficult to get off the ground. Very often, his over-elaborate dialogue coupled with weak plots were obstacles in his drive to succeed as a playwright. However, Guinan was a very determined man and he did everything in his power to become accepted into the inner sanctum of the Dublin literary circle, with a view to furthering his literary ambitions. He attended Holloway's literary soirées and regularly sent scripts to the Abbey, as well as corresponding with the theatre's directors and Holloway regarding his work.

By 1906 Fitzmaurice had made his first submission to the Abbey, but the play was rejected. The Fay brothers were still at the Abbey recruiting and training new actors, although internal battles raged. The directors hired Ben Iden Payne to develop the Abbey, although Willie Fay still continued to direct the 'peasant' plays. Synge was reading new submissions for the theatre and in a letter to Guinan regarding his most recent submission, *Rustic Rivals*, he wrote:

> Once or twice you use expressions like 'I was never any great shakes in a shindy', which at least in their associations are not peasant dialect, and spoil the sort of distinction one can get always by keeping really close to the actual speech of the country people. On the whole, however, your dialect – is it not Kerry dialect? – is very good. If you write any more plays we would be glad to see them.[67]

Although this positive response must have been a great source of encouragement for the County Offaly man, Fitzmaurice's influence is evidenced by Synge's reference to the Kerry dialect. There is absolutely no doubt that both Guinan and Fitzmaurice supported and helped each other in their individual quests to see their work produced on stage. George's influence on his friend is further recorded in a letter of Holloway's to Guinan, when he asks if he had taken George's advice, by 'peppering the dialogue with strange oaths to suit the taste of the Abbey trio'.[68]

Guinan was not afraid to voice his dissension when his scripts were rejected, particularly when he believed that his work had not been given the attention it deserved. Yeats once suggested that Guinan attempt a one-act play, as it was a rigorous and well worthwhile discipline, which Synge had of course gone through. Guinan wrote to Holloway:

> Yeats says I have a splendid gift for dialogue and characterization that I allowed it outweigh other considerations ... I propose challenging Yeats in the press openly.[69]

Guinan's discontentment festered in the fact that he thought the Abbey director had 'read the little play under the impression that it was another anecdotal comedy'.[70]

Holloway later referred to Fitzmaurice's first submission after seeing *The Country Dressmaker* when he 'could not credit how much Fitzmaurice had improved since he sent in his first play last year'.[71] Although Howard Slaughter indicates that the Kerryman's first submission may have been the one-act farce *The Toothache*, there is no available evidence to substantiate this. It is also possible that the full-length play *The King of the Barna Men* was his first submission. This play illustrates his preference for folk drama, while both plays illustrate his early intention to rebuke the red-coated petticoats of the literary revivalists. As both of these scripts lay undiscovered until after the playwright's death, the rejection of either may have been enough for Fitzmaurice to discard them at this point in time. However, following his first rejection, he decided that for the time being, it was better to conform and write within the boundaries of the more acceptable and popular realistic comedies at the Abbey.

On reading the one-act play, *The Toothache*, one is struck by Fitzmaurice's attempts at dark humour and farce, which is indicative of both the music hall and Gaelic folk traditions. Robert Hogan goes so far as to claim that such are the similarities with this play's 'grotesque antics [that they] might have been written by Synge himself'.[72] The play's inherent obscurity displays some of the darker elements of his later folk fantasies. No reworking of this play seems to have taken place, which might indicate that this work was indeed his first rejection. Meanwhile the full-length play, *The King of the Barna Men,* illustrates his love of farce and humour as well as his ability to draw on folk tradition. As is evident from the notebooks found after his death, *The King of the Barna Men* underwent some re-drafting in latter years, and the final draft included a title change.[73] Perhaps this interest in the longer play is further evidence that *The Toothache* had been his first rejection.

The *Toothache*[74] follows Patsey Dunn's ill-fated visit to a village blacksmith's forge in order to have some teeth pulled. Set in North Kerry, the town is one 'with the population near a hundred, five public-houses and the Great House in one fourth of a mile itself'. It is likely that this is an actual description of Duagh, and census records for the time support such a supposition. *The Toothache* is considered a complex and 'strange amalgam of the comic and the grotesque' and a complex absurdist drama in the idiom of Ionesco or Beckett, with the use of music hall songs juxtaposed with the extraction of teeth.[75] The symbolic sexual action and the realization that Patsey is actually a clown victim both support this theory.

Patsey is unable to open his eyes with the pain: 'with a head as big as a pot on me from a belter of a toothache in these three teeth'. Mulcair, the village blacksmith, has come with 'great recommendations' and the fact that Patsey has been told Mulcair is both cheaper than an apothecary and less painful, leads him to the forge. Mulcair is not alone in the forge and is kept company by Jim, Con and Neddy who will all remain on stage throughout the action. All four men see Patsey as little more than a gombeen man when he refers to Jim as 'your honour' and 'sir' after mistaking Jim for the smithy. Jim, Con and Neddy get ready to watch the extraction scene and it is made all the more frightening for Patsey when Mulcair is described as a 'black beist'. Jim explains firstly why it is necessary that they remain, and then explains the importance of Neddy's ballad singing so as to soothe Mulcair. Poor Patsey believes that these men are 'all good sort of people', and he is conned into buying porter for everyone present, handing over a two-shilling piece. However, the game is almost given away when the story of Frynk Sheehy, a previous patient of Mulcair's, is told, and the fact that Sheehy left the forge 'roaring, bawling leppeing down the road and over the fields' after having his teeth extracted.

When the operation commences, Patsey is kept on the flat of his back, as Mulcair kneels on his chest. Neddy begins the ballad *Green Brooms* that tells the story of John who, following his father's threats, goes to the woods to cut branches in order to make green brooms. He meets a lady at 'The Castle of Fame' and asks her if she wants these green brooms. Eventually she asks John to marry her and he consents. At that point, Jimmy ghoulishly and excitedly looks for blood as the first tooth is pulled. Neddy continues his song, and with the words 'John's beauty put her in game', a second tooth is extracted. By now, Jim is completely wound up watching the 'great blood ... coming through his eyes now in style'. Mulcair roars for some cloth to soak up the blood as he continues to slap Patsey around when he screeches. Neddy's song continues as the lady asks John to 'lay by your trade/And marry a lady in bloom, full bloom', while Mulcair misses a third tooth. Jim, still fascinated by the blood, is reminded of a story of a woman's injury after a fall and that he had never seen a pig that bled as much when killed as the woman in question.

The song ends: 'There's no trade like the cutting of brooms', and with it the third tooth is finally pulled. Mulcair is thrilled with himself while Patsey is reeling from the pain and trauma, a victim of a vicious assault made to satisfy the dark nature of the men in the forge. However, the fact is that the three pulled teeth are three healthy ones! So now we ask ourselves, what was the whole point of this play?

As the curtain falls, we have witnessed an obscene desire for blood, suffering and pain at the expense of poor innocent Patsey. The extraction scene harbours a dark symbolic sexual violence, which resonates in the words of the suggestive ballad song. The scene is tantamount to the audience having witnessed a vicious crime that it might surely wish had been stopped. The pace of the action and the innuendo suggested by the song may have been influenced by music hall entertainment, but the underlying current of darkness in the play makes for a great deal of unease. Perhaps then it is not difficult to see why the play could have been rejected. Might this play have coloured the Abbey directors' views regarding his later dramatic fantasies?

The King of the Barna Men[76] is a three-act comedy and a much more acceptable play. Set in 1850, the play introduces the device of a gift from a supernatural character. Dermot Rue Mullarkey, the champion wrestler of the 'Kingdom of Carraweira' for seven years, believes his success could not have happened without the aid of a magic blue ointment given to him by the Hag of Foildarrig. The first act opens in Mullarkey's kitchen, the day before the annual tournament begins. His two greatest supporters, his uncles Teig and Donncha, are unsure as to whether or not he has entered this year's competition. When Polsh tells the pair of 'gommologues' that Dermot is above in his room, this worries them. However, Dermot is acting strangely and has told Polsh of the ointment's part in his past victories, and how the Hag now refuses to give him any more ointment because 'he didn't mind the box he got of it but leaving the cover off and flies and every devil coming at it'. Dermot believes he would be a fool to take part in the next day's tournament, although Polsh is insistent that he takes part anyhow. Aeneas Canty, 'the King's Factorum', or Jester, arrives at the cabin, followed by the two princesses, Maureen and Roseen, to tell one and all of the Tournament. Teig urges Dermot to 'be the man and let the divvle carry that codology of ointment blue' and fight for the sake of prestige. Aeneas announces that whoever wins the tournament will also win Maureen's hand in marriage.

Act Two sees Dermot being urged to forget about the ointment and remember the prize that awaits him, not only marriage to Maureen but the Barna lands also. The Hag, who is in the vicinity, ignores Dermot, and he and his two uncles 'send her rolling to blazes and bumping and hopping down the steep incline'. However, this does not stop her and she reappears to seduce Dermot's rival, Cormac. Cormac is continually mocked as Dermot's supporters urge him not to take part in the tournament. The Hag gives Cormac the ointment and although Dermot makes a dive for it he is accused of carrying out 'a dirty Saxon deed' in doing so. However the Hag rescues the box for Cormac but Dermot vows to fight on regardless.

The King appears with Father Moore discussing the Queen's guests, who are the Protestant bishop and the Duke of Bayrla:

> ... isn't it misfortune was down on me ever to be having dealings with the Duke of Bayrla! It wouldn't do to be having the Protestant Bishop coming down to be making a souper of me darling daughter.

Meanwhile, the Bishop, Gobblebite, is distressed by this 'terrible country', which is 'far too rough for me' and tells the Queen that the King is just like a bold Norman Squire. His only wish is to make a decent Protestant of Maureen. The bickering between the two princesses finds Roseen looking for help from her Texan uncle, as she is none too happy at Maureen's prize: the winner of the tournament.

One and all are in readiness on the day of the tournament as Act Three begins. The King and the priest have plenty to drink and converse in Irish between themselves. When the wrestling begins, the stage directions make this scene deliberately ludicrous. In fact, the fight is not quite a fight, but sometimes a dance, interrupted at times by the farcical notions of the onlookers, as well as the King and Queen's strange and out of character dance. Amidst the furore, the priest gets pins and needles while the Queen sings an Irish ballad. It is quite the pantomime. Roseen then rushes in and tells one and all that her Texan uncle is giving her 'a fine farm with sixty cows and a pair of horses and the grass of thirty heifers or a man'. This means that even the runner-up in the tournament will do well for himself by marrying Roseen. Unlike his later plays, second best is quite rewarding and acceptable, although in coming second Dermot will have to go through the emotions of losing the tournament without having the ointment to help them. He has learned the important lesson that: 'Something great must have been in me surely, and after all it couldn't be the ointment made me do all I ever did'.

The play offers representations from both the Protestant and Catholic communities. In some ways it seems that there is a wider contest happening. Fitzmaurice is illustrating a personal analysis of Ireland within the play's action: the Protestant Bishop wishing to convert the princess, the King speaking Irish to the Catholic priest, and the subtle corruption of the Irish word *Béarla*, meaning English, in the Duke of Bayrla's name. Interestingly, an outside source of help is available to Roseen in the form of her Texan uncle.

Despite our discussions about which one of the two plays, *The Toothache* and *The King of the Barna Men*, might have been the first play rejected by the Abbey, the fact remains that there is only scant information available with regard to George's early submissions. Apart from the few references to Fitzmaurice in Joseph Holloway's journals, little else exists to record exactly what George was writing during those early years in Dublin. However, despite both Guinan and Fitzmaurice's individual difficulties, both men decided at some point to attempt a collaboration on a three-act play, which became *The Wonderful Wedding*. Written some time between 1906 and 1908, it was an obvious attempt to latch onto the type of Abbey play in vogue at the time. It was submitted and subsequently rejected. *The Wonderful Wedding* was first published in 1978 in the *Journal of Irish Literature* Vol. VII number 3, after the only typescript extant was found among Guinan's papers.[77] By incorrectly recording the play as having been completed during the second decade of the twentieth century,[78] the editors overlooked vital evidence in Holloway's journals. Holloway wrote in May 1908:

> Speaking of the three act play he [Guinan] and Fitzmaurice wrote together, Yeats asked him who was it wrote the part in pencil at the end of the second act, for said he, "it was the most dramatic bit I ever read".[79]

Although Guinan owned up to having written this part, it is impossible to indicate from the typescript at least, who contributed what to the play. It contains several minor holograph corrections in Guinan's handwriting, as well as his faint signature, which can be deciphered on the front page.[80] Robert Hogan suggests that much of the third act is Fitzmaurice's own, by referring to its similarities with his later play, *The Simple Hanrahans*. Critically, there is evidence of its similarities in theme and subject already found in Fitzmaurice's earlier short stories. The theme running through *Peter Fagan's Veiled Bride* (1900) is reminiscent of the tricks played in *The Wonderful Wedding* when Francie marries the wrong girl. Indeed, his mother Bridget's imprisonment also calls to mind Lena's suitors being locked in the barn in the short story *The Plight of Lena's Wooers* (1900).

The *Wonderful Wedding*[81] revolves around two brothers, Daniel and Peter Normyle, who live next door to each other. Daniel is the more prosperous of the two while Peter is 'a struggling farmer'. During negogiations with the Hanrahan family regarding a match for his son Francie, Daniel, with Peter's help, has manged to fool the Hanrahans into thinking his farm is bigger by flattening the ditch between his land and Peter's. This, they believe, will result in a bigger dowry being handed over with the bride. Act One opens in Peter's kitchen with both men's wives, Bridget and Maura, in conversation. Peter is wracked by guilt and when his conscience gets the better of him, he confesses the deception to his wife Maura, believing that Aileen Hanrahan, Francie's bride-to-be, 'won't have the pleasant times she has at home'. The couple do not realize that Bridget Normyle has been outside the cottage all along and has overheard their conversation.

Act Two opens with Daniel goading Peter for being so willing to take part in the trick once Daniel had 'put pin to paper' to buy cattle for him. Meanwhile, Bridget begins to show what she is really made of when, despite Daniel's threats, she declares that Francie's marriage will not go ahead. Bridget's odd behaviour has become a mystery as she secretly regrets having married into the Normyle family. As she is 'burnin' to break against the chain' of her unhappy marriage she declares; 'There'll be no marriage. Eighty pounds won't smooth my conscience'. Despite her husband's threats, she is 'strong in the rectitude of my own heart, and 'tis soon I'll prove it'. Francie is just like his father and believes that Daniel was correct in making the best bargain for himself. Before the Hanrahans arrive for the wedding, Daniel locks Bridget in the dairy, leaving Peter to stand guard singing to soothe her. Her absence is explained away by the belief that she is cursed. Peter himself wonders if he will be a changed man as 'his soul has been laid bare' by all the murky business.

As Act Three opens, Peter is still standing guard when local man Jamesie Sinon enters. To Jamesie's surprise, Peter lets on that it's his own wife Maura who is locked inside, thus causing Sinon to believe he has seen a changeling instead of the real Maura. Jamesie also tells of some 'schaymin' that has brought the crowds out to the finest wedding 'for seven years' to see the bride's 'big white veil that fell in a straymer all over her, and another veil inside so we couldn't get a peep at her face at all, at all'.

A delighted Daniel comes in and releases a screaming Bridget who declares: 'I'll show the world at last what I am, and what they should have always thought me to be'. There's a terrible uproar outside as Francie experienced three weaknesses, while Old Hanrahan is 'afeared there has been some confusion over this marryin' as his 'cherished daughter will have three fields short of the due'. Francie has just married Aileen's sister and not Aileen as expected. As the Normyles have been tricked, Bridget comes face to face with Daniel about Francies's 'old hag of a wife'. Francie blames his father: 'look at the wife you have got for me after all your tricks!' Daniel admits to Hanrahan that he is 'willing to forgive and be forgiven' which echoes a similar theme in *The Country Dressmaker*. Bridget brings the play full circle as she concludes: 'for the honest way is the best way'.

This collaboration with Guinan may very well be evidence in highlighting Fitzmaurice's eagerness to see his work on stage, so much so that he was willing to meet the whims of the Abbey directors with a realistic country cottage play. However, his interest in folk drama also becomes evident in this play, as does his attention to the development of themes of deception, the acceptance of second best, and the quest for material wealth. Despite the two playwrights' early rejections, it would be Fitzmaurice who received the first break. In fact, he had two plays produced by the Abbey before Guinan's first play, *The Cuckoo's Nest,* was produced in 1913. Guinan must have been hurt at Fitzmaurice's earlier successes, although there is nothing to indicate any particularly jealous behaviour on his part. Though it is probably true that their friendship petered out naturally given George's years away from Dublin, they did attend plays together. However, there is no doubt in my mind that John Guinan was in the audience on 3 October 1907, eager to give his friend all the support in the world on the opening night of Fitzmaurice's first Abbey production: *The Country Dressmaker.*

6 | *The Country Dressmaker*

When the Abbey Theatre received *The Country Dressmaker*, Lady Gregory wrote:

> A new play has been sent in by Fitzmaurice who works with Guinan – 3 acts – peasant – good speech – rather harsh – wont make us loved. It is I think really good – Fay is enthusiastic about it – Payne is here reading it at the moment. If it turns out well it will really be a godsend.[82]

1907 had brought with it more controversy. J.M. Synge's *The Playboy of the Western World* had caused rioting early that year and audience numbers had plummeted. Prior to the opening of *The Country Dressmaker* in October 1907, Yeats issued a warning that the Abbey 'would require 200 police when they produced his [the Fitzmaurice] play, seeing that 150 were required during the run of Synge's *Playboy*'.[83] He was worried because he felt this play actually gave a worse portrait of the Irish person than *The Playboy* and thus anticipated that more serious riots would occur. The fact that there were no troops required came as quite a surprise to him, and he was little short of astonished that the Fitzmaurice play achieved unexpected public popularity, providing an important commercial success for the Abbey. *The Country Dressmaker* opened on 3 October and among the audience were Jack Yeats, William Orpen and Hugh Lane. It proved such a popular choice that its run was extended, despite the theatre's obstinate no re-run policy. Yeats declared, 'We are putting the play on again next week owing to its success'.[84] It had certainly enticed back the audiences that had stayed away since *The Playboy* riots. It eventually played 134 times between 1907 and 1925.

Essentially a realistic comedy, *The Country Dressmaker* tells the story of Julia Shea who spends her hours dwelling on the ideal notions of love found between the covers of popular English romantic fiction novelettes. Her preference for this type of fiction directs us towards the play's inherent underlying theme: that of dream versus reality – and leads to a comparison with Synge by Fitzmaurice biographer, Carole Gelderman.[85] Although George's play reflects his rather conventional beginnings as a successful playwright, the play clearly displayed his ability to reproduce the authentic North Kerry dialect for the stage.

Julia has been kindling a love for her sweetheart Pats Connor, who has emigrated to the United States about ten years before. She idealizes him as she would the romantic hero in her favourite novelettes. She believes that Pats has gone to seek his fortune in order to return someday to claim her as his bride. A neighbouring family, the Clohesys, has been fooling Julia by telling her that Pats has been writing to them since he left. Why did Julia fail to question Pats on his return for not writing to her directly? She has simply remained aloof from the reality of the situation, unwilling or unable to see the truth. Julia's mother, Norry, is well aware that her daughter's foolish notions are pushing them nearer the poorhouse door and she is left with no choice but to call upon a local matchmaker, Luke Quilter, to organize a match for her daughter. He has a match in mind with local man Edmund Normyle whom he knows to be in love with Julia. The Sheas' neighbour and good friend, Matt Dillane, is none too convinced by Quilter's reputation, although he understands that marriage is the most practical option. Matt himself has been very frustrated by Julia's antics, which have proved far from practical for a very long time. Luke Quilter 'the man from the mountains', being the wily matchmaker that he is, uses every means to complete the match, and by the end of Act One he has succeeded in his plans when his lies result in Julia's decision to marry Edmund in three months' time.

Act Two reveals that the fun is about to begin when Pats returns home from the United States. Michael Clohesy reveals the truth about his great debts and therefore his desire that one of his daughters marry Pats *and* his fortune. The necessity of marriage for both the Sheas and the Clohesys was an economic fact of life. With the imminent arrival of the first Yank on an Irish stage, the lengths to which the Clohesys go to ensure their financial survival become clearer. In gleeful tones Michael reveals to his wife, Mary Anne, the gossip surrounding Pats and his marriage while abroad to a German woman who suffered an alcohol-induced death. The main comic action revolves around the Clohesys as their antics provide much entertainment for the rest of the play.

Although Pats has no particularly deep attachment to Julia, his arrival home brings with it an awful predicament. He makes his way to the Clohesys' farmhouse where he meets Babe, the younger daughter, who has arrived back from the meadow in a foul temper. As the plot unfolds, Babe appears far from sweet in her eagerness to win Pats for herself. In her desperation she goes completely over the top by telling Pats everything her family has done to fool Julia. She gives the Clohesy plan away with amazing ease and in her simplicity appears almost as naïve as Julia Shea. Ironically, it is a letter that causes the Clohesys' downfall when Babe foolishly shows Pats a letter of her father's in which he explains why Pats should marry 'a strong farmer's daughter'. Poor Babe believes she has beaten her sister Ellie to the prize and that the returned Yank is hers. As she departs the kitchen, Pats is allowed the opportunity to burn the letter, and thus he escapes all too easily from the trap that the Clohesys have laid for him.

Whether it is a revelatory sense of guilt or his sense of injustice at what the Clohesys have done, Pats moves to counteract their plans. In the space of seconds, he must decide what to do when Julia and her friend Min walk into the Clohesys' kitchen unexpectedly. He exclaims that he has returned in order to be with his 'darling future wife'. Julia is utterly shocked at her reunion with Pats who is 'So changed, so changed!' Julia doesn't want the older and bald Pats, but the younger man that has existed in her dreams for the previous decade. Later she is upset further upon hearing he has already been married. Once the truth is laid bare, she is utterly appalled by the physical appearance of the older Pats, and her romantic idealism lies in shreds.

Writing about the opening night, Joseph Holloway makes reference to the play's weakness of plot, as 'the second act was not nearly so well constructed nor real to us as the first and last acts'.[86] Despite Michael Clohesy's declaration in Act Two, 'If we could only get him into the clutches of the Clohesys, the script in its original form allows no real reason for a third act. In the 1907 version, Act Two originally ends with Babe's words before her exit:

> It's some harm I did I'm thinking by what I told him. But how could I help it with the cute old sham of a Yank and the way he pretended to be enjoying it.[87]

Later, Fitzmaurice made an important change to this ending and rewrote this section so that Babe's words justify a reason for a third act (and is published in the 1970 Dolmen Press version):

> I have done harm codded by that old sham of a Yank. I'll do more harm or something will give. I'll break the chaney taypot. I'll break the chaney taypot. (*Handles teapot, reflects and replaces it on a little table*). (*Suddenly*). I wo-ant; I wo-ant. (*Bursts out door*

*slamming it after her. As curtain falls the noise of crockery
breaking is heard).* [88]

Strangely Fitzmaurice dropped the words 'withered' and 'old' in the
later version. In hindsight, perhaps these descriptions might have
explained more clearly Julia's reason for refusing to marry the man of
her dreams. However, this version heightens audience anticipation of
the third act and prepares us for the Clohesys' final attempt at getting
their man. Importantly, the smashing of the crockery on the darkened
stage at the end of Act Two was a change Fitzmaurice made in 1921.
This change was influenced by the 'haunted kitchens of his daringly
experimental dramatic fantasies'.[89] The comic attempts to get Pats
once more into the clutches of the Clohesys make for the action in Act
Three. Yet, despite the hilarious fights between the Clohesy sisters, as
well as Mary Anne's firm attempts at proving who really wears the
trousers in the Clohesy family, the play ends on a rather dark note. By
marrying Pats, Julia describes herself as an ox going to the slaughter
as she looks towards an impending loveless marriage. Dreams,
illusions and obsessions become all-important in Fitzmaurice's later
work, and stemmed from this play's theme of having to make do with
second best in life. There are those who, perhaps too simply, have
suggested that Julia's statement, 'I am willing to make the best of it',
became the playwright's personal axiom for the remainder of his own
life.

Just as the play is structurally weak, some of the characterizations
presented are also poor:

> Mr Fitzmaurice is given to sketching his lesser people in a few bold
> strokes without even enough background to furnish us with true
> portraits.[90]

Luke Quilter, a potentially prime comic character, is a far less well
drawn character than Morgan Quille in *The Magic Glasses*. Yet
Fitzmaurice was still at an early stage of his development as a
playwright, and *The Country Dressmaker* is perhaps best seen as an
indicator of a playwright learning his new craft. It is clear from the
play that he had a natural talent for characterization, despite the fact
that he should really have expanded the highly comical character of
Babe. Despite the sisters' jealousies, Ellie Clohesy's participation on
stage is merely one of a cameo role and the script does not allow for
the development of the sisters' relationship in their bid to marry Pats.
In fact their girlish jealousy becomes clear only towards the end of Act
Three when a catfight breaks out. Min Dillane's role, although small, is
important, as she understands the change that has come over Julia

since Pats' return. Luke's final advice to the couple at the end, to make the best of it, merely echoes Min's earlier utterance.

It is only with the very end of Act Three that we are definite as to why Julia has changed her mind:

> because he is what he is and isn't what he was. Love died the first minute I saw him at Clohesys, and my dreams forever were over.

Love's young dream has grown old and her lament continues as she vocally regrets turning her back on Edmund, 'the heart that cherished me'. Structurally, this disillusionment might have better served the audience if it were clear by the end of Act Two and not Act Three.[91] Julia, not unlike Fitzmaurice's later characters, has lived far from reality and despite her obsessions time had not stood still for her as it had done in her novelettes. Not only has Pats aged, but Julia has completely ignored the economic side of marriage for years.

Despite criticisms of the plot's structure and characterizations, critics were very positive:

> The author, has most unquestionably, in his dramatis personae, given us some remarkably true types of Irish character.[92]

The characters were viewed as 'intensely true to human nature in general, and their language's perfect expression of themselves'.[93] Though Yeats described it as 'a harsh, strong, ugly comedy' he admitted that he did 'admire its sincerity'. In the following years Yeats often changed his mind regarding the play and wrote to Lady Gregory in 1913, after seeing the last act and a half of the play: 'I wish now I had seen the whole, it was astonishingly good'.[94] He recognized the value of rural comedy and the necessity for audience support for the Abbey. Although Yeats claimed that Fitzmaurice thought himself 'a follower of Synge', the Kerry man utterly rejected such a conviction.

While Yeats might have been surprised at its success, the press complimented the Abbey for having found a play that no one had the slightest objection to. Meanwhile, Holloway recorded how he believed that Irish people will accept looking at themselves on stage, once it is the truth, unlike the *Playboy* 'and such like foreign tainted stuff'.[95] Holloway also referred to some Kerry people who sat near him on opening night who claimed that Fitzmaurice's dialect was authentic North Kerry, so much so that Fitzmaurice 'won over the audience completely'.[96]

Lennox Robinson later recalled that George wrote *The Country Dressmaker*:

> without the faintest hint of influence from any outside source; his characters are understandably Irish, his situations are natural, and

his dialogue is rich and fluent ... it seemed that he had in his grasp
the popularity achieved by Lady Gregory.[97]

However, despite its popularity, it had been fate that dealt a hand
in Fitzmaurice's career with William Boyle's withdrawal of his own
work in protest at the staging of The Playboy. Although Willie Fay
might have attempted to reason with Boyle, he still believed that
Fitzmaurice's work was better.[98] By this time, the ambitious Willie Fay
was growing tired of having his decisions overruled by the directors,
referring to Yeats and Lady Gregory as 'cocks of the walk'.[99] He was
feeling less in control than ever and had no authority over the actors
and no power to make them obey his orders. Yeats was planning
investigations into Fay's management as players complained of his
violent language. In truth, Yeats was afraid that Fay would use the
popularity of productions such as The Country Dressmaker against
Lady Gregory's and his own work.

Despite the lack of any written evidence regarding Fitzmaurice's
feelings on the situation, he must have been well aware of the whispers
and gossip surrounding the Fays' involvement with the company. As
both of the Fay brothers felt harassed and overworked, it was evident
that a storm was brewing. In December 1907, Willie Fay wrote to the
directors looking for complete control of the contracting of actors,
while at the same time, Yeats was corresponding with Synge about
getting rid of Fay. By that time The Piper by F. Norrys Connell was in
rehearsal, a play that Willie Fay disliked intensely, while the players
spent much time debating this 'burlesque on Irish nationalism set in
1798'. The turmoil in the theatre reached its climax and by January
1908 the Fays had resigned, while the dispute also resulted in actor
J.M. Kerrigan's resignation. As the excitement surrounding the Fays'
departure began to die down, a spark ignited again when The Piper
opened to the public and proved yet another controversial play. The
individuals playing the group of garrulous 1798 Irish patriots found
themselves booed and hissed by an audience that saw the play as
nothing short of the slandering of Irish patriots.

Despite assumptions to the contrary, Fitzmaurice regularly
attended the Abbey during this turbulent period, which raises the
question as to why he did not take stock of all that was going on in the
theatre at the time?[100] It seems Fitzmaurice failed to take note of the
Abbey's political and artistic turmoil. Contrary to production trends,
he decided that his personal success merited a complete change in
theme and play type. Although Holloway may have declared that
George possessed a 'gift of dramatic writing' and echoed Lady
Gregory's words by claiming he was 'a godsend for the company', he

also made a further observation: 'whether he will develop it or not is the question'.[101]

However talented George might have been, it was not simply just a question of whether or not he would develop his gift, but *how* he might further develop it. His memories of the audience's call for him during the opening night a few months previously cloaked him from reality, not unlike the character Julia.[102] Indeed, this theme of unreality would prove to be a strong undercurrent in his subsequent plays. Fitzmaurice ignored the theatre's strong trend towards realism and plays such as *The Man Who Missed the Tide*. Therefore his next submission would prove far from pragmatic or practical and too impulsive by far. Fitzmaurice's strange one-act play, *The Pie Dish*, would mystify and alienate both Irish critics and audiences alike.

7 | *The Pie Dish*

It was with a great sense of excitement that, in April 1908, Fitzmaurice anticipated the opening of *The Pie Dish* at the Abbey Theatre. Described as 'a symbolic fantasy',[103] *The Pie Dish* formed part of a triple bill and was staged with the one-act *Teja,* by Hermann Sudermann, translated from the German by Lady Gregory, and *The Golden Helmet* by W.B. Yeats. Fitzmaurice's short one-act was, of course, far removed from the type of realistic play audiences had become accustomed to and at curtain fall on the opening night it was met with a stunned silence, save for a few handclaps from Synge. Critically, even Yeats seemed to have missed out on the play's themes by his insistence during rehearsals that the words 'dead and damned' be taken out of the play.[104] The fact that Fitzmaurice refused to allow this makes it feasible to believe that, contrary to today's beliefs, Fitzmaurice had indeed attended the play's rehearsals.

Although the small audience was mystified, they laughed uproariously in all the wrong places. Despite these reactions the actors liked the play and it was staged every other year until 1912, owing to the 'extremely credible' lead role it gave to Arthur Sinclair who played the character of Leum, as one reviewer claimed:

> We have seldom seen a piece of acting so extraordinary as the death of Leum Donoghue in the hands of Mr Arthur Sinclair. Simple, unrestrained, unrhetorical in speech and gesture, the writhing of the body, the twisting of the limbs, and the slow stumble of speech, as in paroxysms of pain the old man besought God or devil for time in which to finish his piedish gripped the soul with attention. But it was not in the play, it was Mr Sinclair.[105]

Holloway called the play an insult to the audience and Irish reviewers failed to see any theatrical merits in the characterizations or dialogue, claiming the play to be both grotesque and sacrilegious.[106] Despite the acclaim for Sinclair's performance, *The Irish Independent* described the play as ugly, clumsy and unintelligible with no sympathy for any of the characters portrayed in the play.[107] During its revival over the next couple of years, reviews did not change:

> It was gruesome ... It was realistic in the extreme, so tragic that many eyes were turned away. But the prayers were received with outbursts of hilarity, and the agonizing utterances of the women were punctuated with loud shouts of laughter'[108]

Despite these negative Irish reviews,[109] the play formed part of the repertoire during an Abbey tour of England where *The Pie Dish* and its author found appreciative audiences. When it was performed in Manchester in 1909, critics lauded the play. One review claimed that Fitzmaurice had:

> ... caught the secret of [one of] the greatest pieces the Abbey has staged ... he has that imaginative reach which gets down into the elementary terrors and desires, and hopes and fears, of the world, that insight which pierces through the surface of common life and sees the great forces beneath.[110]

As the *Guardian* newspaper praised the play most warmly, the company also staged Yeats's *Cathleen Ni Houlihan*, Lady Gregory's *Hyacinth Halvey* and Norrys Connell's *The Piper*. Huge profits were made with continuing praise for the actors and the plays. Two years later, when *The Pie Dish* toured London with Synge's *Playboy,* the reviews again praised Fitzmaurice's work. The *Daily Chronicle* revelled in its 'language ... pathos [and] humour'; while *The Daily News* reported:

> Its representation is delightfully even and unaffected in its well-controlled and well-harmonized spirit. [111]

However, it was during the Oxford tour that same year that Fitzmaurice received the critical acclaim he deserved:

> that a playwright should set out to write a play like *The Pie Dish* is in itself a justification of the Irish movement.[112]

A darkly comic play, *The Pie Dish* reveals the last hours of Leum Donoghue, who at 'eighty years or more' has long since turned his back on his farm work in order to concentrate on his ornamental clay pie dish. Leum lives with his daughter Margaret and his two grandsons. When the play opens we find Leum asleep. Having suffered a stroke, he is 'pure wild' at the notion of dying without having finished the pie dish. Meanwhile, Margaret's only wish is that he would prepare, as a Christian should, for his imminent death, thus saving the family from the neighbours' ridicule. She has instructed her two sons, Jack and Eugene, to make their grandfather respectable for the priest's visit.

It seems Eugene is the only relative who understands Leum, as his own physical disability – a limp – and his imagination make him just as much an outsider as his grandfather has become. Leum exclaims that the 'great wonders that are in the pie-dish' will not be revealed until the pie-dish has the last 'figario' applied to it. Soon afterwards, when Jack leaves to get the priest, Margaret's sister Johanna arrives and confronts her over the care of their father. Leum had lived with Johanna twenty years previously until he left 'over his being cut short in the butter'. Ultimately, both sisters are afraid that Leum's actions will result in their families being ostracized in the community and that they will be unable to find suitable matches for their children, such as had happened when the family suffered an outbreak of consumption some years earlier.[113]

With the arrival of Fr Troy we learn that Leum's obsession began when he slept in 'the big fort below our house' on the day he left Johanna's house. When Fr Troy stands over Leum's bedside, his pious sentiments to reconcile the dish-maker with his own Maker are utterly rejected. In a last ditch attempt at survival, Leum calls on the devil to give him time to finish the pie dish:

> Good God in heaven, it's time I must get – if it isn't time from God I'll get, maybe the devil will give me time! Let the devil himself give me time, then, let him give me time to finish my pie dish, and it's his I'll be for ever more, body and soul!

A distraught Leum dies screaming with rage and the dish crashes to the floor. The lifetime's work and the lifetime itself end together.

Despite certain comic elements, such as both grandsons' pathetic attempts at moving Leum to the settle bed early in the play, or the two daughters' bickering, audiences failed to comprehend the dark, macabre and violent elements at work in these scenes. The language itself is violent, spiteful, rage-filled and hateful, while an interesting juxtaposition is that the dark, sombre play is set on a bright June day. One might suggest that the theme of the play is simply the futility of wasting time on a useless project. Yet by ignoring other themes one can miss much of the play's meaning. The overriding struggle between Christianity and paganism is illustrated by means of the importance given to both the material items and the family's social status in the play. However, first and foremost, the pie dish was always another world away. Its unattainability might have made Leum's endeavours so much more exciting, but, sadly, it also reflects all that is mortal about its maker. The pie dish made of putty is expendable, like its maker, and neither the forces of light nor darkness can save Leum from himself or the certainty of death.

Father Troy's entrance towards the latter half of the play was a satirical look at the constricting influence of the then contemporary church. Though this theme lends itself time and time again to Fitzmaurice's work, Irish audiences took exception to his caricature of the church, its flock, and society itself. At face value, Leum's dreams and unrealistic attempts to bring some beauty and meaning into his life, were surrounded by meanness, fear, violence and narrow-mindedness. Sadly, Eugene's imagination is sustained by his grandfather's obsession, while both grandfather and grandson simply sought respite from the 'slush – same old thing every day' and the mundane existence of everyday life.[114]

Leum is symbolized as a disgrace to the family and the loss of respectability, the play's secondary obsession, is evident in his daughters' fears. Despite the preparations for anointing him, they are not one bit worried about his soul or his salvation, but consumed by the prospect of being disgraced 'through the length and breadth of Europe'. The play was seen as advocating devil worship and was lambasted as being blasphemous. The critics' failure to investigate the family's violence towards their father and grandfather is not surprising. Leum, who should have held the all-important patriarchal role in the family unit, despite his foolishness, should never have been treated in such a disrespectful way.

Eugene, who is 'emayshiated' from his bad leg, will be left to pick up where his grandfather finished, wondering about the possibilities of finding a way out of the ordinary, such as his grandfather had sought. Leum's brutal scream at the end underscores all the violence he has suffered from the others around him. The final question posed in the play 'What was in this at all?' takes on a larger significance in the face of things to come for the playwright himself.

This strange one-act was produced as the trend towards realism soared and the Cork Realists[115] were looming on the horizon. By now Fitzmaurice had been seven years or so in Dublin, and city life seemed to have taken its toll. Directly after *The Pie Dish* completed its first short run, he began his absence on sick leave from the Civil Service, although he did return to Dublin for a short time in October, where he saw Lennox Robinson's one-act *The Clancy Name,* which he felt was one of the strongest pieces of drama in the Abbey repertoire, and Thomas MacDonagh's play, *When the Dawn is Come.*[116]

On 30 January 1909, Fitzmaurice began a further period of sick leave due to a 'congested liver' complaint and in March wrote to his supervisor from Duagh:

I beg to state that the doctor who usually attends to me was away when I called, and owing to the inclemency of the weather, I was unable to get to see him today. I will forward medical certificates as soon as possible.[117]

He sent on a medical certificate shortly afterwards, but when he was due to return to work in April, he failed to show up and ultimately lost his job. He was not reinstated until December 1913. Somewhat disillusioned with the Dublin scene, he had more important things on his mind.

The negative Irish reactions to *The Pie Dish* continued every year it was staged at the Abbey up until 1912, while the excellent English reviews spurred him on in his quest towards fantasy. During his years in Kilcara Beg he would spend his days wandering around the farm, passing time chatting with neighbours while forming new characters in his head. Although he might have completed the realistic play, *The Moonlighter*[118] during his early months on sick leave, he took encouragement from the English reviews of *The Pie Dish*, which resulted in his beginning to write what are probably his two best plays, *The Magic Glasses* and *The Dandy Dolls*. Unfortunately, with the rise of new dramatists, in particular the Cork Realists, prose melodramas began to replace the type of work that Fitzmaurice was ultimately trying to bring to Irish audiences. These more realistic plays would become the Abbey norm. Perhaps George's years away from the Dublin scene made him rely too much on the hope that Irish audiences could learn from the more enlightened English audiences and critics. In due course, he would take the eventual decision to submit his new fantasy plays to the Abbey. A terrible outcome lay in store.

Despite Abbey realism, Roger and Jaymony and a host of supernatural characters were seeking creation, and Fitzmaurice sought to answer their call in an environment he loved and one that was conducive to writing. His plays would once again take precedence over everything: even his sense of duty to his family or to himself.

8 | Two Dramatic Fantasies

From early 1908, George Fitzmaurice established himself at home in Kilcara Beg for more than five years, his imaginative creations spurring him on. In *The Magic Glasses*,[119] the first of his two greatest dramatic fantasy plays, Jaymony Shanahan has spent most of his life, since he was 'in the fifth book', above in the loft at his parents' house.[120] He stays there contemplating life as seen through a set of blue, red and brown glasses that he bought years ago from a 'brown woman' at a fair. It is clear from the opening minutes of the play that Jaymony's parents, Maineen and Padden, have failed in their attempts to get him down from the loft, which has resulted in their peeler[121] sons 'lighting with shame on account of it' and therefore refusing to come home on a visit.

Maineen and Padden have sought the help of a local faith healer and quack doctor, Morgan Quille, and as the play opens, so begins the careful build-up to his entrance. The discourse on Quille sees Padden admitting his fear of this impending visit, which is not helped by the fact that they have enticed Quille to their cottage 'on a false pretence that Jaymony has his breast bone down'. The build-up is tense and Padden describes Quille as having 'the notions and capers of the devil' and being 'a variegated rogue', although Maineen regards Quille as 'a fine respectable man'. We suspect that Padden may be correct, but are entertained with descriptions of Quille's colourful cures. Maineen tells of how he 'cured Mary Canty of the dropsies and the swellings with his dilution of the white heather that does be growing in the bogs'. Padden, however, believes it was nothing

> but a bully ball of wind in her stomach, that came up in a hurry ... at the fright Mr Quille gave her, he to coagle her into a corner, gave her a thump in the middle and stuck out his tongue at her in the dark.

When Padden sees a strange man and he 'rising like a cloud over
the gap in Peg Caxty's bounds ditch', we are in no doubt but that this
'huge man with a long black coat on him, and a hat like a parson' is
Quille. Maineen soothes her terrified husband by encouraging him to
be 'brave ... for the sake of having Jaymony cured' so they can welcome
their peeler sons home.[122] So Padden thinks of his two emigrant sons,
with Robin 'sitting down to his bread, butter, tea, and two eggs' and
Frynk 'the way he made an ape of Poet O'Rourke in the argument
about Dublin and London'. His fear of the supernatural results in his
bravery being short-lived and Maineen has to physically struggle with
him to keep him in the kitchen. As Padden hides behind her, she tells
Quille the truth about Jaymony and begins by pacifying him with
punch and, of course, his payment. Padden's doubts as well as his
pathetic attempts to please Quille only annoy their visitor who flings
Padden across the floor. As Quille begins to rant and rave, music like
that 'in Teernanogue or what they hear them that do be drowning to
their death', begins upstairs. Quille asks to hear 'the exact rudiments
of the case', because it is time to see if this being in the loft is a fairy or
a Christian.

When Jaymony calls from the loft asking is 'the tea drawn yet?' we
are introduced to a selfish thirty-eight-year-old man threatening to
'smash every mug in the dresser' if the tea isn't ready on his descent
from the loft. When he appears, he sits down to eat and drink rapidly,
while Quille studies him from the corner. It is only when Quille rises to
light his pipe that Jaymony is made aware of his presence and
becomes embarrassed. As Quille is about to begin his exorcism he
orders the 'haunted thing' down on his hands and knees and, taking
the reddened tongs, begins a long psalm-like monologue, concluding
that Jaymony is 'some sort of a Christian anyhow'. However,
Jaymony's ailment is a pure mystery and his withdrawal into the loft is
incomprehensible to Quille. When Quille asks him why he stays in the
loft, Jaymony's reply is a realistic one: that it is 'better than being in
the slush ... same old thing every day ... this an ugly spot, and the
people ignorant, grumpy and savage'. When Quille explains the
advantages of being outside under the 'sunny sky', he is speaking as
someone who has spent time in Tralee Jail when falsely accused of
participating in the Agitation of the time.

Quille is spellbound by Jaymony's story of buying the glasses from
a fairy woman at a fair. He is in awe on hearing of 'the pleasure and
diversion of the world' that Jaymony witnesses, and is mesmerized by
the talk of his visions: 'the seven wonders of the world ... gold and
white money ... palaces ... the purtiest women ... and the dandy army
in the grey of the night'. Suddenly, Quille exclaims that he can see

visions similar to Jaymony's. As soon as Jaymony sees himself 'on a noble horse ... leading the army on', Quille falls into convulsions, the 'two terrible eyes rolling in his head, he having no sight in them at all'. Returning to reality, he leaves a bottle on the table instructing Jaymony to go and do the ordinary everyday things such as digging, discussing crops and cattle with his neighbours. Quille also prophesies that on 21 March Jaymony will find his future wife, who will be a woman with 'a slight impediment in her speech'.

Jaymony is temporarily elated and rushes out to begin digging. As Padden rushes out to tell everyone about what has been done for Jaymony, Quille hastily announces his exit: 'no time have I to waste'. However, while Maineen follows Quille to thank him, she meets Jaymony coming back inside shrugging his shoulders, having become tired and disillusioned after hearing that his brothers are coming home. Maineen urges him to take the medicine in the bottle to 'prevent the charm from being cancelled'. Relapsing into his gloom Jaymony refuses to carry out these instructions, but he says he will do so the following day: 'and it's a great effort I'll make entirely, if it isn't too far gone I am to be cured by quackery or the power of man'.

Padden arrives back with Aunt Jug and Aunt Mary and they drink whiskey to celebrate the cure, news of which has been shared with the community. Maineen then tells them that Jaymony has gone back up into the loft playing his music again. Padden knows they will be well and truly 'scandalized' and he goes to the bottom of the ladder, urged on by Jug and Mary, roaring at Jaymony to come down.

As if under a spell Padden finds he can't move and the same happens to Jug and Mary. As all three are by now 'dazzled drunk', Maineen implores them to let go of the ladder afraid they will 'pull the top loft down'. Maineen then believes she sees Jaymony on the table in the loft his eyes 'gone curious mad'. In his stupor Padden sees the devil with horns and hoofs and can smell brimstone. The ladder gives way eventually and the loft tumbles down. Amidst the rubble, all that is seen is Jaymony's legs sticking up and his 'jugular cut by the Magic Glasses!' Padden's immediate worry is that they will be arrested for murder or manslaughter and urges everyone to begin keening. Padden and Mary rush out shouting that 'the house fell down on Jaymony', while the stage directions have Maineen and Jug begin to 'ullagone and keen (from the Irish "caoin", to cry or lament) louder and louder as tumultuous voices are heard approaching'.

This play is so heavily invested with the supernatural that a rational explanation of its ending is next to impossible. However, elements of the play are quite realistic in the sense that local quacks were quite common in rural communities at the turn of the twentieth century. Fitzmaurice would have known of the local cures available from men of learning in the North Kerry area who had the powers to set charms and make medicines from herbs found growing by the roadside. The 'quack' would be called if a person broke a hand or leg, for example, and would take a briar in his hand and holding it over the broken bone would say the words of a charm before binding the broken limb.[123] Having finished this play, Fitzmaurice would take the theme of the supernatural to a higher level with *The Dandy Dolls*, his most important dramatic fantasy.[124]

In *The Dandy Dolls*,[125] Roger Carmody is a man obsessed with eating the priest's geese and making dandy dolls. In this play we are introduced to the supernatural characters of the Grey Man, the Hag of Barna and her Son. Roger has spent the last forty years of his life trying to make the perfect dandy doll, but each time he finishes one the Hag's Son comes and rips out the doll's windpipe, rendering it useless. The play is set on the Eve of May, one of the quarter days in the pagan calendar. In the first scene we find Cauth sitting knitting in the kitchen, and a child on the hob. The Grey Man enters on a visit. Not recognizing him, Cauth tells him she has nothing to give him, as 'there is nothing in the house but the red raw starvation'. The Grey Man, who later identifies himself as 'one of the Counihans of the Isle of Doon', is looking for Roger. We learn that Roger is in the 'practice of making dandy dolls', as well as being 'well engaged by his marauding after poultry in the dark'. Cauth explains all about her suffering and her family's resultant starvation because of Roger's antics. She cannot understand his 'booby game' when he is unable to save any of the dolls from the Hag's Son. The Grey Man tells her how Roger's antics are known of far and wide and he tries to soothe her. But she becomes suspicious of this 'old fairy' out on this 'haunted eve of May'. He tells her that he wants to warn Roger of an impending visit by the Hag's Son, and because he and his own family are 'bauble makers to the King and Queen of Spain', he has a personal interest in protecting the doll.

Cauth calls to Roger, who comes in raging at the noise from the 'rasp in your old windpipe that would frighten a horse from its oats'. An argument ensues but Roger won't engage in it because 'the joy is upon him' with his new doll. He recognizes the Grey Man and wants to know why he is there. The Grey Man hands him a bottle and orders that he drink from it when the Hag's Son comes to rob the windpipe from his new dandy doll at ten o'clock that night. Roger smells the vile liquid and refuses to drink it until the Grey Man warns him of dire consequences if he does not do so. Before leaving, the Grey Man takes time to admire himself in the mirror.

Roger claims that 'the heart and soul is gone out of me entirely', knowing something is going to happen to his latest dandy doll. He hides the doll as we hear Keerby, the priest's clerk, and Fr James approaching. Keerby warns the priest not to have 'hand, act, or part' with the dandy dolls. Keerby does not want to go in to Roger's kitchen on account of the 'bad name on the house' and he tells the priest how Roger was seen with 'two black ravens' on either shoulder in his younger days. Fr James is unimpressed by such pagan pishogues: he simply wants to know where his geese are. He is also afraid that Roger will get his 'new clutch of goslings' or his 'fine young grey goose with the cuck on her'. Demanding to see the dandy doll, he insists that if the dolls are responsible for Roger stealing his geese, then he is 'going to baptize it a good Catholic by the grace of God'. They name the doll Jug, after Roger's aunt, and Fr James and Keerby leave immediately after the baptism. Relieved to think that this might work against the Hag's Son, both Cauth and Roger doze off and, as the curtain falls, the child sings to the air of *It's mourn to hope that leaves me*.

Scene Two opens at one minute to ten and Cauth and Roger are still asleep. The Child is playing marbles on the floor, and imitating the clock's ticking. Cauth wakes up and warns the child to stop. The Clock strikes the hour and a voice outside calls 'open, quick'. Roger's friend Timmeen has come to warn them of the Hag's arrival. As Timmeen enters, the Hag's Son appears from a room, having come in through a slit in the window or a hole in the thatch that Roger has not fixed. He claims that baptizing the doll was useless against the power of his mother and himself. Timmeen and the Hag's Son rush at the doll and drag it off the table. Fr James and Keerby re-enter and neither their fighting nor praying will get rid of the supernatural characters. As Fr James tries to help Timmeen, the Hag's Son dodges the priest's blows.

The sound of a fife playing outside warns of the Hag's imminent arrival. She enters, fantastically dressed, and playing a flute. When she strikes Cauth with the instrument, her son is encouraged to join in the fray. Roger awakens to the sound of the priest roaring: 'the power of man shall conquer ... the power of the witch!'. Believing he is hitting the Hag, the Priest is actually hitting Timmeen. The Hag's Son grabs the windpipe from the latest doll, and Roger is immediately consumed with the desire to find a goose or a duck or even a turkey to eat. The Grey Man appears and only then does Roger remember the bottle. When he drinks from it an explosion occurs, and in the ensuing darkness we hear the noise of a struggle. The dimly lit figures of the Grey Man, the Hag and her Son are seen dragging Roger along.

Keerby claims to have witnessed the bottom of the bottle opening, as if on a hinge, and seeing 'the finest horse, black as jet, with red eyes on him, prancing and paving fit to be off' as well as a 'bully army, and captains, general, soldiers, with their cannons, swords and carabines, all in full bloom for war. Fr James reckons, 'Tis mysterious surely, and fantastic strange'. Keerby tells him what he wants to hear: that his geese are now safe because Roger has been carried away by the Hag and her Son 'riding on two Spanish asses ... galloping like the wind ... to their woeful den in the heart of the Barna hills'.

The theme of supernaturalism in *The Dandy Dolls*, which began with *The Magic Glasses*, has developed into a most fantastical tale, 'a glorious free-for-all where the imagination runs riot in a swirl of colour and a welter of words'.[126] Whatever about the lack of serious explanations for the incredible occurrences in *The Magic Glasses*, Fitzmaurice was adamant that in the *The Dandy Dolls*, the development of his dramatic fantasies was first and foremost a lesson in wild dramatic entertainment. The play is macabre and grotesque and wickedly humourous, but it is also accurate in its illustration of the Irish oral tradition in rural areas and telling fantastic tales around the fireside. It was only with the coming of electricity during the fifties and sixties that this tradition began to wane. An old neighbour of mine, referring to his younger days growing up in the countryside, often says, 'when we got the light, we lost the Banshee'.

Sadly, Fitzmaurice's five years in Kilcara Beg had shaded him from the realities of Abbey Theatre life. His return home had already caused his family to suffer a deep sense of frustration. His siblings worried about him. His dreams of free and easy days conducive to writing did not necessarily meet with the family's approval. It is unfortunate that these, his most creative years, would not result in the success that Fitzmaurice so desperately wanted to achieve. He was convinced that success with the Abbey Theatre would finally make his family proud of him. He wanted to prove that dreams could result in success unlike the dreams of his father. While today it is evident that Fitzmaurice was correct in believing in the excellence of these two plays, little had changed with Irish audiences or the Abbey directorship, as Fitzmaurice would find out.

9 | George Fitzmaurice's Drama: An Interpretation

It seems somewhat odd that while Fitzmaurice was most comfortable in the theatres of popular music hall entertainment, he strove for a career in a genre that was the polar opposite. Nonetheless, whether it was stubbornness or naivety, it is difficult to understand why he had not been sensible and followed the overwhelming success of *The Country Dressmaker* with another similar realistic comedy. Within a few months of his success with *The Country Dressmaker*, he was attempting to develop his writing into a more energetic source of entertainment: high drama, farce, humour and darkness. Looking back retrospectively, it seems to defy logic that his playwriting should deviate so quickly from his previous endeavours, particularly in light of the fact that he should have been more than aware of the demands of Dublin audiences. The result of his deviation, however, was his marginalization as a playwright. Yeats, who utilized the fact that the Irish individual was readily given to mingling the rational and the superstitious, concerned himself with how an idyllic Irish life could be portrayed. For his part, Fitzmaurice never intended denying the Irish person's rich cultural inheritance, but he refused to hide from the harsh realities of early twentieth century life. He saw a narrow-minded, priest-ridden, intolerant society, too taken up with materialism, and he was particularly offended by how public opinion could impinge upon people's personal lives.

The Pie Dish, The Magic Glasses and *The Dandy Dolls* are all set in farmhouses in North Kerry, their basic theme being the obsessive following of personal dreams. Leum Donoghue in *The Pie Dish* and Jaymony Shanahan in *The Magic Glasses* pursue dreams which result in death. Roger Carmody in *The Dandy Dolls* does not die but disappears over the hills of Barna having been kidnapped by the Hag, probably never to be seen again. All three individuals illustrate a determination to follow their dreams to conclusion, despite the pressures and influences of family, church and society. As the protagonists' imagination separates them from their families and society, their obsessions lead them to ignore the passing of time and everyday life. Roger, Jaymony, and Leum portray acts of individual thinking and conscience more readily identifiable in the Protestant ethos. The eccentricity portrayed by Fitzmaurice's dreamers was far from the dogma of the Catholic Church, which was an authoritative and all-powerful institution. The Church's influence on matters in the spheres of health, education, politics and culture was enormous.

During the dreamers' attempts to attain the impossible, the supernatural elements of the folk mind burst through the rational world into Fitzmaurice's drama, reflecting human traits such as greed, violence and wickedness. These supernatural characters are really versions of human failings 'blown up and made strange'.[127] It was in his Gaelic heritage that Fitzmaurice found his dark humour, love of fantasy and the grotesqueness of vision. In later years, his own description of his characters as *wicked old children* would describe in a nutshell his attempt at satirizing Yeats, the Catholic Church, and the nation itself. It may even seem at times that Yeats and the co-founders of the literary movement were just too grown up for Fitzmaurice's liking.

George's artistic dreamers, the Old Couples, the Quack Doctor and the Wise Child are all characters that can also be found in the mumming plays. This was a vibrant aspect of Irish tradition which the founders of the Irish Literary Theatre Society had ignored. The mumming tradition was undoubtedly a source of spectacle, poetry and strange action, where the natural order is disturbed. This sense of strange and disorderly spectacle is felt in Fitzmaurice's plays, where individual dreamers like Leum, Jaymony and Roger refuse to accept this social order that their families wish to maintain. Nothing matters but the completion of the pie dish or the dandy doll, and the amount of time spent in imaginary worlds is of no consequence to Jaymony. In these plays the interrelationship of supernatural and human worlds defies all logic and the old fairies' intrusion brings with it a complete breakdown in the natural order of things. The rural Irish tradition of accommodating supernatural or otherworldly dimensions as part of normal life militated against the acceptance of Fitzmaurice's plays. He insistently wove his characters around the inter-relationship between the supernatural and the human world, which embraced both primitive and contemporary society as being equally relative.

In Ireland at that time politics and culture were so inter-connected that art for its own sake was neither a necessity nor a priority, and ancient mythology was a framework in which uprisings could be explained and encouraged. As Fitzmaurice's protagonists fight a hopeless fight for their unrealistic dreams, their families are depicted as being totally devoid of imagination. For them the power and influence of church and society take precedence over all else, which would have proved difficult for a Protestant individual such as Fitzmaurice. However, he had immediate access to a world of Irish rural life, a life that Yeats, from his elevated status as an Anglo-Irish gentleman, could only romantically acknowledge. Frank Fay recognized what Fitzmaurice was doing when, in 1909, he said of the Abbey playwrights:

> These dear people don't know how to write plays: they can do dialogue and character, but except for Boyle and Fitzmaurice, they don't know how to write what will really act. Synge gets nearest to it, after Boyle and Fitz.[128]

Reacting against the Literary Revivalists' portrayals of legendary heroes and noble peasantry, George's personal circumstances dictated his greater ability to portray the rural reality than many of his Anglo-Irish literary counterparts. Not unlike Yeats's Countess Cathleen 'selling her soul to save her people', George illustrated that selling one's soul to the devil in order to gain more time to carry out one's selfish and unrealistic ideals was as dramatically relevant. However, while Yeats took the demons out of folklore, Fitzmaurice insisted they remained. Fitzmaurice satirizes the ideals of the Literary Revival, and by relating to the ancient Gaelic society's true heritage and culture, he attempts to free the literary movement of its nonsensical ideals. While he spent hours dreaming of an idyllic literary career, he feared that Ireland's rich cultural inheritance was being replaced by the Catholic Church's edification. The Church's teachings on sex and morality were anathema to him and he was unafraid of portraying what he perceived as being the replacements of the old and noble order in his plays.

Through the illumination of imagination, Fitzmaurice's fantasy illustrates the consequences of the dreamers' individuality. Without patronizing them, he simply wished to encourage audiences to be transported to the realms hidden somewhere between the rational and the superstitional. Fitzmaurice was also prepared to break from the acceptable theatrical vein and to magnify stage life to the extreme. He built his drama on movement, poetry, violence, terror, humour and delight. As Fintan O'Toole correctly surmises in his essay *The Magic Glasses of George Fitzmaurice*, too much was taken at face value when it came to Fitzmaurice's work; and too little was made of its sophistication and downright mischievousness.

Fitzmaurice's dreamers are a type of 'anti-hero' and he never offers them sympathy, but portrays them as being equally greedy, fearful and selfish as those characters surrounding them. Lest we forget, Roger, Jaymony and Leum are as capable of the same wickedness, greed and violence as their own families inflict on them. Roger insists on giving all his time to creating his dandy dolls and robbing the priest's geese, eating them 'bones and all', despite his wife's nagging and his family's starvation. Jaymony nags and berates his mother for not actually having the tea made before he descends from the loft. Leum Donoghue is a selfish, deluded old man who has never been there for his family since he took to creating the perfect pie dish. Audiences were shocked and declined to accept Fitzmaurice's male characters as tolerable images of the Irishman, who had fought oppression for centuries. The portrayal of the Irish male as selfish was simply not one that conformed to the mythical heroes of old.

Today's theatre accepts the invocation of 'a world of terror and awe, where reality is painful and myth the escape route of the deluded'.[129] This prompts us to ask if reality is too painful for Jaymony, Leum, and Roger? Are these characters deluded by their ideals, or disillusioned by reality? Early twentieth century audiences may have thought Fitzmaurice was deluded. He affirmed his beliefs by marrying the supernatural and human worlds so closely that the results were viewed as an insult to the ancestral and mythical elements of Irishness.

Ironically, the only receptive audience for Fitzmaurice's experimental drama was an English one. His works, taken in the contemporary context of the literary revival, were far too explosive for all concerned, and truthfully, George Fitzmaurice's work was so packed with explosives that it is surprising that any of his plays were staged at all. In creating his own dramatic entertainment he relied greatly on his knowledge and love of the commercial theatre. He realized that melodrama, farce, action and physical movement were elements that had audiences coming back for more. However, his plays were interpreted as being closer to the stage Irish 'buffoonery' and were disliked by Yeats because of that. Fitzmaurice had his dreamers face the condemnation of their families and a more potent retribution by the larger and external society or institution. No one escapes the dark ridicule in his plays, and he not only parodies the wrath of the priest, but also his protagonists' selfish idealism as well as their families' behaviour. Sadly, Fitzmaurice did not escape the condemnations of those who completely misunderstood his drama.

Leum screams for the devil's help in front of a Catholic audience; Jaymony lives in the loft peering through the glasses at the naked women of Tír na nÓg; and Roger lives in his world consumed by dandy dolls and his addiction to the priest's geese. The question most often asked by his detractors, who viewed these plays as little more than blasphemous nonsense, was the same as Fr Troy's question in *The Pie Dish*: 'What was in this at all? What was in this at all?'[130] It is little wonder, then, that the reaction to Fitzmaurice's work was one of potent denial and rejection.

10 | 1913: Rejection of *The Dandy Dolls*

It is probable that the long five-year period at home in Kilcara Beg without paid employment resulted in the early development of George's alcohol addiction. When life did not meet with his expectations, he escaped his disappointment and his family's deep-set annoyances by spending long periods of time in the pubs of Duagh and Abbeyfeale. Whatever savings he might have had did not last long and one wonders how George could possibly have afforded to survive at all, as the miniscule royalties he had received from *The Country Dressmaker* were probably put towards the mortgage of the house and farm at Kilcara Beg.[131] Locals readily acknowledge George's alcohol addiction by recalling the many times he was found staggering along the roads late at night unable to recall the direction of home. Indeed, it later became a common and pathetic sight to see him falling from the bus that had brought him from Dublin. These incidents, like his eccentricities, were often related in a humorous fashion. Just as Jaymony is forever captured peering into his red, blue and brown glasses, Fitzmaurice can be pictured staring into his pint glass, perhaps in search of the elusive success he yearned for, and in later years, in search of the reasons why it all went wrong.

At this point Ireland was facing turbulent times ahead as the political temperature rose dramatically. While the country witnessed social and political disturbances, the Abbey was attempting to continue without Annie Horniman's subsidy, which she had withdrawn in 1910 when, through a lapse in communication, the theatre failed to close on the day of Edward VII's death. The Abbey was forced to tour England and America to try and keep the theatre afloat. Synge had died in 1909 and new playwrights such as T.C. Murray and Lennox Robinson began to reveal a new theatrical realism, which stemmed from the typical Abbey-type play. Meanwhile, the Abbey was facing up to criticisms of its policies. For instance,

Ernest Boyd went to great lengths to lambaste the theatre for its lack
of programme variety, accusing it of merely confining attention to
plays that attract good houses'.[132] It was the attempts to attract good
houses that resulted in annual revivals of *The Country Dressmaker*.
These, as well as the positive English reviews *The Pie Dish* had
received, heralded an opportunity for Fitzmaurice to consider writing
new work. By the end of 1912 he was so assured of the quality of *The
Magic Glasses* and *The Dandy Dolls* that he sent these two plays to
the Abbey Theatre in November that year.

As *The Country Dressmaker* was still financially important to the
theatre's survival, Fitzmaurice's trip to Dublin during the early months
of 1913 coincided with another of its revivals, as Holloway records:

> Fitzmaurice told me he considered the present performance of his
> play better than the original one – he had not seen the play since. He
> liked [Fred] O'Donovan as Luke, and thought Eileen O'Doherty
> grasped the subtleties of the conflict of Julia Shea.[133]

His attendance at the Abbey was not, of course, his primary reason
for visiting Dublin. His double submission pointed to his intention to
have both plays produced simultaneously. This remains an important
factor in their interpretation today. However, the Abbey directors
considered that it was too volatile a time to stage. *The Dandy Dolls*
and it was decided to wait until a later date. Fitzmaurice seems to have
accepted this at the time. Although there are no extant records of this
decision, Fitzmaurice allowed the production of *The Magic Glasses* to
go ahead, content in the knowledge that he would see *The Dandy
Dolls* produced at a later date. March saw *The Country Dressmaker*
staged once more, though it is not known if George attended or not.
One has to wonder if he might have stayed in Dublin to support John
Guinan, whose first Abbey production, *The Cuckoo's Nest*, opened that
same month.[134]

Once again, Fitzmaurice utterly defied and confused critics and
audiences alike when his one-act fantasy, *The Magic Glasses,* was
staged for three nights beginning on 24 April· The play was one part of
a double bill, the other play being the two-act *Broken Faith,* by Cork
women, Suzanne R. Day and Geraldine Cummins. Produced by
Lennox Robinson, Fitzmaurice's latest offering received less
newspaper column space than *Broken Faith* and was deemed 'a piece
of unmitigated nonsense, capitally acted and productive of a good deal
of amusement but not worth detailed examination'.[135] According to
one reviewer it was 'a clever little joke', while another claimed it to be
'an extraordinary farce, which in its quaint and rich vocabulary, keeps
up the best tradition of the Abbey Theatre'. The latter more positive
review had, however, missed the play's theme. Perhaps critics were by

now predisposed to expect strange and incomprehensible drama from Fitzmaurice, so that the playwright's themes and idealistic definition of drama were not properly considered. The play was, however, staged again that October, probably because Robinson liked it.

Despite these negative reviews, Fitzmaurice remained positive in light of the expected production of *The Dandy Dolls*, which always remained his favourite play. An Abbey Theatre English tour in June 1913 which included *The Magic Glasses* and *The Country Dressmaker* in its repertoire, also kept his hopes high.[136] Incredibly, vital evidence regarding the submission and eventual rejection of *The Dandy Dolls* has never been critically analysed until now and is significant in any analysis of Fitzmaurice's relationship with the Abbey. Yeats and Lady Gregory eventually rejected *The Dandy Dolls*, and Fitzmaurice was utterly disgusted by the way in which he had been treated. The Berg Collection housed in the New York Library contains a letter from George Fitzmaurice to Lady Gregory written from Kilcara Beg on 21 September 1913. It reads as follows:

> Dear Madam,
>
> As I have already informed you I returned *The Dandy Dolls* to the theatre at the request of Mr Yeats. The reasons you give for his rejecting it were such as he gave himself, but I did not accept them as valid, nor the criticism in general which he was pleased to make on the play, inasmuch as he was utterly at sea as to the inner meaning and drift of the piece, and I wrote two letters to him explaining this. The second rejection, however, I took as final and I did not intend to bother further about getting it taken at the Abbey. Shortly afterwards I got a letter from the Abbey asking me to send on the play, stating that Mr Yeats thought it and *The Magic Glasses* the best plays I had given them but that *The Dandy Dolls* could not be produced at that particular period – about Easter. If this was not an intimation that the play was accepted and would be played in due course, I don't know what to think.
>
> I am, Madam.
> Yours faithfully,
> Geo. Fitzmaurice.[137]

Apart from the fact that this letter illustrates the writer's ability to defend his work, it also proves the importance of the play to the playwright. He was happy that his five years or so in Kilcara Beg had resulted in two extraordinary one-act dramas, and he was confident that both plays should have confirmed him as one of the leading playwrights of his generation. George had come to Dublin in Dick Whittington fashion, carrying with him a notion of a literary fortune because of his two brilliant new plays. The rejection was a bitter blow to his self-belief and confidence. He was not willing to heed Yeats's criticisms of the play, especially when he believed the Abbey director was 'at sea as to the inner meaning and drift of the piece'. It must have been a bitter pill for him to swallow as he watched Yeats actively encouraging other playwrights such as R.J. Ray. The Abbey director had never shown the slightest interest in Fitzmaurice's career and George knew he was being treated as nothing less than a rural fool. Yeats's to-ing and fro-ing with this play proved too much to bear for the Kerry man, particularly when his lack of understanding regarding it was so evident. A culmination of this bitter rejection, combined with the utter embarrassment it brought, was to have a terrible impact on him throughout the following years. Fitzmaurice now faced the humiliating prospect of having to return to paid employment, thereby conforming to his family's wishes and expectations. By 29 December 1913, he was reinstated in the Civil Service: the nightmare was set to continue.

Fitzmaurice returned to Dublin on a full-time basis at a difficult time in the city's history as the Lock Out spanned four months of the particularly harsh winter of 1913-14. The 1914 Abbey season saw the inclusion of Fitzmaurice's popular *The Country Dressmaker* during an American tour. The *Chicago Examiner* records the evening performance of the play along with Lady Gregory's *The Rising of the Moon*, on 14 March, although it is strange that it only played for one night.[138]

Now back in his dead-end job, it was only a matter of time before there was a dramatically noticeable physical change in Fitzmaurice's demeanour, which was duly noted by Holloway during 1914:

> I saw Fitzmaurice cross from Clare Street to Merrion Square, his hands buried deep in his brown top coat pockets, and a cigarette in his mouth. He had on a tweed cap. His very sallow complexion and small insignificant figure completed the picture as he sneaked along, rather than walked – a strange lonely little man.[139]

The results of the earlier rejection were tellingly obvious. There is no doubt but that Fitzmaurice's deterioration had begun, and the bitterness and loneliness he felt culminated in his delight at the Abbey's recent bad fortune:

> I bet that Fitzmaurice would be pleased with the play *The Cobbler* and its interpretation. He always is when the play is horrid and the acting of the same quality – and sure enough he was delighted. I often wonder how it is the same people can only see merit in the meritless: Fitzmaurice is a case in point.[140]

Even the 1914 publication of Fitzmaurice's *Five Plays*, (*The Country Dressmaker, The Dandy Dolls, The Magic Glasses, The Pie Dish* and *The Moonlighter*), had little impact on his career.[141] In fact, it seems that the number of complete volumes of the Dublin edition that were produced numbered only a few hundred.[142] In 1917, Little, Brown and Company published the collection in the United States, but again with little or no impact. We can be certain that Fitzmaurice was very unimpressed with a review in *The Irish Times* in 1914, which read:

> Unlike many authors, Mr Fitzmaurice is, in our opinion, superior in his longer drama ... hence one may come to the conclusion that the development of character, or rather the play of character, as different circumstances affected it from time to time, is well worked out ... The shorter plays do not give an opportunity for such character-drawing ... As regards the last piece The Dandy Dolls...the abusive language...is repulsive, and coming close at the close of the book, the piece cannot fail to leave a sense of disappointment with the reader.[143]

Throughout Europe, nations such as Germany, Russia and Austria were in a power struggle and war was brewing. By 6 August Britain had entered the First World War and although the Home Rule Bill had received royal assent, it was postponed. Many of Redmond's Irish Volunteers left Ireland to serve in the British Army, while militant nationalists, such as Pearse and MacDonagh, saw this period as an opportunity for the advancement of Ireland's political struggle. As the First World War began, it brought economic prosperity to Ireland. Nationalists believed that England's necessity was Ireland's opportunity and that Home Rule could not be very far away. However, it seemed to Fitzmaurice that he had no future in the theatre and that he had reached a personal stalemate in his temporary Civil Service position. With the outlook bleak, he felt there was only one option open to him: to be amongst the 200,000 Irish men who joined the British army to fight in the Great War. Much would change dramatically in Ireland while Fitzmaurice was away and these dramatic changes, coupled with his experiences of war, would affect him most profoundly in the years to come.

11 | The Return from France

There was at least one production of *The Country Dressmaker* at the Abbey during Fitzmaurice's war years in France. The 1917 revival saw an almost entirely new cast. One reviewer considered this cast 'could give useful points to the original impersonators'.[144] It was during this time of bloodshed in Europe that opportunists in Ireland saw a chance to advance their own republican aspirations. This culminated in the 1916 Easter Rising, when Padraig Pearse and his six fellow conspirators signed the Proclamation which he read aloud to an astonished audience outside the General Post Office in Dublin. It led to bloody fighting between British and Republican forces throughout the city centre. The Abbey was in the middle of the battle zone, situated between the GPO and the headquarters of the Citizens' Army at Liberty Hall. It seems, however, that it was one of the few undamaged buildings left standing, though a number of staff and actors at the Abbey took part in the actual fighting.[145] During the General Election of 1918, the Irish party neared collapse as Sinn Féin secured seventy-three seats and 48% of the votes cast.[146] Those who remained unincarcerated convened at Dáil Éireann in 1919. Between 1918 and 1920 class conflict was a major localized problem, while sectarianism intensified in Northern Ireland. In January 1919, Dáil Éireann ratified the establishment of an Irish Republic and additional British troops and Black and Tans were rushed to Ireland. The country would not see an end to the bloodshed until 1923.

It had fallen to Lady Gregory to try and provide the theatre with some semblance of continuity during these years when it had endured a succession of managers. Actors were beginning to respond to the call to Hollywood and worldwide fame. The Great War had reduced audience numbers, while players' reduced salaries resulted in actors and actresses leaving. The financial position of the Abbey was appalling and the contemporary trend was towards rural comedies as audiences eagerly sought light, comic rural pieces during these dark times. All the while, cinema was forcing changes in theatre-going habits and picture houses had been opening in Dublin, Belfast and Cork since 1910. Yeats's detachment from the Abbey became obvious, as he had begun to drift towards staging his plays for audiences in the drawing rooms of the rich. Although Yeats would write six new plays between 1910 and 1920, most of them were staged privately, as his work was not in tune with popular drama; not unlike the fantasies of George Fitzmaurice. His response to the Easter Rising was the 1919 play, *The Dreaming of the Bones,* which he held back from production, believing it to be 'too politically explosive'.[147]

Although there are questions regarding whether or not Fitzmaurice saw active service during his time in France, his wartime experiences were not without their serious psychological effects. He had been a member of 'Kitchener's Army' and served as a private in the Third Echelon Army Service Corps, of the B.E.F. with a salary of less than seven shillings a week. Fitzmaurice was known to have participated in heated discussions around the topics of religious bigotry and national politics.[148] His fears regarding the changes Home Rule might bring for the minority of the populace were already heightened before his departure for the Front.

The affects of the Great War on soldiers are well documented, and the quietly spoken Fitzmaurice endured great suffering during his time away. The unfortunate writer's experiences would continue to haunt him for the rest of his life. His mother died just a few months before he came home and he erected a headstone over her grave in Duagh on his return.[149] He was already thirty-seven years old when he first joined the British Army, and the horrendous five years in France aged him greatly. He returned a much weaker man. Although by now he was forty-two years of age, physically he appeared much older. The rejection he had felt before his departure in 1914 still simmered beneath the ravaging wounds of war, though he attempted to resume a normal working life in his Civil Service position. His mental suffering, however, would become all too apparent, and by 1921 even his inability to 'sit out plays' in the Abbey is recorded.[150] Later records refer to his having to walk around at the back of the theatre during his favourite music hall shows.[151] By 1923, Holloway records that Fitzmaurice did not read as much as he once did and if he read at all, it was 'by the light of an unshaded lamp and a candle – finding such a light very soft and soothing to his eyes'.[152] As he still attended music hall shows, it is possible to surmise that his fear of attending the Abbey may be the result of an innate fear of the anti-treaty troops' presence there during performances.

Fitzmaurice was amazed at the lack of any great welcome for British soldiers in Ireland and hurriedly rid himself of all recognizable associations with the Army. An Irish man in a British soldier's uniform was by no means a hero, but rather, he was identified as a traitor and a servant of the Crown that had denied Home Rule to the Irish. The Irish Republican Army regarded ex-soldiers as potential informers and Fitzmaurice was well aware of the IRA's stronghold in North Kerry and its takeover of the old Fitzmaurice ancestral home of Duagh House during 'the troubles'. Amazingly, the catastrophic world event that Fitzmaurice had played such a courageous part in was ignored to such an extent that the Irish population was content to accept that the First World War had little or nothing to do with them, despite the war-time economic boom at home.

Post-War Europe began to experience the flowering of Expressionism in the realms of theatre, art and literature, as artists responded to the complete devastation and loss caused by the War. Europe began to recognize a lack of cultural stability as all European empires, excepting the British, had crumbled during the War. Fitzmaurice, for all his experimental theatrical forms was, at this point, as much stifled by his inability to express himself after having fought in the war as he had been by the condemnation and rejection of his pre-war dramatic fantasies. Ireland would remain very much outside the new wave of artistic expressionism engulfing the rest of Europe. The horror, despair and intensity of his wartime experiences should have shaped him as a playwright of significance, but it was difficult to cope in a country where he already felt an outsider, both culturally and artistically.

An important development in Irish theatre had occurred in 1918, with the foundation of the Dublin Drama League by Lennox Robinson. Under Yeats's presidency, its primary objective was to produce the work of foreign writers, such as Pirandello. The League's foundation resulted in a vitally needed alternative and a second serious form of theatre for Dublin. The League succeeded beyond its original expectations and sufficient demand for continental drama would eventually herald the opening of the Gate Theatre in 1928.

Despite his ambitions of resurrecting his career as a national playwright, George became paranoid at being identified with the British Empire. He did not take a place in Trinity College, as was the prerogative available to ex-British soldiers, because the College represented the raw face of the Empire and Protestantism to the Irish. University was not a financially viable option for him at any rate, as he would have lost his temporary Civil Service position and the meagre income it offered. In terms of his Civil Service career, his position was already extremely insecure. He returned as a temporary clerk to a Civil Service infiltrated by the IRA, at a time when such appointments could be highly politicized. As a member of a Protestant minority living in an overwhelmingly Catholic country, Fitzmaurice could derive little comfort from the increasing power of conservatism. He decided the best course of action to take was to keep his head down and be patient in order to safeguard his personal security while he was attempting to resume his playwriting career.

There is certainly no evidence that his joining the British army was out of a sense of allegiance to the Empire. Like many thousands of his fellow Irishmen who fought on the British side during the Great War, Fitzmaurice, afraid of what might happen to him as a Protestant once Home Rule became a reality,[153] sought an escape route from a country where he felt rejected. Now with his fresh ambitions of resuming his playwriting career, he would attempt to break back into the Abbey, albeit during a particularly dark and desperate time for the theatre.

Lennox Robinson was back at the helm once more, but the Dublin curfew caused the theatre to close and as the War of Independence drew to an end, Ireland was finally partitioned. The Free State would consist of twenty-six counties and the six counties comprising Northern Ireland would remain British. This Treaty, as it was called, led to a most bitter Civil War, where brother was often pitched against brother, and father took up arms against son. Yeats became totally disillusioned and spent most of his time living in England. Despite Lennox Robinson's best efforts, the affects of the Civil War had a disastrous effect on the National Theatre. It was a dangerous time to chance a night out to the theatre, and audiences dwindled further. Thomas MacGreevy wrote in *The Irish Independent* during September 1922:

> We seem to have practically no theatre enthusiasts. A week or so ago I went down to the Abbey on a Saturday night ... and found myself one of fourteen people in the stalls! The pit was full and the circle was nearly as empty as the stalls.[154]

During the Treaty negotiations and the Civil War, comedy and farce were the only sure ways of attracting audiences at all. Unfortunately, without the European influences, Irish drama was proving very stale as its subject matter never varied. *The Country Dressmaker* was still enjoying revivals during this time and was staged in January and September 1920; February 1921; January and December 1922 and again during November 1923. Was this a motivating factor in writing new work that George intended for Abbey production? Certainly, enjoying regular success with *The Country Dressmaker* must have been at least one influencing factor. When

Maunsel reissued *The Country Dressmaker* in 1921, Fitzmaurice had a further incentive to write and it was in one of these reissued copies, found in Fitzmaurice's room after his death forty-two years later, that he had made handwritten changes to the second act. This is the version that appears in the Dolmen Press Volume of Fitzmaurice's *Realistic Plays*, published in 1970.

After returning to work in the Civil Service, Fitzmaurice began writing once more. However, fearful of the political tensions in the city during 1920, he returned to Duagh for a period of extended sick leave – an incredible 190 days. Since his return from the Front he had steadily increased his writing efforts. It is speculated that he began to write any of the following three plays: *The Waves of the Sea*,[155] *Twixt the Giltinans and the Carmodys*[156]and *The Enchanted Land* in 1921. However, I believe that in his attempts to cope with life on his return, he turned firstly to the genre of fantasy that he loved most, by writing *The Enchanted Land*. Despite the 1913 rejection of *The Dandy Dolls*, Fitzmaurice was willing to bow to pressure and write a play that would be acceptable to the Abbey. Because of this reality and his desperate need to see his first post-war production, on the completion of *The Enchanted Land* he compromised and scripted *Twixt the Giltinans and the Carmodys*.

According to Holloway, George's realistic play, *Twixt the Giltinans and the Carmodys,* was submitted to the Abbey in late 1921, and after a conversation with a Mr Perrin in 1923, he wrote:

> ... it is about a year and a half since Fitzmaurice brought us the play ... Fitzmaurice is one of those fellows whom one never gets to know ... Fitzmaurice had been written to several times to tell him of his play being in rehearsal but Fitzmaurice never took any heed![157]

This information, as well as the fact that he spent a further seventy-nine days on sick leave in 1921, leaves us with ample evidence that he completed *Twixt the Giltinans and the Carmodys* in 1921. It seems likely that he submitted this play to the Abbey on his arrival back to Dublin from Duagh.

During 1922 Fitzmaurice was still only a temporary clerk on much reduced wages by comparison with permanent staff. It is amazing that in the political climate of the time he managed to keep any position at all, given his prolonged absences. He became friends with his new supervisor, Mr Frank Lyons, who described George as a gentleman. Fitzmaurice appreciated others who were gentlemanly and although he was not particularly outgoing himself, he had a good sense of humour – that same sense of humour still spoken of in Duagh. Politics and music hall shows were his favourite topics of conversations and rarely, if ever, would he speak of his own body of work.[158]

Ireland was somewhat of a cultural and artistic vacuum during the 1920s and 1930s, and Fitzmaurice's failure to look elsewhere for an audience was, perhaps, his greatest downfall. Lady Gregory and Yeats had been very much on the Free State side during the Civil War and a new relationship between the national theatre and the State was in its infancy. As post-Civil War Ireland moved eventually into a period of relative calm, so also would the Abbey attempt to follow suit by allowing time for things to settle. George Fitzmaurice was prepared to compromise the true potential of his writing in the hope that a new realistic comedy of his would bring him the success he craved. Once again he illustrated the problem he faced all of his life: 'whether to write to please an audience or to write what he knew to be true'.[159] However, his sole ambition at this point was to see his new play, *Twixt the Giltinans and the Carmodys*, on the Abbey stage.

12 | The 1920s

Although academics agree that *Twixt the Giltinans and the Carmodys* is one of his weaker plays, it has some similarities in theme and character to *The Country Dressmaker*. It also calls to mind some of the darker elements of his earlier folk fantasies. The Abbey accepted the play and Lennox Robinson was one of the few people who liked it, which is reflected in an interview during September 1922. Speaking of the Abbey's plans for the following season, Robinson boasted that the Abbey was about to give audiences 'a wild, match-making one-act comedy by George Fitzmaurice'.[160]

Lennox Robinson produced *Twixt the Giltinans and the Carmodys* during 1923. [161] It would be the last of Fitzmaurice's new plays to be staged by the Abbey during his lifetime. One of his longer one-act plays, this work tells the tale of a shrewd and greedy matchmaker's tactical manoeuvres and a rather innocent middle-aged man recently returned from the United States, it is rumoured, with a fortune. In order to make his own fortune, matchmaker Michael Clancy must make sure that this Yank, Billeen Twomey, is married by 5pm that same evening.

The scene opens in the kitchen of Shiwaun Daly, (Billeen's aunt), where she sits sewing her death shroud. It is rumoured that Billeen is a millionaire who keeps his money in a locked suitcase and has promised Clancy £2,000 when he marries. Clancy is determined to get Billeen to marry either the 'graceful' Bridie Giltinan, or the 'gamey' Madge Carmody, and even manages to convince Billeen that Tomaus Brack will kill him if he is not married by 5pm that same evening. Meanwhile, the servant girl, Old Jane, broods over her thoughts of all the gold in the case. While Billeen does not seem to care about his wealth, it is what keeps Old Jane going as she childishly dreams about the 'jingle of it and the bing! bing!'

Clancy instructs the Giltinans and Carmodys to call to the cottage, albeit at different times, as he does not want either family to realize his plans. Anticipating that Billeen will marry one of the women he has chosen, Clancy has a priest 'planked nice and snug for himself in the little barn waiting to be called as soon as he's wanted'. When both families finally realize the tricks Clancy has been playing, they converge on the cottage looking for an explanation, where a catfight breaks out between Madge and Bridie. Clancy loses his temper and threatens everyone with a pike as Billeen tries to act as peacemaker. With just six minutes to go before the 5pm deadline, Billeen is under severe pressure. He surprises one and all by deciding that the woman for him is in fact 'our darling Jane'. It turns out that there is only three years between herself and Billeen and that 'Old Jane' is merely a nickname. Clancy agrees that she has more reason to marry Billeen having suffered a lot of drudgery down through the years.

The once 'suspended priest' Fr Dansell, who has been 'taken back again' by the church, is called in. It was not uncommon for a priest to be temporarily suspended, for example, because of an alcohol addiction. This allusion to addiction might possibly be a reference by Fitzmaurice to his own problems with alcohol.

Billeen and Old Jane exchange vows and the priest is paid his £10. Old Jane now looks for the keys to the case holding Billeen's fortune. All is revealed and the fortune is considerably smaller than anticipated because of Billeen's difficulty with arithmetic. Old Jane is thoroughly disgusted as she sees her dreams come crashing down about her feet. Clancy is also enraged at not getting exactly what he had been promised. Yet, despite this strangest of weddings, the couple decide to make the best of their marriage. They make the occasion a celebration and buy a ring the next day. We are left wondering about the outcome of the marriage when, at the final curtain, 'a loud kiss is heard'.

The usual Fitzmaurice themes run through the play: materialism and greed, unreality, and making the best of a bad situation. However, the suspended priest, the strange marriage and the couple's antagonism towards each other are darker elements introduced into the play. J.D. Riley believed there was much more to it than 'met the eye' and summed it up by saying; 'the rather ghoulish undertones leave the reader wondering'.[162] Maurice Kennedy believed the play followed *The Country Dressmaker* in theme, although without the original touches.[163] Indeed, it crosses one's mind that Fitzmaurice may have been suggesting comparisons between marriage and death as the play begins with Shiwaun's shroud sewing, and concludes with a marriage that might eventually become a very antagonistic one. Although it is described as a realistic play, one cannot help wondering if the priest's 'curious little smile' is an allusion to the supernatural world. With an excellent producer, the elements of farce and dark humour might outweigh the simple comic aspects of the play, thus overcoming its inherent weaknesses and allowing it come to life. A more serious study of this play might also shed some light on Fitzmaurice's disposition after his return to Ireland.

After its opening night, Holloway recorded that the 'Company played the farce with high spirits' although he felt the players could make nothing out of it.[164] *The Irish Times* reported the play to be of 'little dramatic merits or values' yet, 'the mere fact of its being a bright comedy ... [is] something of a relief after Mr Ray's gloomy play'.[165] When Holloway told Fitzmaurice that he had already seen the play twice, Fitzmaurice's reply was 'I pity you!' That remark probably reflects his personal disappointment at the script as well as the production standards. Holloway records that after their meeting, 'he left him [Fitzmaurice] going up the stairs to the balcony to his play for the first time'.[166] It is now generally believed that this conversation between Holloway and Fitzmaurice records the very last time that George ever set foot in the Abbey.[167]

Dáil Éireann had narrowly approved The Treaty in January 1922 and a bitter election campaign followed. The result of that election, in June 1922, ratified the pro-Treaty position and a national government was set up under the leadership of Arthur Griffith. Griffith died shortly afterward and William T. Cosgrave succeeded him. A bloody Civil War ensued. (The Fianna Fáil party under de Valera would not enter the Dáil until 1927). Despite the Civil War and the pervasive doom and gloom, the Abbey remained open for thirty-four weeks during 1923, producing fifty plays, ten of these being new productions, although some of the older material was 'rather roughly handled'.[168] Almost all productions were poor as both writing standards and production illustrated 'frequent shoddiness'. By now, Dubliners identified the Abbey as a source of great fun and gossip. Brinsley MacNamara condemned the theatre's directors for concentrating on plays of Irish life, as he believed that this resulted in the 'stultification of all their aims and almost complete obliteration of the force ... , which at one time the theatre bade fair to be'.[169]

Just as 1922 and 1923 were turbulent and difficult times for the country, life at the Abbey was no different, with troops regularly visiting the premises. According to Abbey Theatre 1923 records, Fitzmaurice's last submission to the Abbey was a one-act play, *The Green Stone*, which was subsequently rejected. The political situation was, more than likely, a critical factor in the context of Fitzmaurice's decision not to submit further plays. The theatre was regularly raided by de Valera's anti-treaty forces, which often forced it to close. A month after *Twixt the Giltinans and the Carmodys* ended its run, Sean O'Casey's *Shadow of a Gunman* opened for a three-night stint. The staging of this play resulted in the Abbey receiving renewed threats from the anti-treaty forces.

Meanwhile the Free State government was faced with an uphill struggle as it tried to regenerate the economy and establish law and order. Yeats became a Senator for the duration of the Cosgrave-led Cumann na nGaedhael government, and with Lady Gregory he petitioned the government to take over the Abbey, believing there was little more that they could achieve. By this stage the Abbey was on the verge of bankruptcy and after much discussion and consultation it was announced in 1925 that the theatre would receive an annual government subsidy of £850.

Republicans despised the Minister for Finance, Ernest Blythe, who would later become a central figure in the Abbey, for his betrayal of ideals, as he had once stated that Ireland would not accept the partition of the country. However, as Yeats proudly announced that the Abbey was to become the first state-subsidized theatre in the English-speaking world, Blythe took a certain amount of pleasure in being seen as its patron. A government-appointed individual would now have to sit on the Board of Directors. This effectively meant that the autonomy of the Abbey Board was artistically compromised. The subsidy also meant the revamping of part of the premises into the Peacock Theatre, which Yeats hoped would be an experimental theatre for poetic drama. This small theatre was often leased because of financial considerations and provided the Gate Theatre with its first home.

When Fitzmaurice's department came under the jurisdiction of the Department of Agriculture and Fisheries in 1924, he received a slight salary increase. Already quite stooped, he was finding working life extremely difficult at this stage and, because of his infirmity, he was unable to lift the heavy record books. In 1925, at the age of forty-eight, he finally became a clerical officer. He received a salary increase in his new position, where his supervisor found his work 'accurate, reliable and competent'.[170]

With the new state involvement, it is no surprise that George Fitzmaurice refused to allow the Abbey to revive *The Country Dressmaker* in 1925, a refusal that he would not withdraw until his retirement in 1942. His disappearance from the Abbey has for far too long been attributed to Yeats's jealousy of him, an accusation fuelled by Austin Clarke. One must apportion some of the blame to Fitzmaurice himself for his seeming indifference towards his own advancement and, apart from his fear of State involvement in the theatre, his apparent lack of motivation in seeking other theatrical outlets for his work. This combination led to his virtual disappearance from the theatre. Fitzmaurice had never enjoyed the luxury of a literary patron and had to rely on a mundane job that left him without the luxury of making personal choices in life. He found another outlet for his work through the medium of print in the *Dublin Magazine* publications, when *The Linnaun Shee* was published in 1924. His good friend and editor Seumas O'Sullivan (James Starkey) was a vital link for Fitzmaurice down through the years.

The reason for Fitzmaurice's disappearance from the Abbey stage is understandable in view of the political upheaval of the time. The ex-British soldier did not feel comfortable in the new Free State. He also felt that he had not received enough recognition for his pre-war folk fantasies. However, as he turned his back on the Abbey Theatre, it is almost incomprehensible that he chose to disregard the Dublin Drama League, and later on, the Gate Theatre. A relationship with a theatre was crucial if he was to have any chance of revitalizing his playwriting career in an experimental vein. It is a mystery as to what he thought he might achieve by having his work published yet unperformed. Perhaps he lived in the hope that his discovery would come sooner rather than later, when some visionary producer might read this work and herald him as a genius.[171] His aspirations in this regard proved unfounded, and it is frustrating to consider his disregard for any alternative to the Abbey, such as the Gate, which might indeed have welcomed his experimental drama.

Meanwhile, the Abbey Theatre was still reliant on popular drama, and staged new plays such as *Professor Tim* by George Shiels. Shiels was, along with other writers including Murray, MacNamara and Robinson, responsible for good box office returns. During 1926, the Abbey staged a production of O'Casey's *The Plough and the Stars* on the tenth anniversary of the Easter Rising. Attacks on the play came from veterans of the republican side and also from George O'Brien, the State appointed member of the Abbey Board, who urged Yeats to cut various scenes.[172]

The Abbey was put in a position of defending itself against those who saw both O'Casey's play and the Abbey as undermining the very basis of the State itself. Such was the nationalist feeling that men armed with revolvers plotted to kidnap Barry Fitzgerald (who played Fluther), so as to stop him appearing.[173] When *The Plough and the Stars* proved to be Yeats's last stand against the nationalist mob, O' Casey left for London in March and many were glad to be rid of him. During 1928, the Abbey Theatre took a critical decision to cause no

further controversy: a decision that resulted in the rejection of O'
Casey's *The Silver Tassie*. Its second act which displays a mix of
expressionism and naturalism in its use of plainchant and
expressionistic devices, was deemed both stark and disturbing.
However, O' Casey's international reputation allowed him to find
outlets in London and Broadway, while Fitzmaurice remained
detached and adrift from every theatrical opportunity back in Dublin.

Yeats had by now become heavily influenced by Japanese Noh
theatre, and his plays were very much outside the Abbey experience.
He premiered his plays privately. This period was a bleak one, not only
for the theatre in general, but also for many writers and artists in
Ireland.

As a result of the success of the Dublin Drama League, the Gate
Theatre opened its doors in 1928 and offered a programme that was
an explicit alternative to the Abbey by presenting foreign drama as
well as encouraging Irish playwrights. Ironically, its first production
was Ibsen's *Peer Gynt*, a play that Fitzmaurice's *The Dandy Dolls* is
often compared with as an almost 'distillation of that early Ibsenite
urge'.[174] Yet why did Fitzmaurice ignore this critical dramatic
development? Is it simply the case that he was not invited to have his
work produced there, before Lord Longford's 1950s' request to stage
The Enchanted Land?[175] Equally there is no proof that the Gate did not
issue an invitation to George, whose experimental work must have
been familiar through the reissuing of his plays, as well as their
publication in the *Dublin Magazine,* during that decade.[176] Indeed,
The Magic Glasses and *The Dandy Dolls* would have proved much
easier productions than the full length *Peer Gynt*.

The Censorship of Publications Act was introduced in 1929, which
restricted the publication of much serious fiction. A public taste had
formed for English Mills and Boon type romance novels and American
cowboy fiction.[177] A distinct Irish literature failed to emerge from
Ireland's obsession with a national culture and identity. Apart from
Ireland's few success stories from this era, for example, James Joyce,
young writers were being subjected to terrible ridicule. In the sphere
of visual art, a government commission to design and create a gift for
the League of Nations was awarded to Harry Clarke, who created a
stained glass piece, the Geneva Window, depicting characters from
plays by great Irish writers. In one section of this magnificent window,
Clarke chose to include Fitzmaurice's Jaymony and his Magic Glasses.
However, the government rejected the completed work as highly
unsuitable. Its depiction of naked women was deemed offensive and
this incident is indicative of all that was insular and conservative in
the Irish State. This magnificent work of art was ignored, and for years

hung in a dark corner of the Municipal Gallery for Modern Art, until it was sold to The Wolfsonian: A Museum for Modern Art and Design at the Florida International University at Miami Beach.[178]

Importantly, critic, reviewer and fellow North Kerry man, Thomas MacGreevy, who had directed for the Dublin Drama League in the early days, was familiar with Fitzmaurice's work. Although he may not have known him personally, it is a strong possibility that he would have suggested Fitzmaurice's work for production.[179] Is it possible that, at this point in time, Fitzmaurice was indifferent to any or all approaches made to him by the new theatre? We can be certain, at least, that his terrible bouts of paranoia, which he began suffering from in the post-war era, were getting worse. His distrust of State involvement in the Abbey is already clear: therefore, could he really trust an alternative theatre that utilized the Peacock Theatre premises?

His seemingly odd behaviour at this point in his life may very well have been influenced by his worsening addiction to alcohol. Certainly, post-traumatic stress, the result of his participation in the First World War, his innate fear of the Free State and the government's involvement in the theatre, as well as his sense of entrapment in his job, all contributed to his behaviour. He was almost predestined to seek solace in alcohol. The only place he could find any sort of peace was the public house. By now a very lonely man, he no longer found joy or real comfort in writing his folk fantasies. Unfortunately, life was to become even lonelier for George Fitzmaurice.

13 | The Post-War Plays

Chronologically, it is easiest to group Fitzmaurice's plays in two categories: his pre-war and post-war plays. The post-war group comprises four plays that were written before 1926: *The Enchanted Land, Twixt the Giltinans and the Carmodys, The Linnaun Shee* and *The Green Stone*. Fitzmaurice struggled to deal with the memories of living amongst his comrades-in-arms in the trenches. Surrounded by filth and squalor, this muck-filled, rat-infested, claustrophobic world was incomparable to the carefree years spent roaming the North Kerry countryside. He began writing on his return in an attempt to obliterate the horrors that he had witnessed and lived through.

His first play, *The Enchanted Land*,[180] is set in two dramatically different worlds. Although completed quite shortly after his return, it was, for some reason or other, not published until 1957. Fitzmaurice was compared to Lewis Carroll in style, having 'created an Irish never-never land rivalled only by that of James Stephens'.[181] It was premiered in the United States in 1966 and produced by Howard Slaughter. Its Irish premiere occurred ten years later, when the Abbey staged it as part of a double bill along with *The Pie Dish*, which starred Eamon Kelly and Maura O'Sullivan.

Dolmen Press published *The Enchanted Land* in the first volume of plays in 1967. Although it opens in a pure fantasy world, the play is rather more conventional than his previous fantasies.[182] The first scene takes place in an underwater chamber where we meet Grey Marse of the Whirlpool and her husband Diarmuid. The drama tells the story of how Eithne, a commoner, was exiled to the underwater world five years previously because she was in love with Aeneas, the King of Ireland's son. Now that she has completed her stay, Aeneas has come to take her back to Ireland to be his bride. However, Diarmuid and Marse's daughter Elaine, the twelve-toed mermaid, wants to be Queen of Ireland. Not content to make do with being second best (unlike the

Julia Sheas of the world), Elaine steals Eithne's magic ball of yarn that was given to her by a brown woman. It will transform Elaine into a beautiful earth woman so that she can take Eithne's place in Ireland.

Act Two is set in the real world of Ireland eighteen years later. It has proven difficult for Elaine to adapt to human ways, as she has always lived in fear of her true identity being discovered. The ball of yarn is all but depleted of its magic and, as Elaine's beauty fades, she compensates for this by surrounding herself with hideous hags.

The third act, set in the Palace of Aeneas, finds Aeneas playing host to many visitors, who have all come to see Elaine's famed beauty. They are shocked by the reality of what they find. Aeneas then rejects the ugly Elaine by sending her away, and marries Peg the Dairymaid instead. However, Elaine may have lost her beauty but she has not lost her ingenuity and practicality. It turns out that she has been putting away some money in case of emergencies. It is this ingenuity that helped her outsmart Eithne in the first place, and there the play ends.

In this play, George turns the usual fairytale storyline on its head. It is Eithne who should have been rewarded by marriage to a Prince after the years of imprisonment she spent in the Underworld. Instead, she does not want anything to do with him. Elaine may have outwitted Eithne by marrying the Prince, but she loses Aeneas in the end. Aeneas is depicted as nothing more than an imbecile and a coward, and is told at one point in the play to 'Pull yourself together for once and be a man'.

There is nothing romantic or sentimental about the main characters and Elaine survives on commonsense, her cleverness winning out in the end. Unlike the protagonists of Fitzmaurice's shorter fantasies, Elaine is willing to compromise her ideals and get what is best for her.

Strangely, all that is regal in this play is seen in terms of food. Echoing Roger Carmody's gluttony and addiction to the priest's geese in *The Dandy Dolls,* the play describes each of the characters' obsessions with the consumption of food and alcohol. *The Enchanted Land* illustrates elements of music hall farce, in scenes such as the hags' dance and the speeches by the courtiers. Perhaps Fitzmaurice was attempting to find a new balance between fantasy and realism, music hall and theatre, which might have been acceptable to Irish audiences.

When he turned his back on the theatre, his first *Dublin Magazine* publication was *The Linnaun Shee* (1924).[183] Though not as wildly exuberant and fantastical as *The Dandy Dolls*, this play is still categorized as a dramatic fantasy. Set on May Eve, the play tells the story of Jamesie Kennelly's all-consuming love for the imaginative folk

figure, the linnaun shee. Jamesie and his wife Hanora are very well off
with everything they could wish for. Yet there hasn't been 'a stir or
move' out of the foolish fifty-five-year-old farmer as Jamesie is so
besotted with the linnaun shee, that he spends 'all the time above in
the loft'. This behaviour is utterly incomprehensible to everyone else
who sees the linnaun shee as an 'old, yellow, withered, wrinkled,
screed'.

The play opens with Bids, the servant girl, making butter, and her
uncle, old Denisheen Canty, joining her in the kitchen. Denisheen's
regular repetitions and rhyme remind us of the strange wisdom of
Mogue in *There are Tragedies and Tragedies* and also of the Child in
The Dandy Dolls. His repetitive lines come at important times in the
play and are akin to a mantra bringing the play full circle:

> Cures I have for the culligreefeens and cures galore for the
> garradhuv; but ... bad luck to it ... I have no cure at all ... for there's
> only one cure ... for a servant girl that's in love.

The neighbours, Julia and Mary, call for the customary exchange of
the news with Hanora over tea. Hanora has not been herself lately.
The two women's curiosity is really getting the better of them and they
believe that Hanora is breaking a sacred bond by not revealing to them
what is wrong. They believe that Hanora's bond with them is more
sacred than the privacy between husband and wife: that of being
'jointed in butter'. Both women accuse her of being 'dishonourable'
although they later backtrack on this accusation and assure her that if
they had anything to tell, they would do so: 'for whatever we might
keep close, we never keep back'. When Bids discloses there is a
problem with Hanora 'the way you are over whatever's in Jamesie',
Hanora realizes it is May Eve, and gives the game away about
Jamesie's love for the linnaun shee. Her two visitors are utterly
delighted at the news of this infidelity, 'the likes of which have not
occurred in the parish for ages'.

The linnaun shee eventually rejects Jamesie and, as a fog descends,
leads him to the edge of a sixty-foot quarry filled with dark water.
Jamesie is totally unaware of what is happening and sees 'something
teetotally different' in the quarry: 'the little high green field at the
other side of the quarry lit up with a marvellous light'. The linnaun
shee wants to turn her attention towards the physical pleasures to be
had from a younger man. While one might be reminded of Julia's
regret at not choosing the younger man in *The Country Dressmaker*,
the Hag's choice represents a darker and more disturbing vision.

It is left to Daniel Tobin to report the off stage action to the
audience, as it is his future son-in-law who is instead wooed by the

Hag. Jamesie returns silently and begins to carry on his everyday life as if nothing has happened. Before Jamesie's entrance however, Hanora is directed as 'sitting facing auditorium, with clasped hands and fixed look' as if this is her nightmare alone: 'It could be a dream you had yourself, Hanora, your mind on one thing', she is told. This direction is a very important technique utilized by Fitzmaurice, as it seems that all the action is, in reality, going on inside her head.

The Lyric Theatre first staged the play in May 1949 and Austin Clarke used yellow hues for the set due to the numerous references to butter and the yellow hag.[184] Critics like A.J. Leventhal congratulated the Lyric on this production, considering that the play had 'lain forgotten far too long',[185] while Benedict Kiely wrote that:

> Fitzmaurice's play ... now produced for the first time, survived some awkward opening moments, to attain an entrancing beauty and terror and mystery'.[186] Austin Clarke recalled the play as 'delightful and gay.[187]

Fitzmaurice confirmed to Clarke that the play was really a satire of Yeats's cult. The play might be a parody of Yeats's *Cathleen Ni Houlihan*, while the linnaun shee's song calls to mind Yeats's poem *The Stolen Child*.

There are issues in this play that have gone unanalysed as commentators preferred to compare it with Fitzmaurice's previous dramatic fantasies. It is not generally believed to be the equivalent of *The Dandy Dolls*, but nonetheless, similar themes occur. The American academic and Fitzmaurice biographer, Carole Gelderman, is less than enthusiastic about this work because it lacks that wildness of the pre-war folk fantasies. Indeed, she insists that the play's collapse occurs because the audience does not meet the protagonist, Jamesie, until the play is about two thirds of the way through.[188] It may be that fantasy is not the central element of the play. With Jamesie's return, the play's ending might also be seen as more optimistic than previous fantasies. However, the future is not so optimistic for Daniel Tobin, as his future son-in-law is lured away. Hanora's action in staring blankly at the audience is unnerving, in light of her husband's return.

J.D. Riley believed *The Linnaun Shee* was one of Fitzmaurice's finest plays because it was a 'presentation of a simple theme of wide application', placing it second only to *The Dandy Dolls* because the technique was "less adventurous and perhaps a little less certain."[189] In fact, such was the importance of this play to Maurice Kennedy that he grouped it with *The Pie Dish* and *The Magic Glasses*, by naming them 'the strange trio'. By comparing the three plays' characters to the 'frustrated poets' of the great school of Gaelic poets around Sliabh Luachra, the last remnants of the old Gaelic culture, he claims that the

importance of the three plays has 'not been generally recognized'.[190]
Riley was in agreement. He believed the great school had been
replaced by the passion for land as well as the struggle to survive at
any cost. This, he believed, had led to the strangling of creative art in
rural Ireland.

After its Abbey rejection three years previously, the *Dublin
Magazine* published the one-act play *The Green Stone* in 1926. [191]
There are no records of the play having been staged prior to a
performance by the Rathmore Drama Group in County Kerry fifty
years after its publication. The 1978 production was runner-up in the
All Ireland One-Act finals. The play conveys the story of another
dreamer, Martineen Collopy, and the magical green stone he got from
a mermaid some twenty years before. It is more modern in that it is set
at a time, which was contemporaneous with its actual writing. This
setting is qualified by the mention of the Yank's arrival by motorcar
and references to 'national taychers', etc.

The action takes place in the Collopys' kitchen and we soon learn
that Martineen's uncle Shemus, the rich farmer, believes his nephew's
capers reflect badly on his family and hinders any attempts to make a
match for his own daughter: 'Shemus is getting terribly ashamed lately
of even being related at all to a gentleman with a fad about a green
stone'. Martineen is bone-idle and a 'big expense' for the family. His
mother, Eleanor, believes it is her family's destiny to 'continue to
suffer' for his tomfoolery. It seems that the green stone is helping
Martineen foretell the future, but only when one sits for 'three hours
before it without moving'. Martineen's brother believes 'the whole
thing pure imagination'. The family desperately searches for a way to
finish this 'curious and chronic affair' that 'all the doctors in Europe'
cannot cure.

Meanwhile, Martineen has been filling his cousin Jimmeen's head
with nonsense, thereby endangering Jimmeen's vocation to become a
priest. Shemus decides the green stone must be gotten rid of and
suggests they firstly try hiding it in the skillet in the kitchen. Enter
Martineen, who, glancing around calmly, finds the stone easily, and
also tells Shemus that he has foreseen his forty cows escaping out 'a
gap in the soft meadow'. Martineen goes out and although this time
they hide the green stone in a pot of boiling water, Martineen returns
to find it again, and foretells another local happening. When he
disappears a third time, Eleanor offers to hide it under her skirt, but
again without success.

Shemus puts the stone in the fire and then takes it out with a tongs,
placing it in the middle of the floor. When Martineen comes in he
begins a long discourse on how the 'divvles of farmers do be going

on...acting the swank'. Eleanor has put up with enough and loses her patience. At that point, Jimmeen comes rushing in telling everyone about a yank who has declared an interest in buying the green stone for 3,000 dollars. The yank duly arrives by motorcar and Martineen is nowhere to be found. The Collopys know that time is against them. The ensuing farcical action has the family display its wonder at the American, as they play real stage-Irish characters. Although Jimmeen reckons Martineen has been 'swept off by that mermaid', he comes up with the idea of giving the pagan yank a false stone 'out of the glosha'.[192]

Martineen arrives back claiming to have foreseen the yank's arrival. Suddenly, a mermaid's 'queer cackle' is heard outside and Martineen bangs the stone on the hearth and in the semi- darkness it explodes, turning to gold. The family is gleeful except for Martineen. Thade, his father, begins to brag about buying the Great House, cars, clothes and horses, but suddenly becomes afraid of people knowing of their good fortune. He then begins to talk about hiding the money.

Their good fortune turns out to be a wasted opportunity and nothing will change for them because all they are left with is merely 'great trouble in guarding goold'. Although Martineen has given his family everything, they only give him five shillings. He wants to escape by going to the pub, but becomes caught up in his family's pretence, and so pretends to go for tobacco. As Martineen is left on his own at this point in the play, it has been suggested that this is a deliberate device by Fitzmaurice to give expression to his own dilemma. The play questions whether Martineen might have been better off with his dreams and carefree existence, rather than giving in to the everyday 'slush' that Jaymony complained about in *The Magic Glasses,* and having to worry about people knowing his business.

Completing four plays between 1919 and 1926 was quite an achievement for Fitzmaurice, especially in light of the fact that he lost interest in pursuing his career with the Abbey during this time. It is staggering to consider that, after the publication of *The Green Stone* in 1926, Fitzmaurice would virtually disappear from the Abbey and the theatrical scene. Fitzmaurice's name was not seen in print, or on an Abbey programme, for another sixteen years. This led Slaughter to surmise that George may even have given up writing for some of those years, although this cannot be substantiated.

Fitzmaurice was never in a hurry to complete his plays: the years following the publication of *The Green Stone* resulted in the completion of some of his lesser known plays: *The Waves of the Sea; The Terrible Baisht; The Simple Hanrahans;* and *There Are Tragedies and Tragedies.*

The Waves of the Sea[193] was discovered only after the playwright's death and was first published by Dolmen Press in the 1967 volume of *Dramatic Fantasies*. University students at Altoona, Pennsylvania first staged it in 1966 with Howard Slaughter as the producer. It has yet to receive an Irish production. Although Carole Gelderman records Austin Clarke's presumption that Fitzmaurice wrote this two-act play shortly after returning from the First World War, there is no definite proof to substantiate this claim. Clarke may have made this conclusion because of Fitzmaurice's attempts in the play at utilizing a talismanic device – a ring – which might also indicate his wish to return to writing fantasy.

Set in North Kerry in 1900, *The Waves of the Sea* features two factions of the Danagher family; the Red Danaghers and the White Danaghers. Much to the disgust of the White faction, Rich Danagher of North Cork has been left six farms by the 'fogey Yankee Pete'. Wise James of Scartaglin, the leader of the White faction, has acted immediately by getting Rich extremely drunk. So, as the play opens, Rich Danagher is asleep in a drunken stupor after three days of drinking. With his new-found wealth, Rich has become a desirable match and the plan is to trick him out of his wealth by making him believe that they have found a sophisticated lady as a wife for him. When James and his sister, Minnie, learn of Rich's proposal to their servant girl, Slanty Mane, Minnie whisks her around the kitchen by the hair, threatening Slanty to be 'all severity and virtue' and warning her to ignore her love for Rich.

Wise James, who arrives with his three nephews and Delia, declares that Rich has only become wealthy because of the 'witchcraft of a three-halfpenny ring he bought from the ugliest divvle you ever see of a black and grey gypsy hag'. James has also managed to buy falsified documents for £5, with the intention of persuading the drunken Rich to sign over the farms. Rich will then be sent into exile to the island of Dhoul-na-Ferris, with the savage island native, Donal Bluebeard, for company. Rich staggers down from the bedroom, and having dreamt about 'some papers I put my name to above in Kanturk', he declares 'there's some treachery on the move'. He refuses to sign the papers and is overpowered and bound, as Donal Bluebeard enters to take him away, leaving Slanty to lament his departure.

Act Two is set on May Eve, thirty years later, and the ill-gotten gains have resulted in the White Danaghers becoming 'morose and cross and queer'. The little fellow, who thirty years previously had told Wise James of the magic ring, now translates a French inscription on the ring: 'When the owner drops the ring six feet in the sea, on a certain May Eve strange things you will see'. The whole fantasy element of the play is further explored where Minnie's granddaughter plays 'The Silvery Waves' on the piano and Wise James knows this is a bad omen on May Eve. The music reminds Minnie of 'the sea coming moaning and rumbling around Dhoul-na-Ferris on a wild night', as Delia, Long John, Mossie and Sonny arrive, having felt something move them towards the cottage.

Some measure of retribution has taken place. It turns out that Sonny, a solicitor, would have been as well off if he had to 'struggle for a living', because 'he can no longer eat' despite having the best cook in Ireland. Mossie's problem, on the other hand, is that his 'appetite is too big' and people think him a terrible pig. Long John, a doctor, is plagued by hypochondria, while Delia, who now owns a pub, must listen to her own son, Fr Pat, telling her that she is damned, while he gives all his money away. However, Wise James has nothing afflicting his conscience.

Having already introduced the ring as a fantasy device, Minnie hears a noise like a big river, as the island of Dhoul-na-Ferris moves towards them, with Donal Bluebeard standing on the island 'like on a prow of a vessel', with Rich beside him shouting. After eating wild mushrooms, both men are talking in riddles and rhyme, while the Danaghers are livid because sand now covers everything they own. The farmhouses are destroyed and all the hoarded money is washed away. The ring prophecy introduced during the first act is revealed; the farms were left to Rich because the ring he bought from a hag was inscribed: 'Who buys this ring buys charms and alarms, / But the first benefit coming in six bully farms'.

Wise James instructs one and all to begin shovelling the sand off everything it has buried because it will 'be good healthy exercise curing loss of appetite and too much appetite, fancy diseases and scruples'. Ironically, the hard lessons resulting from their greed look like being repeated when Rich ignores Slanty Mane because she is still only a servant girl. The ring might have fetched Rich the fortune he desires, but blinded by greed, he has overlooked the real fortune in Slanty Mane.

The ring device points the play in the direction of the folk tradition. However, the magical movement of the island in Act Two could never excite an audience as much as the Hag of Barna's appearance in *The Dandy Dolls*. The talismanic ring device weakens what might have also been a half-hearted attempt at recreating a play similar to *The Country Dressmaker*. George wanted to create a dramatic balance between realism, comedy and fantasy that would somehow satisfy theatre audiences. The fact that the play remained unpublished during his lifetime may indicate his possible disappointment with the overall results.

Originally published in 1954, *The Terrible Baisht*[194] has yet to receive a production. Fitzmaurice may have begun to write the play much earlier, perhaps during the 1930s, although J.D. Riley points out that some of the play was written during or after the Second World War.[195] Riley made this assumption on the basis that one character in the play, the grocer, Daly, makes reference to the First World War. The use of the word *First* indicates that, at the time of writing, World War Two had already begun and possibly ended. Its publication date might, therefore, point toward the possibility of a number of revisions.

The play revolves around an urban setting called Barravale. Shannessy, the local butcher, is a hopeful candidate for the Dáil, and leader of the 'Bunch', which is made up of the town's business people. The scene is set outside a public house on a fair day. Maura and Kate, two locals, are sitting on empty boxes in front of the pub. Two farmers, the 'right sponger' Faley and the 'miserly' Dennehy, emerge from the pub discussing the Department of Agriculture leaflet, number 156, which legislates that 'in-calf heifers that are narrow between the hind legs' are inferior.

Maura and Kate share a little drop of alcohol and some snuff, and voice their suspicions about the strange events in the town. The Bunch are strangely absent from their shops – an unheard-of situation on a fair day. The play reveals their involvement in 'blackguarding the strange youth' that was living in a cave for the past three weeks on Crowley's land. Later described as having a 'sententious little glint in his eye', the grocer, John Daly, is reminiscent of the greedy fairy folk in Fitzmaurice's other plays. It is he who has put about a story that this 'terrible baisht' with a 'woeful' carbuncle on his nose is the devil himself. Although Daly's stories are eventually proven incorrect, he suggests that the youth is actually the local Canon's clerical nephew. Following Daly's entrance, a curious character, Hollyhocks, comes through on his way from Lyre. Drunk as usual, he addresses no one in particular about an 'awful grievance': the fact that there is no good porter around Barravale. He then promptly leaves.

Shannessy, whose sights are firmly set on leaving butchering behind for life as a T.D., enters with the Bunch. He begins by attacking the miserly Dennehy who, as a result of the new information in leaflet 156, got a poor price for his cattle at the fair. Shannessy and the Bunch have found out about Daly's 'overplus of imagination', and decide to tackle him before the Canon learns of the gossip about his nephew. Confronting Daly, they want him to admit his actions to the Canon but he refuses. Shannessy reminds him that, being from Cork, he is not a native of the town, and that his admission to the Canon would make him 'as good a native as any native'. Daly is furious at this suggestion, claiming his success is down to his 'honest dealing across the counter', and points out that he had 'neither hand, act nor part, in the blackguarding of the Canon's nephew'.

The man believed to be the Canon's nephew enters, and Daly hands him a £10 note as a bribe. In the face of this gesture, the generosity of the Bunch seems boundless and they all give the 'student' something to keep him quiet; a leg of mutton, a new harness, alcohol, barn bracks, butter, a gold watch, apples, etc. Overcome by all this, the 'student' asks the Bunch to be friends with Daly by quoting the only Latin phrase he knows: 'Vis Unita Fortior' although he is unable to translate it. He exits, delighted at his newfound luck. Doctor Jim arrives and questions Shannessy about the leg of mutton he has ordered. He is expecting the Canon, and the Canon's nephew, who is due to arrive by train that evening, for dinner. Of course, it then becomes clear that the Canon's nephew, who has left laden down with gifts, was really only a tinker who had been living in the cave.

Maura and Kate are delighted when everyone turns on Shannessy. Daly is left to reflect on where his imagination has gotten him and the fact that he must 'surely be some sort of poet' for having come up with these stories. Dennehy and Faley follow him into the pub. Dennehy will buy Faley another pint, although Faley has £5 more than his friend. Hollyhocks enters once more, and again, addressing no one in particular, begins making utterances once more decrying the bad porter: 'The country is going to the dogs. Ah, but the devil to it and that's what I say'.

It is somewhat thrilling to see Shannessy's fall from grace, as he had been so confident of his election to the Dáil. His character, that of the would-be politician, is being parodied by Fitzmaurice. He is exactly the type of person that the country does not need – someone with his own interests at heart and who has no real concern for the town that supports him. The play is a satire aimed at the smug, self-satisfied merchants and politicians who were to be found throughout Ireland at the time. Meanwhile the tinker has revealed the townspeople's incredible gullibility and the fact that they know nothing of friendship or loyalty and ultimately deserve what they get. The play ends as it has begun, with the two women keeping a watchful eye on procedures, knowing that little, if anything, will change. Faley will continue to make a fool of Dennehy; Hollyhocks will continue to complain about the porter and the country; Daly will find some other story; and the Bunch will find another leader; while Dr Jim will continue with his entertainment of the clergy.

The Simple Hanrahans[196] was published for the first time in the
Dolmen Press edition of the Realistic Plays, and is also, as yet,
unproduced. Liam Miller recalls seeing a draft of the play about 1948
and believed Fitzmaurice intended submitting the play to the Abbey
around that time. George may have begun writing it during the mid
1920s or early 1930s[197] and his decision not to allow further revivals of
The Country Dressmaker after the 1949 production may have
impinged on any decision to submit the new play. He had submitted
the play for publication in the *Dublin Magazine*. Seumas O'Sullivan's
wife came across a typed copy of the play around 1948, after her
husband's death.[198] Drafts of the play still survive and were found
among Fitzmaurice's belongings after his death.[199] The script is quite
short for a full-length play and any performance would definitely last
less than an hour and a half. Despite being more contemporary, in that
it uses more sophisticated modern language, the inherent difficulties
regarding the malapropisms found in the play would result in
difficulties for any producer, and severe editing would be necessary.

Act One is set in a public house and we are introduced to two
customers, Gunn, a national school 'Taycher', and Roche, who are on
their way to Peter Munnix and Lena Hanrahan's wedding. Both men
have collaborated in this match, and Roche, who was encouraged all
the way by Gunn, deliberately left open a gate to a five-acre field on his
own land, which lies between the Munnixs' and Hanrahans'
homesteads. This plan was carried out so that the Hanrahans would
believe it was the Munnix family's five-acre field, which has resulted in
a more substantial dowry from Lena. Both men were adequately
compensated and Roche received 'loads of turf and a load of bog-deal',
while Gunn's wife got 'six pounds of butter and a goose the next day
from Mrs Munnix'.

Michael Hanrahan and his brother and wife come into the bar and
begin celebrating Lena's marriage by swallowing pints of porter. Gunn
and Roche are delighted that these 'simple' folk, the Hanrahans, seem
to have taken the bait. When the Hanrahans get up to leave they are
unable to control their laughter, leading Gunn and Roche to believe
this behaviour merely illustrates their ignorance regarding the
'attyteeket (etiquette) of a wedding'.

Act Two takes place in the Munnixs' kitchen and the Hanrahans
seem broken-hearted at losing their daughter Lena. There is an
emotional farewell. Shortly afterwards, the Hanrahans make a quick
exit, 'galloping away ... laughing their lights out'. Then Peter dashes in
to tell one and all of Lena's wooden leg, false teeth and wig. The
Munnixs declare that a deputation will force another £1,000 out of
Michael Hanrahan when they bring Lena back home. While Mrs

Munnix weeps for her 'innocent boy', Peter hoists Lena on his back in order to bring her back home.

In the third act the Munnixs arrive at the Hanrahans and Peter deposits Lena on the floor. Gunn demands an extra £1000 'for the loss of your daughter's whole leg'. When Munnix again demands satisfaction he threatens that Lena 'will be thrown to you in a heap in the corner'. Hanrahan reminds him of the 'most disrespectful way' in which Lena was treated already. Meanwhile, it appears Peter has been visited by Cupid and doesn't seem bothered anymore by Lena's imperfections. He begins whispering with Lena 'with some tickling, little giggles, etc' and reveals he has fallen in love with her. Peter refuses to be paid for Lena's missing leg and is blind to the material greed of his parents. He prefers to make a go of this relationship that will be based on love and not economic gain. Lena has always been in love with Peter. The play ends as Mrs Munnix tries to console her husband with the possibility that their other children might turn out better than they think.

While reading this play it is possible to be encouraged by some elements that make for effective comedy. Peter and Lena's reconciliation appears to be the correct end to the play. One weakness in the script, which any producer would have to contend with, is that Gunn, who is by no means a central character, has the majority of the play's spoken lines. The creation of humour by utilizing malapropisms is sometimes overdone, resulting in sections of the play becoming stale and drawn out. With sharp production this comic play is not without potential.

Although Slaughter states that *There are Tragedies and Tragedies*[200] was completed in 1940, it was not published in the *Dublin Magazine* until July 1948. Premiered in 1952 by the Fortune Society, Dublin, it was also presented by Druid Theatre Company, in 1977 and 1993.[201]

Early on in the play we learn that for some reason the local bank has become broke and Humphrey Doolan and his wife Kytie have lost their life's savings including an unexpected legacy. His greedy brother Geoffrey, and sister-in-law Maura, call to the cottage, hoping to find that the shock of this loss will cause the couple to be either dead or dying. Humphrey is however, 'Dazed, dazed but not dead', and Geoffrey and Maura feign sympathy. Although they live nearby, it has taken them six weeks to visit, their lame excuse being that they had not heard the news, since they are cut off from civilization by a mountain to one side and a grouse moor to the east. When the 'misfortunate creature', Humphrey, hears them, he reveals that he is down but not out, while Maura attempts to comfort Kytie, who exclaims loudly: 'It's a wonder there's a bit of me left at all and the tortures I have been through for weeks and weeks and for months and months'. Comically, she reveals that her agony comes not from losing the money, but from 'her corns', while Humphrey astonishingly reveals his love of fashion and the tragedy of not having 'proper buttons' on his coat.

The irony in this play lies in the fact that characters are taking serious issues far too lightly indeed, while trivia take on stupendous proportions. It is little wonder that Geoffrey and Maura, having a very practical outlook on life, are 'utterly confounded'. The strange character Mogue enters, she speaks in elusive rhyme and veiled meanings stating her belief that old Kytie is really 'purty' and not fit for Humphrey.

Kytie has refused to condone what she considers to have been a foolish plan by Humphrey, namely, to invest money in a public house. With his fashionable notions and 'patent leather low shoes and two pairs of dandy socks with primroses painted on them', she thinks he is the 'champion booby of the world'. Whatever Humphrey's dreams are, Kytie's negativity is sure to doom them. Although Humphrey is able to put manners on his brother Geoffrey with his 'high-diddle gas bagging', he cannot do the same with Kytie. Humphrey and Kytie argue away while Geoffrey considers them 'bad as well as mad', fearing his own reputation because of this nonsense. He tells them what he thinks of them while Mogue announces, 'There's a reason in reality but there's more reason in love'. The news arrives that in reality their money is still safe and the bank was never broke, although the script never reveals why it has taken six weeks for this news to come through.[202]

Humphrey's inability to distinguish between actually owning a pub and dreaming of owning one makes him one of Fitzmaurice's dreamers. Geoffrey and Maura are the materialists, disgusted by the loss of money, while at the end of the play, Mogue disappears and Humphrey and Kytie kiss, which proves that their love is still alive.

Although the reviews for the Druid Company's production of *There Are Tragedies and Tragedies* were good, it is not easy to know how well the other three plays might be received by audiences today. All four plays invariably illustrate production and scripting weaknesses, a result of Fitzmaurice's irregular attendance at any productions after 1923. However, with a good director, these plays might well prove successful.

The Simple Hanrahans is a relatively short three-act play; *The Waves of the Sea* is a two-act play; while *The Terrible Baisht* and *There Are Tragedies and Tragedies* are one-act plays, the latter of which would not run for more that fifteen or twenty minutes. These plays have been virtually ignored for up to sixty years and most amateur or professional theatrical groups will, in all probability, ignore them for the foreseeable future.

Figure 2 This photograph is believed to have been taken about 1930 and includes, from left: Mr Creagh Hartnett (Abbeyfeale); Georgina Fitzmaurice, playwright's sister; George Fitzmaurice, playwright. Other individuals unknown. Author's own.

14 | The 1930s

By the 1930s there was a considerable shortage of good plays being submitted to the Abbey and a competition was launched in 1932 to rectify this situation. A great many entries were received and first prize was divided between Paul Vincent Carroll and Teresa Deevy for their plays, *Things that are Caesar's* and *Temporal Powers*. Carroll's main thematic interests lay in the relationship between ordinary people and the clergy, and the latter play was said to have been the first of its kind produced at the Abbey actively to portray an anti-clerical stance. There were those who believed that Carroll was a possible Abbey saviour, though the now aging Yeats did not agree. Instead, Lennox Robinson believed this title was due to George Shiels, whose plays were staged due to huge public demand, despite their 'vulgarizing influence on the Abbey'.[203]

Lady Gregory died in 1932 and in the same year Ireland elected a new government. The fervently republican Fianna Fáil came to power and the Abbey now found itself on 'the wrong side of the political fence'.[204] Eamon de Valera, the new Taoiseach and leader of Fianna Fáil, pursued a policy of economic nationalism. This meant cuts in areas such as the arts, as spending in such domains was considered less than worthwhile. The Abbey had its subsidy reduced by £100 during de Valera's first year in office. Lennox Robinson was ultimately managing an Abbey in decline. Production standards fell further when revivals of old comedies found players ignoring direction and gagging lines just for laughs. Robinson fell victim to alcohol addiction, while the Dublin public was simply engrossed in the gossip and stories surrounding theatre life. Yeats's realization of his failure to make a successful theatre out of poetic drama had come too late and there was simply no going back. Over the years, both realistic drama and the prose melodramas had superseded the earlier poetic fantasies by becoming the typical Abbey play. F.R. Higgins asked if Ireland had truly 'lost the spiritual zest for the making of poetic drama?'[205] Although Yeats was thoroughly disillusioned by it all, he still wrote obscure plays such as *The Cat and the Moon*, which was performed in the Peacock. However the audiences that had applauded the ultimately poor Abbey productions were sickened by the obscurity of Yeats's plays.

Whereas the Abbey was, perhaps, far from the literary theatre it was supposed to be, there were still some memorable moments, with productions such as Robinson's *Drama at Inish* in 1933. Financial pressure however, meant that the Abbey spent many months on tour in America during which Irish-American societies called for the withdrawal of plays that gave the wrong impression of Irish life. Being sensitive to Irish-American relations, the Government and the Abbey eventually reached a compromise: an addendum was included in the programmes stating that the Irish government did not accept responsibility for the selection of plays, despite its Abbey subsidy. As the State was now effectively Catholic Church controlled and deeply conservative, de Valera made representations to the Theatre that the government should be involved in deciding the repertoire of plays for the 1934 Abbey American tour. *The Playboy of the Western World* would meet with angry reactions from Irish-Americans during this tour.

The Abbey remained closed for long periods during the 1930s, and when it did open, performances were by the inferior Second Company while the First Company was away on tour. Yeats believed that the Abbey had to make a fresh start, and by 1935 he believed that Robinson did not have the strength of character that was a prerequisite for a good manager. While Robinson was away on tour, he decided to create a larger Board of Directors and proposed the appointment of F.R. Higgins, Brinsley MacNamara and Ernest Blythe. He also brought in Hugh Hunt, a new producer from England.

Following these changes, one of the first decisions taken was to produce *The Silver Tassie*, which had been rejected seven years earlier. This production shocked pious Catholics and resulted in accusations of blasphemy. As a Catholic, MacNamara added his voice to the many objections, after which Yeats compelled him to resign, and Frank O'Connor was drafted in to fill his place. Hunt's new interpretations of *The Playboy* and *The Plough and the Stars* also met with disgust and his eagerness to make substantial dramatic changes to such productions were in vain. Blythe, who knew nothing at all about drama, had a life-long attachment to the Irish language, which would result in his directorship being associated with the Abbey kitchen farce, pantomimes in Irish, and with his demands for compulsory Irish. By now acrimony was rife, and during Yeats's absences the Directors all vied with each other to become his successor.

Other changes began to take place in Irish rural society as people began to channel their energies into organizations such as the GAA and amateur drama. By the 1940s, towns such as Tralee, Listowel, and Killarney in County Kerry would follow this trend and the first amateur Kerry Drama Festival opened in 1943, following other festivals that had been launched countrywide. These amateur festivals were used as springboards for new playwrights and new plays flowed in to the National Theatre. One of those playwrights most successful at this time was George Shiels, whose plays were staged during the late 1930s while the power struggle in the Abbey boardroom continued.

While Blythe had encouraged the writing of one-act plays, the tradition was fast disappearing, though during the years 1934 to 1938, one-acts such as *The Resurrection,* by Yeats; *In the Train*, by Frank O'Connor and Hugh Hunt; and *A Spot in the Sun*, by T.C. Murray, were produced. One of the most powerful of the one-acts was staged in 1938 when Yeats's farewell play, *Purgatory,* was presented to audiences for a single performance during the Abbey Theatre Festival that August. Some seventeen plays in all, many of them one-act classics, were staged, and audiences were made up of Irish people and individuals from America, Britain and the Continent. Fitzmaurice's great fantasies were nowhere in sight.

The fact that Fitzmaurice was not included in this revival of one-act plays must have rankled with him. He had always keenly observed the theatre's attempts to revive the art of the one-act. However, because he was still very afraid of the anti-treaty government association with the theatre, he had approached no one with his work. Instead, both Robinson and MacNamara added what Fitzmaurice believed was insult to injury, by ignoring his classic plays and encouraging the revival of *The Country Dressmaker.* A man full of contradictions throughout his life, the deeply felt bitterness at the 1913 Abbey rejection of *The Dandy Dolls* surfaced from within. The revival of his one-act plays might have heralded a wonderful new beginning for Fitzmaurice, were he included in the repertoire. While he tormented himself regarding the lack of any invitation by the Abbey to revive his favourite one-act plays, the Gate Theatre was going from strength to strength in offering an alternative theatre to the Dublin public. The plays of Fitzmaurice were absent from both theatres.

His contradictory state of mental health during this time can be determined from the existence of three letters written by him in 1935 and 1939.[206] He was now in his sixties and fast approaching retirement from the Civil Service. The requests for a revival of *The Country Dressmaker* resulted in replies that illustrate a deep-rooted fear of the political situation which pertained at the time, while the critical tone of the letters may very well indicate his disgust at the lack of preference for his one-act plays. He refused permission for any revivals of *The Country Dressmaker* even though he knew this popular drama would draw good crowds and put his name back in the limelight. Although the Abbey had its new playwrights as well as a new management structure, it still concentrated on the drawing power of plays such as *The Country Dressmaker*. The three letters of Fitzmaurice's available to us illustrate his vehemence in declining these invitations.

Lennox Robinson and Brinsley MacNamara wrote two letters to Fitzmaurice in 1935, while F.R. Higgins wrote a third in 1939, all requesting permission to stage *The Country Dressmaker*. Fitzmaurice's reply to the first request by Robinson opens with an explanation of the 1925 withdrawal of the play, as it was:

> due to the fact of my working in a govt. office and therefore fair game for the attention of the public who you are aware take an absorbing interest in the Abbey ...

Fitzmaurice was, of course, acutely aware of the public's love for theatre gossip in Dublin society, probably having listened to it as he sat sipping his Guinness in the city's pubs. He had, after all, referred in his letter to the fact that the Abbey had already seen a 'famous play' cause 'general hysteria' after the war, no doubt a reference to *The Plough and the Stars* in 1926. Fitzmaurice continues his explanation:

> When one has a play produced at the Abbey Theatre, the public seem to think they have a moral right ... of making an Aunt Sally of the culprit, and in a general office the strategic advantages are all on their side.

Fitzmaurice's sensitivity as a Protestant, a minority of the populace, may have given rise to these beliefs. It is a strong indication of the paranoia that had begun to fester in the playwright's personality. It is interesting to note that George's friend and work supervisor, Frank Lyons, never mentioned any unpleasant behaviour by other staff towards Fitzmaurice:

> Fitz had a good sense of humour, but was not concerned with trivialities. Two of his favourite topics of conversation were politics – which he often ridiculed – and music hall shows ... He seldom mentioned his plays to me in private and never discussed them at work.[207]

By now, Fitzmaurice expected and feared the worst behaviour in everyone around him. He was drinking heavily to counteract the loneliness that resulted from his subconscious exaggeration of what may have been simply the gentle banter that can occur in any work situation. Ironically, given his earlier dreams of literary fame, his letters reflect a certain resignation that his dreams were now at an end. He wrote that it was 'better once and for all to bring this little affair down from the realm of fantasy to the plane of ordinary life and fact'.

The sharp tone of this first letter indicates his resolve to leave his dreams behind him. This harshness may have resulted in his not being included in the repertoire of one-act plays at the time. Despite his hostility and staunch defiance in not wanting his work revived, he surely secretly wished for further invitations when he ends the letter by requesting that any further communication 'be enclosed in a plain envelope without the superscription "Irish Plays, Abbey Theatre".' He did, however, return the forms of agreement that Robinson had so presumptuously enclosed.

When he receives a second request from MacNamara that same year, his second letter of reply seems less bitter than the first. He states that it 'is regretted that it is not considered desirable to enter into an agreement of this nature at present'. From this correspondence we also learn that he and MacNamara had chatted about the issue, which George felt should have resulted in the matter being made 'quite clear'. Yet the fact that there is a third letter extant, in reply to F.R. Higgins' invitation, may suggest the utter confusion and rancour in the Board of Directors at the time, as they all fought to succeed Yeats. Before this third invitation was issued, Yeats died and it was Higgins who was appointed Managing Director. On 5 May 1939, a staunchly firm Fitzmaurice replies to Higgins:

> I regret to state that the reasons furnished to Mr Robinson some time ago as to the inconvenience which might result from the revival still hold good.

As Robáird Ó Faracháin, in the 1972 radio documentary, *The Wicked Old Children of George Fitzmaurice*, described him as a 'fiery old man', it seems there can be no doubt but that Fitzmaurice was still adept at standing up for himself. However, this third and final letter of 1939 does end on a more conciliatory note as Fitzmaurice states he was 'prepared to meet some representative of your theatre so that the misconception – if any – might be removed'. The letter goes on to state that there were 'no ideological reasons against the reproduction of the play at your theatre', which seems to infer that this refusal was not because he disliked or mistrusted the Abbey itself. By 1942 he would relent when another invitation was issued to revive *The Country Dressmaker*. This may reflect his financial fears as he retired that same year. For once he may have felt it was time to forego all principles and humbly accept the revival. He had, after all, no further reasons to fear the perceived ridicule of his colleagues in the workplace.

The Second World War broke out in September 1939 and Ireland declared its neutrality. The War would have huge consequences nationally, and would indeed affect the Abbey Theatre. As in the First World War, Irish writers would find themselves cut off from Europe as the unfolding events shaped a very different world. At this point, there was little to encourage playwrights to experiment with new forms. The 1940s would result in a significant decrease in the number of new plays being produced, although Abbey audiences would increase. The Abbey was deemed to be providing a good night's entertainment with the same type of popular comedies that had gone before. In 1941, F.R. Higgins died suddenly at the age of forty-four and was replaced by Ernest Blythe. For the next thirty years Blythe would control the theatre in the confines of his own narrow artistic views.

By now Fitzmaurice was spending more and more time in the pub. He was known always to stand at the counter, and he always wore his hat. He liked to stay out of conversations for the most part. Life was lonely in Dublin and George missed the comings and goings in Kilcara Beg. His feelings of failure and his growing fear of travelling inhibited any chance of regular visits to Kerry. Yet life in Kilcara Beg went on even without him. All he had left now were memories of his younger days travelling to neighbours' houses, and nights in the pub with his few good friends. That carefree life where he and his family were so readily accepted into the community seemed so far away from the impersonal hustle and bustle of city life. The letters that must have been exchanged between him and his siblings no longer exist, but memories of the Fitzmaurice family in Kilcara Beg remain etched in the local people's memories to this day.

15 | The Fitzmaurice Family in Kilcara Beg

During the late nineteenth and early twentieth centuries, the locals in Kilcara Beg were familiar with a beautifully whitewashed farmhouse, the entrance to which is still known as Bateman's Gate. The farmhouse, though not visible from the roadside, was surrounded by row upon row of raspberry bushes, strawberry beds and an orchard heavy with the fruits of early autumn. Cherry trees also coloured the surrounds, while the front garden was reserved for a stunning array of roses that constantly seemed in bloom. This was home to the Fitzmaurice family after the Parson's death. Though George would spend his working life in Dublin, except for his extended periods of sick leave, life went on in Duagh for the rest of his family.

Throughout the year the house was a magnet for local children. All of the Fitzmaurices were fond of their young visitors and though they offered local children fruit from the orchard, their kindness never deterred the children's raiding parties, which the family secretly enjoyed. During one such raid, a young girl stayed very still on the bough of an apple tree as Mr George passed beneath, head bowed, unaware of the child's presence above him, or so it seemed.[208] There was much fun to be had for George. His maternal uncle, Brown Batt and his wife Joanna lived in a mud cabin near the farmhouse. Batt was in charge of the farm, and George loved to watch him scolding and chasing the children away from his gooseberry bushes. George never lost his deep appreciation for the characters, the lore and the colour associated with Duagh. His closest friends were Mickeen the Yank (Mick Galvin) and Jer O' Connor, who was better known as *Jer Lop* because of his limp. Jer lived with his sister Joanna near the entrance to the Fitzmaurice's farm and Joanna, who was quite small, was known locally as *Tu'penny*. Jimmy Joy, another great friend and neighbour, also owned a pub in Abbeyfeale as well as a farm near the Fitzmaurices. On the radio programme *The Wicked Old Children of*

George Fitzmaurice, Jimmy recalled Jer's and George's regular drinking habits, as well as their conversations on topics such as dogs, horses and women and how both men often had to find their way home unsure as to whether they were 'coming or going'.

Among the regular visitors to the Fitzmaurice home were young Tom, Bridie and Margaret Relihan, whose mother Catherine (née Morrissey) ran a small shop nearby in Creggane. Catherine was a dressmaker and some say that her presence so near to the Fitzmaurice household resulted in George's inspiration for *The Country Dressmaker.* Margaret followed in her mother's footsteps by becoming a dressmaker and, ironically, she played the part of Julia Shea in a local production during the 1940s.[209] Catherine made some of the Fitzmaurice's clothes and regularly served the family members in her shop where they bought the essentials. Winifred Fitzmaurice also bought her regular supply of snuff there and Catherine, like other locals, described her as an intelligent but quiet and reserved woman.

Without fail, the Fitzmaurices had the daily paper delivered to their doorstep. The paper was collected for them at J.D. Hartnett's of Abbeyfeale and then dropped in to the shop at Creggane for delivery to the Fitzmaurice household. It was either Bridie's or Tom's job to make the delivery by following a track from their own house through the fields of red and white clover. The children never left without a coin for their trouble as well as the previous day's paper, which their mother then read. In those far off days when people knew how to recycle almost everything, each and every word of the two-day-old newspaper was read before being passed to another household.

All the family gathered at Kilcara Beg each Christmas and appreciated the annual present of a hare from a neighbour.[210] Though the locals always maintained the utmost respect for the family, who came from the other side of the religious divide, the move to Duagh had exacerbated their feelings of being on the periphery, and never truly belonging there. Their experiences resulted in a total lack of any credence towards the Protestant religion in which they had been raised. Winifred remained a practising Catholic all her life and travelled to mass on Sundays by pony and trap, her black silk hooded cape blowing in the breeze.[211]

Winifred welcomed the contributions from Ollie, Mossy, and George that supplemented the household income, which consisted of remuneration from land leased to graziers, as well as money from the sale of eggs and home-made butter.[212] Little if anything is remembered locally of Henry, Ulysses or even Mossy. Ulysses died tragically in 1916 at the age of thirty five.[213] It is said that he and George had been very close and Ulysses had been in receipt of George's earnings while he fought in the First World War. It is believed that Henry emigrated to the USA, although no records have been discovered despite exhaustive research. It makes sense, though, that he may have emigrated to Oregon where his uncle Mossy and his family had settled during the 1880s. The family must have received letters and photos from him, yet nothing has survived and it has always been assumed that Henry died there, unmarried.[214] The eldest brother, Mossy, died in 1930, at the age of sixty-six. According to local man, Dan Flynn, he died in Sligo and the local coursing fraternity hired cars to travel there in order to bring his remains home. When the hearse was deemed to be travelling too fast, Willie Stack ordered it to go no faster than fifteen miles per hour.[215]

Ollie worked for a number of years as a storekeeper in St Finan's Hospital in Killarney, returning at weekends to Kilcara Beg. Miss Una, the eldest of the two sisters, spent much time in Killarney with him. Although it is unclear as to how often and for how long she might have stayed, it is unlikely that she was ever employed while in Killarney.[216] Ollie was perhaps one of the only family members who really became involved in the community. According to locals he was a lovely man and his great love of coursing greyhounds was influential in the formation of Duagh's coursing committee in 1926.[217] Coursing was held in a large field on the Fitzmaurice farm and Moll Dillane, a relative of Winifred's, made sandwiches for these events, while Han Sheehy sold sweets. A very quietly spoken gentleman of medium height, Ollie was never seen without his top hat and he was addressed by one and all as 'Sir'.[218] He loved to visit the local rambling houses, as well as Lyons's Pub in Duagh village, or else Joy's or Joe T.J. O'Connell's pub, in Abbeyfeale, along with his friend, Jackie Creagh Hartnett.[219] It was a familiar sight to see him in the farmhouse parlour telling stories to one of the neighbours' children sitting on his lap. As a young girl, Sr Labouré and her spinster aunt were regular visitors to the farm, and on one occasion, Mr Ollie, her great friend, gave her a present of a watch. On arriving home, she was taunted by her older sister for accepting the gift, as it meant her engagement to an older man. Needless to say, the poor child was horrified by this cruel suggestion.

One of the outstanding memories of the children who visited the house was the books, journals and magazines found in every corner, nook and cranny.[220] It seems that George's plays were also a part of the family's library as Dan Flynn's father, Jack, used to call there in order to read them and declared *There are Tragedies and Tragedies* to be George's best play. Dan's father said that Ollie was also a voracious reader, who used to sit and read beside the fire in his room that was

his alone until George came home from Dublin, when a bed was set up
for him there. Ollie's books were always stacked on the wide window
sill and he never entered the kitchen, considering it a 'women only'
domain. George might be found reading in different corners about the
house or by the firelight in Ollie's room. Originally, George's bedroom
had been the very small one behind the kitchen. It had been a familiar
sight to see a young George in his long nightgown and cap spending
the clear bright nights sitting on the window sill reading by moonlight.
Each family member had his or her own room. The large room
opposite Ollie's was once divided into two, and while Winifred slept in
the upper section that had a fire, her eldest daughter slept in the lower
section nearest the hallway. Other rooms at the back of the kitchen
were more than likely occupied by the Stacks when they moved into
the farmhouse.[221]

The late Fr Edmund Stack has alluded to the fact that George may
have had a girlfriend before he left for Cork. However, what has never
been disclosed before is that George may have had a son that he may
never have acknowledged, or perhaps may never even have known
about. It is a difficult subject and one that the older people are still
hesitant in talking about. But around some areas of North Kerry it is
believed that George's son lived well into his nineties. There are,
perhaps, reasons why this story should be told, but there are other
reasons why discretion is preferable. I have decided on the latter.

Miss Georgina and Miss Una were the only two sisters of seven to
survive into old age. There is no evidence that they had ever sought
employment, spending their lives tending to the daily chores about the
household, as well as looking after Winifred. The ladies' pride was
evident by the fruit and flower gardens, which they lovingly tended, as
well as the fresh flowers placed in the parlour daily. The housework
had probably always been left to the two sisters, as Winifred is
remembered as having been a terrible housekeeper.[222] The two sisters
used to cross the road to Catherine Morrissey's tiny shop and
occasionally travelled as far as Abbeyfeale to Monday's market,
making purchases in McDonnell's grocery shop and sometimes at
Eggleston's Drapery.[223] Georgina's exquisitely beautiful brown eyes
and lovely smile were her defining features. In fact, Miss Georgina
proved quite a follower of fashion, as she was one of the only women
in the locality who used to wear a hairpiece![224] Miss Una was known as
the more prim and proper of the two, though both sisters enjoyed their
favourite tipples[225] and sometimes attended parties given at Ellis
Mansion, where they played the piano.[226]

Miss Georgina was a familiar sight in her fawn raincoat and
autumn colours. George's friend, Jer Connor, who would take her to

places by pony and trap, always warned her that if she was not ready at the specified time, he would leave her walk home. Dan Flynn also recalls his first trip to Listowel races, which he attended with Miss Georgina and the local priest. After Georgina sought Dan's help in backing horses, they ended up coming home with thirty shillings' winnings after their horse won the last race at odds of fifteen to one! On one occasion at least, Georgina also accompanied George and Una to London to see music hall shows.[227] It is also known that Georgina gave birth to a stillborn baby. Much of her love affair is lost to time, and the discretion of locals still holds strong. There is little evidence available to us today regarding this tragedy. We will probably never know the full circumstances of Georgina's affair. All that is certain is that her pregnancy left the family feeling embarrassed and hurt.

Whether they had stayed in Bedford or not, the two sisters probably had little chance of ever marrying. In Act One of *The Country Dressmaker* in an argument between matchmaker, Luke Quilter, and dressmaker, Julia Shea, Luke insists on the necessity of marrying young or else one's chances are 'gone for ever more'. It is considered rather strange that none of the family ever married, especially when the two spinster ladies were only in their twenties at the time of their father's death. The family's history, the scandal at Bedford, and the humiliation endured, had not helped matters. Marriage might well have been too formidable a move for both sisters in terms of the security and assurance they so obviously lacked all of their lives. The sisters regularly made the sad journey back to Bedford to visit a former neighbour, Harry Owens, who allowed them to stand at a window and look down on their former home. Their lack of prospects and their reclusive lifestyle in Kilcara Beg stifled any possibility of leaving the past behind. They were destined to remain spinsters, tending to the house and garden in Kilcara Beg, making a little butter, some jams, and looking after the wildfowl. While Dan Flynn says he 'drank more tea in the Fitzmaurices than any other house', the sisters also enjoyed the customary visits of other neighbours on Sundays. Local woman, Eileen Galvin, recalls visiting the sisters with her aunt, and being given strawberries and cream.[228] Despite the custom, there seemed to be an unspoken local understanding because the sisters never ever returned these Sunday visits, although Georgina did call to the Sheehys on the morning of the marriage of one of their daughters.

Despite the differences between themselves and the locals, the respect for all the Fitzmaurices is possibly summed up best in the words of the local priest at Ollie's funeral: ' ... it was my duty as a parishioner to be at the funeral'.[229] Long after George had made

Figure 3: Georgina and Ollie Fitzmaurice outside their cottage in Kilcara Beg, with, it is believed, an American cousin on holiday. (Date unknown). Courtesy of Bridie O'Connor, Finuge

Dublin his home, the family's routines were accepted as part and parcel of this community's daily life. Ollie was a familiar sight in the rambling houses and pubs and at all the coursing events. Despite their somewhat limited participation in the ordinary life of this close-knit community, a watchful eye remained on the sisters. George's dreams of a literary career had been forged in Duagh and its surrounds, and doubtless his siblings were quietly proud of his achievements. Duagh was a place he loved dearly, respected and missed a great deal while he was away. Locals, to this day, recall with great fondness, the Fitzmaurice family, the immaculately kept cottage, and all the comings and goings. Despite their reserve, which lasted all of their lives, respect for them in the locality is still evident to this day. The cottage's magnetic attraction still remains, even if it is now just a memory.

As Fitzmaurice approached retirement age, he wondered what life would bring. Kilcara Beg seemed a lifetime away and his reasons for having stayed in Dublin in order to pursue a writing career were now meaningless. As he feared his ability to cope with retirement, these happy and colourful memories of Kilcara Beg flooded into his mind. Although Fitzmaurice was an all but forgotten name for theatre audiences, the 1940s would rectify this, at least to some degree.

16 | The 1940s

Throughout the 1940s the Abbey saw a decrease in the number of new plays performed. There were only sixty-two new plays, unlike the previous decade's total of one hundred and four. However, audience numbers increased dramatically during the Second World War, which was, in part, a result of the fact that Dublin was virtually cut off from the rest of the world during this time. A change in Abbey Theatre policy resulted in the ending of limited production runs, which meant plays ran for longer periods of time. Business at the Gaiety and Olympia was also thriving and it is surely certain that Fitzmaurice was amongst the regulars attending these music hall venues. There were new dramatists at the Abbey, such as Joseph Tomelty and Louis d'Alton. Blythe was now the Abbey's Managing Director and he dreamt of a Gaelic-speaking theatre. From 1942 onwards, junior players were accepted only if they could perform plays in Irish as well as in English.

The Abbey was still reviving popular plays and *The Country Dressmaker* made a welcome return to the repertoire in 1942. Fitzmaurice retired from the Civil Service that same year, which meant he was free to enjoy the play's revival. It is probable that financial necessity encouraged him to allow the revival, as he now had to survive on a small pension. Strangely, he would not make any new submissions to the Abbey, despite the fact that he certainly considered submitting *The Simple Hanrahans* a few years later.

Reviewing *The Country Dressmaker* on 6 October, 1942, *The Irish Times* recorded:

> There was almost a first night atmosphere in the Abbey Theatre last night for the revival after eighteen years of *The Country Dressmaker* which from its first production in 1907 proved for years one of the most popular plays with Abbey patrons. Last night's reception suggests that the taste of the present-day audiences is no whit different from that of a previous generation.[230]

Bríd Ní Loinsigh played Julia Shea, and gave 'a fine study of the part of the dressmaker'. Ria Mooney, (who subsequently left the Abbey, only to return as Play Director in 1948), played Norry Shea, while other famous thespians of the day included Michael Doolan, Eileen Crowe, F.J. McCormick, and Cyril Cusack, who played the returned Yank, Pats Connor. *The Country Dressmaker* also enjoyed a short revival the following year, while *Twixt the Giltinans and the Carmodys* was published in the *Dublin Magazine*. However, Fitzmaurice was an almost forgotten figure in the Abbey annals and apart from these revivals and the irregular *Dublin Magazine* publications, the majority of audience members were probably unfamiliar with his name, not to mind his body of work.

The decline at the Abbey of the one-act play – despite the revival attempts during the 1930s – had also brought about the decline of the verse play, a tradition that the poet Austin Clarke claimed had been abandoned by the Abbey. Clarke had been mesmerized by the first verse play he saw at the Abbey years before, which had encouraged him to write a cycle of plays about early Christian Ireland, in much the same way that Yeats had utilized characters from the heroic sagas. Thus Clarke and Robáird Ó'Faracháin founded the Dublin Verse Speaking Society in 1943 'so that broadcasters and actors might have practice in lyric, choral and rhythmic speech'.[231] Independently of the Verse Speaking Society, the Lyric Theatre was founded in 1944 'to save from neglect the tradition of verse drama left to us by Yeats',[232] and was well served by actors such as Cyril Cusack, Ria Mooney and Eithne Dunne. It produced twenty-seven plays in eight years, for example, Clarke's *The Viscount of Blarney; The Kiss; The Second Kiss*; and *The Death of Cuchulainn*.

When Austin Clarke came across some drawings by Norah McGuinness of figures from *The Dandy Dolls* published in the *Dublin Magazine*, he borrowed a copy of *Five Plays* from Seumas O'Sullivan. Clarke read the plays and then began a search for Fitzmaurice in the hope of gaining his permission to produce them. The Lyric Theatre eventually played a vital role in the continuation of the Fitzmaurice revival by premiering three of his plays; *The Dandy Dolls, The Magic Glasses,* and *The Linnaun Shee.* The Earlsfort Players and Liam Miller also played vital roles by producing *The Moonlighter, The Magic Glasses* and, later, *One Evening Gleam.*

Despite Clarke's earlier interest in Yeats's work, his experiences with Yeats were generally unhappy: he suffered humiliation at the hands of the Abbey Director during earlier years. Unfortunately, Clarke had become extremely envious of Yeats and everything he had. Apart from an Abbey rejection of a play he once submitted, Clarke had also, without success, approached Yeats regarding writing his biography. The ultimate rejection came when he had to bear the humiliation of not being included in the *Oxford Anthology of Verse* edited by Yeats.[233] At this point, it seems only fair to point to the simultaneous importance of Fitzmaurice's work for Austin Clarke. In seeking to find an alternative to Yeats, Clarke had indeed utilized Fitzmaurice's dramatic work as a model.[234] In this regard, Clarke's indebtedness to Fitzmaurice has been long overlooked. Clarke's seemingly gallant attempts at denouncing Yeats's jealousy of Fitzmaurice as the reason for Fitzmaurice's disappearance from the Abbey is grossly exaggerated, and has resulted in biographers exonerating Fitzmaurice from any blame that should rightly have been apportioned to him. Fitzmaurice's 'disappearance' is attributable, at least in part, to the confusion that had always surrounded his fantasies; to the decline in interest in one-act plays at the Abbey; to his subsequent swing towards publication rather that production; and ultimately, to his increased paranoia. Inevitably, his name was almost completely forgotten as a direct result of his stringent refusal to allow the revival of *The Country Dressmaker* between 1925 and 1942. It cannot be emphasized strongly enough that Fitzmaurice alone was responsible for this.

It was *The Dandy Dolls'* premiere in 1945 that perhaps gave him the greatest pride and satisfaction. Clarke had begged him to allow the Lyric Theatre to stage this masterpiece, and eventually he yielded. By now Fitzmaurice was absolutely terrified of critics and refused to attend the opening night. The company therefore arranged a special dress rehearsal of the play, for which he was extremely grateful. It was, after all, his favourite work and in later years he told his cousin Wilfred Fitzmaurice 'I like this play'.[235] Furthermore, the fact that the Lyric rented the Abbey for its productions indicates that Fitzmaurice had no direct problem with the Abbey Theatre per se. The play was staged on two consecutive Sundays, 2 and 9 December 1945. Indeed, Clarke had understood Fitzmaurice's intention and later wrote that the play:

> must depend a great deal on production since it would have to be treated as a verse play, the rhythm and movement and grouping ... the unity one finds in a ballet.[236]

John Chichester, an acquaintance of Fitzmaurice, saw this production and commented to George that he had felt it was a sinister play. In a rare comment on his own work he retorted; 'It is not sinister!' and claimed that he had 'used words as a musician uses notes in composing a piece of music'. He refused to elaborate and instead asked Chichester not to breathe a word of the conversation until he, Fitzmaurice, had died. [237]

Reviewing *The Dandy Dolls'* production, A.J. Leventhal thought the only instance that held the production back from being 'a triumph' was the lack of 'mimetic magic' in Maurice Selwyn's interpretation as the Grey Man.[238] He went on to state:

> There is music in his prose which many a poet might envy and his symbolism, born of Irish legend, has roots in human understanding more effective than the Maeterlinckean dependence on a piling of atmosphere through seemingly unrelated episodes.[239]

When the Lyric Theatre staged *The Magic Glasses* in 1946,[240] critic A.J. Leventhal, who found it incomprehensible that the play had not been produced since 1913, described it as 'outstanding'. The following year, the amateur group, the Earlsfort Players, revived *The Magic Glasses* once more, while two years later the play was performed at the Green Circle Theatre Club in London.[241]

In 1948 the Earlsfort Players staged a premiere of his longest play, the realistic four-act *The Moonlighter*. Producer, Liam Miller, took on this onerous task. Miller also managed an effective discussion with Fitzmaurice about tightening the play:

> over a few jars and a few pipefuls of Bendigo tobacco, [they] made the necessary cuts to combine the first and second scenes into one act.[242]

They agreed to make it a three-act rather than a four-act production.

It is likely that, as a young boy, Fitzmaurice first heard stories of an infamous North Kerry moonlighter by the name of Canty.[243] A tragedy in four acts, *The Moonlighter*[244] is his longest and most intricately plotted play. It questions the political ideals of nationalists at the time, and contains 'many minor motifs, themes and character features which point forward to O'Casey's Abbey plays'.[245] Fitzmaurice began writing the play after being influenced by other revolutionary-type productions, such as *The Piper* and *When the Dawn Has Come* in 1908. Although he did submit the play the fact that the Abbey failed to produce it at the time was, according to W.A. Henderson, simply because of the suggestive scene where some sweets are shared between the two couples in the third act.[246]

J.D. Riley argued that the title *The Moonlighter* was incorrect and merely the result of a printing error by publishers Maunsel and Roberts. Riley claimed the title was in actual fact *The Moonlighters*.[247] However, there is no record of Fitzmaurice's objection to the former title when Liam Miller produced the play with the Earlsfort Players in 1948.

The play is set in North Kerry and the plot revolves around four families: the Guerins, the Cantillons, the Driscolls, and the Carmodys. The major focus is on the abstract cause of patriotism. Secondary themes include matchmaking, conflict, cowardice, revenge, honour, loyalty, guilt, love and death. Commentators fault the play for its large number of characters and various subplots as they are viewed as weakening the work. However, a satisfactory analysis of this intricate and complex play is beyond the scope of this volume.

Apart from the production problems, *The Moonlighter* is an example of Fitzmaurice as a fine realistic dramatist, questioning the definition of a true patriot. This theme forms the main undercurrent of the play.[248] Despite the fact that the play is, overall, a tragedy, it ends with a sense of moral victory when the moonlighter, Tom Driscoll, is described as follows:

> But it is for him and the like of him that the flowers smile, and always smiled, in the green soil of Ireland.[249]

Critics tend to differ in their overall interpretation of the play's success and A.J. Leventhal felt that the 1948 production illustrated that *The Moonlighter* was 'not one of his best plays', though he did believe the plot difficulties could have been ironed out with professional direction. He wrote that the director, Liam Miller, 'was not without feeling for the finer points of the dramatic purpose',[250] and believed the play illustrated a mastery of what was once known as 'Anglo-Irish idiom'. Not wishing to denigrate the Players' ability, he thought the production had proved too big for the amateur cast who 'could not rise to the demands inherent in the text'. Therefore the production fell 'short of its ambition'.[251] He suggested that a revival of *The Pie Dish* might have resulted in a better outcome.

In contrast to this rather harsh review, other critics were more positive. The *Irish Tatler* wrote: 'Why the Abbey has overlooked work of such quality is one of the greatest literary mysteries' and went on to describe the Peacock production as 'most heartening' and hoped it would lead to 'a general revival of Fitzmaurice's work'.[252] The *Evening Mail* also deemed the play 'an unquestionable triumph for the author' asking 'why should the National Theatre have rejected and suppressed this play by a fine dramatist for all these years?'[253]

Tragedy struck when George's older brother Ollie died in June 1948.[254] His death cast a long shadow over George's life in Dublin and during the following months may have influenced some of the decisions Fitzmaurice had to make. As the decade drew to a close, the Lyric Theatre premiered its last Fitzmaurice play, with a production of *The Linnaun Shee* some twenty-five years after its initial publication.

There was a further revival of *The Country Dressmaker* by the
Abbey Theatre in May 1949. Produced by Ria Mooney, it was to be the
last time Fitzmaurice's work would be seen on the national stage
during his lifetime. *The Irish Times* reviewed the performances as
outstanding and the play's production was described as a 'romantic
comedy to a point just this side of burlesque'.[255] Bríd Ní Loinsigh again
played Julia and was 'superbly controlled in her performance', while
Walter Macken as Quilter was the sloothering matchmaker, who
'rocked the house and dominated the stage while he was on'.[256] Vere
Dudgeon and Sean Barlow's set design was described as 'a novel and a
pleasant breakaway from the stereotyped Abbey cottage interiors'. Yet
it seems this change in settings might not have met with Fitzmaurice's
approval. Having put his trust in another Abbey production, the
playwright did not find this more modern set acceptable, and
Professor Brendan Kennelly claimed that this led to the end of any
further associations with the Abbey.[257] Perhaps Fitzmaurice's
insistence in later years, regarding the Abbey's inability to produce
plays, stemmed from the Abbey's changes to the set.[258]

The Irish Times review also claimed that the play was:

> enjoying a well-deserved airing ... Fitzmaurice exploits with gusto his
> talent for combining dialogue as fully flavoured as Synge with the
> natural dialect of the play's place and time, to frame his own folk
> version of the Cinderella theme.[259]

The review did not stop there as it stated that Fitzmaurice 'shows
an uncanny comic facility for reproducing the romantic clap-trap of
the feminine penny dreadful of forty years ago in the mouth of his
Cinderella'.[260] However, Fitzmaurice's fear of critics led him to
concentrate on the negative and, as he was apt to do, he ignored the
warmth of the reviews. The fact that he had not seen a dramatic
production of *The Country Dressmaker* as a member of the audience
for many years may have inhibited his understanding of the need to
move with the times and make changes. Brendan Kennelly suggests
that Fitzmaurice may have seen these set changes as an insult,[261] but
paradoxically the critics, whom he despised, loved the changes. With
Kennelly's theory in mind, is it to be assumed that Fitzmaurice learned
about the set changes through the newspaper reviews? Or, is it
possible that the elderly man slipped into the theatre unrecognized, in
1949, in order to see the set for himself?[262]

Since the mid 1940s, the Abbey had begun to produce pantomimes
in Irish. However, despite the fact that audiences also saw popular
plays such as those of George Shiels, and Brinsley MacNamara, there
was an acceptance of mediocrity in the theatre. There was a certain
'colour and excitement' lacking in the Abbey which frustrated people

like Ria Mooney.[263] As the decade drew to a close, Fitzmaurice had brought down the barrier between himself and the National Theatre once more. Yet he continued to write.

Though it is unlikely that readers of Fitzmaurice's work will ever be furnished with an exact chronology of his plays, it is certain that two new plays he began writing during the mid 1940s marked a change in direction regarding his beloved genre of folk and fantasy drama. This was the decade during which George wrote two plays set in Dublin: *One Evening Gleam* and *The Coming of Ewn Andzale*.

17 | The Dublin Plays

Liam Miller credits the Lyric Theatre's production of Fitzmaurice's plays between 1945 and 1948 with having encouraged Fitzmaurice to write his last plays.[264] J.D. Riley states that *One Evening Gleam* was written in 1945, at the end of the Second World War, though it was not published until 1950. Calling it 'a small and perfect masterpiece', he states that it seemed to transcend 'the realistic method and extends the limits of the one-act form'.[265] The play was staged by the amateur Fortune Society in 1952, and produced by Liam Miller with décor by Nevill Johnson.[266]

The first of his two Dublin plays, *One Evening Gleam*[267] is set in a Dublin tenement in Great Longford Street, in the home of Agnes Cleary. Her forty-year-old son Jim, blind since he was five, is asleep in a corner bed after suffering a recent 'nervous fit'. It is revealed that twenty years earlier, an 'old Agyptian doctor' prophesied that if Jim ever regained his sight he would die in an hour, though his doctor now dismisses this as mere 'quackery'. His mother is considered a good Christian woman for having cared for Jim all his life. Yet he has become totally dependent on her, and she still refers to him as a child, which has resulted in his almost total seclusion from the world. He has never been able to attempt to make a life for himself.

Mrs Hannigan, a neighbour, appears on stage. Known as a talkative woman, she is drunk, having spent the money she got from her daughter in England, on alcohol. She and Mrs Cleary start to talk about the parson's daughter, Phoebe Tollemache, who lives upstairs in the same building. An unmarried daughter of a once landowning family, it appears she may have inherited some of this land that is now leased to tenants. She is 'of a different class' and a total mystery to the women. Phoebe often disappears for a few days at a time, which mystifies the ladies. Mrs Hannigan does not like Phoebe because of her 'aires' and her upbringing and, ironically, thinks of her simply as a gossip, despite her own gossiping. Mrs Hannigan claims Phoebe has notions about Jim, saying she has seen them 'on a seat in the green one day and he put his hand in hers', and believes that Phoebe is in love with Jim. She also is adamant that this love is not reciprocated, though Mrs Cleary believes 'Aging spinsters are often easily affected by these things'. When Mrs Hannigan continues her chatter regarding her merry life and visits to the music halls with her husband, it is hinted at that this merry life might be a figment of her imagination.

Phoebe Tollemache is often heard 'rattlin' on that oul' pianner of hers with the wires screechin' that wasn't tuned for forty years'. Mrs Hannigan points out that her piano playing is a result of her selfishness. When she begins singing, Mrs Hannigan believes she is drunk though Mrs Cleary disagrees. The women are happy to discuss how Phoebe ignores a Protestant bachelor in their building, who would suit her 'down to the ground', a man whom gossip mongers believe is a 'woman hater' who 'was jilted in his young days'.

As the 'ups and downs of life do be queer', Phoebe finds solace in her piano, just as Miss Una and Miss Georgina had done. There is much hidden biographical detail in this play and Phoebe Tollemache's character is based on elements of George's two sisters. It is also probable that the question of the Protestant bachelor is an allusion to the type of man that would have been an acceptable match for either sister. Perhaps this old bachelor also depicts a caricature of himself. Phoebe's disappearances may also be a reference to Miss Una's 'disappearances' to Killarney.

Phoebe knows that Jim is about to die. Yet, in this short one-act play, so much goes unsaid and is left to our imagination. What is Phoebe's real story? Why is Mrs Hannigan so unhappy? Why has Jim always remained secluded? The play ends when Jim wakes up and claims he can see the moon. In seconds he is dead and the earlier prophecy has come true. It is only when Mrs Hannigan leaves that Mrs Cleary demonstrates the depth of her grief, as Phoebe plays Tom Moore's, *She is far from the land*. In contrast, the penny whistler outside on the street plays the more upbeat popular ballad, *The Men of the West*. The contrast reflects the tragic action of the play.

This is a pessimistic play and the fact that it was written as the Second World War ended also indicates how the happenings in the tenement reflect the larger world. The play reveals a sad lack of honesty. Though Mrs Cleary seems a good Christian woman, it is Phoebe who reveals the truth about her life as a pickpocket. She also reveals Mrs Hannigan's fondness for alcohol. If Jim's vision is seen as just the 'glame from an ould lamp' (whether it is true or not), then what hope can the future hold for Agnes Cleary, Mrs Hannigan or

Phoebe? No glimmer of hope from Jim's vision or even the fact that he died a happy man will satisfy. Therefore life will go on, and perhaps Jim's death will have been in vain.

The last of his plays was *The Coming of Ewn Andzale*. Slaughter believes this play illustrates a certain lack of thought on Fitzmaurice's part, and sums it up by stating that, 'Too much ink and too little blood runs through the veins of the characters'.[268] However, Arthur McGuinness disagrees and is adamant that both this play and *One Evening Gleam* deserve more critical attention than they have received to date.[269]

The Coming of Ewn Andzale[270] was published in 1954 and tells the story of the Davenport family who are from the Anglo-Irish ascendancy class. [271] Their country house has been burned by the Sinn Féiners and they now live in reduced circumstances in Monkstown in a house that they were given by a clergyman relative. This long one-act play is set in the family's drawing room and the language is one of 'polite formality' resulting in 'a stiff and self-conscious speech'.[272]

The play revolves around a letter Mrs Davenport has received from Ewn Andzale who has promised to visit and help them out financially. As the play opens, he is due in a half an hour. The Davenports have two daughters, Queenie, who is 'getting near thirty, and no proposals', and her sister Cissie, who is four years younger. The Davenports' son, Popham, is hoping that the money will set him up in his dream garage. However, Queenie throws the story into disarray by claiming that her mother's obsession with crosswords has resulted in this fictitious letter, when the name Ewn Andzale turns out to be an anagram for New Zealand.

Queenie is the educated one in the family, and believes the letter is merely 'a wish to by-pass by some fluke or other the intolerable and seemingly unjust workings of fate'. She accuses her mother of being just like the 'old authors of the fairytales'. The rest of the family blame Queenie's outburst on the fact that she has not received any marriage proposals, which is, in reality, a result of the family's reduced circumstances:

> Girls in Ireland, young or old, and no matter how beautiful they may be, have no chance of getting married nowadays unless they have money.

Echoes of the two spinster Fitzmaurice sisters abound uneasily throughout this play.

Despite Fitzmaurice's move from the folk idiom, the fairy world is not altogether ignored in the play. The title itself alludes to a 'coming', and later there is a reference to a 'satyr', a representative of the fairy and mythical worlds. However, Queenie's formal education and Mrs Davenport's books on religion remove the family from any sense of a Gaelic folk tradition. When a knock comes to the door, coincidence arrives at their house in the figure of Silas, a half brother of Mrs Davenport's who has been living in New Zealand for years. He reads the letter and offers to help them. The family is left to celebrate their good fortune, although as the play ends a sob is heard.

Fitzmaurice's family had to move because of reduced circumstances just like the Davenports. The experience of the two unmarried sisters and Popham's possible emigration reflect similar traumas the Fitzmaurices had to deal with. Mrs Davenport epitomizes the visionaries of George's earlier plays by the fact that the letter alludes to similar devices in the dramatic fantasies. She has been prone to hallucinations since childhood, while the content of the letter is indeed 'outside our ordinary experiences of life'. Yet, what would have happened if Silas had not arrived? Queenie does not blame her mother for her games, as she knows if her 'mental balance had been stronger the worry would not have caused such a brainstorm'. Mrs Davenport is really a version of Fitzmaurice's visionaries. When Queenie uses the words 'borderline cases', Fitzmaurice is giving a description of himself. He blamed his 'brainstorms' for his erratic behaviour, as we shall see in chapter eighteen. This suggests Fitzmaurice is passing judgement on his previous body of work. Is he stating that his dreams of a literary career were just foolish notions? Are the references to fairytales his way of admonishing himself for having thought about making a career of such nonsense? Was he really reduced to doing 'Crosswords, puzzles, reading', etc., while sitting in St Stephen's Green, in order to make his 'existence more pleasant and bearable'?

Jim, in *One Evening Gleam*, and Mrs Davenport, in *The Coming of Ewn Andzale*, are characters that reflect the glimmer of imagination Fitzmaurice once tapped into in writing his earlier plays. He would have believed Jim's vision was really the moon, while Mrs Davenport's letter was a method of escaping the mundanities of ordinary life, for some period of time at least. Perhaps this is what poverty, reduced circumstances and city life did to one. Yet both plays reveal two prophecies having been fulfilled, although this fact is, for the most part, ignored in both instances.

Apart from Jim and Mrs Davenport, all other characters are blind to the fact that some supernatural happenings have occurred. These plays reflect a Dublin world cut off from the imagination of the rural folk tradition. They are suggestive of Fitzmaurice's sense of isolation in the city and his severance from the traditions he enjoyed within the confines of his former life in Kilcara Beg. Both these plays deserve more critical attention because they undoubtedly reveal much about the playwright which has heretofore gone unnoticed.[273]

18 | The 1950s

Sometime during the 1950s, and already in his seventies, Fitzmaurice decided to move from his Stamer Street lodgings to Rathmines. It had not been unusual for George to move about the city from tenement to tenement, although his move to Rathmines seemed an unusual decision for a man who was afraid of travelling on buses or trams. However, this move out to the suburbs coincided with his purchase of a burial plot at Mount Jerome Cemetery. Although he never recorded a desire to be buried in his native Kerry, it seems surprising that he wanted to be buried in Dublin. 1950 was a particularly difficult year for him following the death of his sister Georgina, with whom he had always been very close. It is believed that a disagreement between George and the Stacks arose around this time, and some locals say it was never resolved satisfactorily. Perhaps the memories of his father's behaviour while at Bedford came back to haunt George at this time. We will probably never know. However, George had resigned himself to dying soon after his sister Georgina, and his death would be in Dublin.

In the intervening years, his cousin, Minnie Mulcaire, did her utmost to coax him to move to a nursing home in Ballybunion. At one point, everything was organized and ready.[274] A car was being sent to collect him, but Fitzmaurice changed his mind and declared that he was unwilling to travel. Although there would be further unsuccessful attempts at getting him back to Kerry, even the promise of free room and board in a Listowel nursing home did little to convince him.[275] Meanwhile, Rathmines was very far away from his beloved St Stephen's Green, and both the *Winter Garden Palace*[276] and *Mooney's* pubs. Not surprisingly, there is nothing known of his time spent in Rathmines. He seems to have done his utmost to avoid people who offered him any friendship at all, and even those who knew him well

had no idea where he was. A letter from Seumas O'Sullivan found in
George's room after his death read:

> I have been chasing you for some weeks past but failed to find you in
> any of your usual haunts. I hope when you handed me your play, you
> meant to allow me to print it ... for I took it for granted that I had
> your permission to do so, and have set it up.

The Abbey Theatre burned down in 1951 and the company was
forced to rent the Queen's Theatre for the following fifteen years.
Theatre size and the economics of this situation changed the theatre's
policy. From a repertory theatre with a number of plays it could revive
in order to fill out those weeks spent rehearsing new plays, it
developed into a theatre whose economic survival depended solely on
long runs of new plays. The Queen's Theatre was much bigger than the
Abbey premises and a revival of popular plays was simply no longer a
viable option.

The early 1950s witnessed a continuation of some semblance of
interest in Fitzmaurice's work, as Liam Miller produced *One Evening
Gleam* in September 1952, which was staged along with J.M. Synge's
The Tinker's Wedding and Lady Gregory's *The Gaol Gate*. The day
before the opening, George wrote to Liam Miller, granting his
permission for the staging of *One Evening Gleam:*

> I agree to the production by Liam Miller of my play ONE EVENING
> GLEAM commencing Monday 15 September 1952 at the Studio
> Theatre Club, 43 Upper Mount Street, Dublin.[277]

Tragically for George, the Lyric Theatre would perform no more of
his work, as it disbanded in 1953, the same year in which the final
broadcast of the Dublin Verse Speaking Society occurred.

The last known productions of his work during his lifetime were
staged by St Mary's Musical and Dramatic Society Dublin, with the
premiere of *There are Tragedies and Tragedies* in 1953, and *The
Magic Glasses*, which was produced by the Listowel Players in 1954.
The *Dublin Magazine* published three plays during this decade: *One
Evening Gleam* in 1950, *The Coming of Ewn Andzale* in 1954, and *The
Enchanted Land* in 1957.

Both Miller and Clarke had attempted to reassure Fitzmaurice of
their belief in his work, and they were not alone. Bryan MacMahon
also expressed an avid interest in his plays and was a member of the
Listowel Players who won the All Ireland One-Act Drama Finals in
1954 with *The Magic Glasses*. MacMahon had often cycled out to
Duagh during the earlier years in an attempt to meet, or even catch a
glimpse of George while he was home from Dublin. He eventually
succeeded in finding him at home although the elderly playwright

would only speak to him through a dimly lit window because he was suffering from a cold. Some years later, Bryan was given a conscience message for Fitzmaurice by a local person, and carried it in his wallet on the off chance he might meet George on one of his trips to Dublin. Walking up a busy Grafton Street one night, he suddenly had a feeling that Fitzmaurice was somewhere in the crowd. Eventually he found a small man, bent almost double, in a doorway. He called to him gently; 'By any chance are you George Fitzmaurice?' The old man 'pivoted slowly' like a train on a track and said that he was. Once George realized who was speaking to him, his apple-shaped face lit up and the two men enjoyed a wonderful conversation as they walked towards St Stephen's Green. Bryan told him of the Listowel Players' All Ireland win and spoke of the magical characters Fitzmaurice had created. He appeared somewhat taken aback when MacMahon told him that all in Kerry were very proud of him. He became very emotional and with his eyes brimming with tears replied, 'Well, that's something anyway'.[278] They talked for over an hour until they finally stopped at Harcourt Street, where George was living, having moved there in recent months. They said goodbye and as Bryan watched Fitzmaurice go in the front door, George looked around slowly as if to say goodbye to the night.

Harcourt Street was the last tenement in which he made a home for himself, around 1956. Ironically, it was next door to the hotel where MacMahon used to stay. Fitzmaurice had moved firstly to number one, a larger tenement, but eventually had to move to a smaller room when it proved too expensive to remain in the larger room. A couple of years later, when MacMahon called once again to Fitzmaurice at number three, George opened the door with a milk jug in his hand. He was delighted to see his Kerry visitor. Bryan tried to persuade George to join him at the theatre on the opening night of one of his own plays, but it was to no avail.[279] MacMahon was anxious to rekindle the Abbey's interest in Fitzmaurice's plays and hoped that by introducing George to these theatre figures it might indeed spur their interest. George was having none of it and eventually said to MacMahon, 'Don't take any notice of those people down there. They can't produce plays'.[280] It seems George was unwilling to take any more chances with the Abbey.

Despite his enthusiasm for the Lyric Theatre's previous productions, he appears to have been less than enthused by any other approach made. Mícheál Ó hAodha, producer at Radio Éireann, became an avid enthusiast of his short works. Yet Ó hAodha's desperate pleas to gain George's permission to produce and broadcast *The Magic Glasses, The Dandy Dolls,* and *The Country Dressmaker* on its fiftieth anniversary, fell on deaf ears. Ó hAodha had made several trips to Kerry in search of the elusive Kerryman and recalling one such trip to Kilcara Beg, remembered asking a neighbour if George was at home. He was informed that; 'He wasn't here since the last time'.[281]

Ó hAodha never managed to meet him in Kerry. He wrote to George on 18 May 1961, still attempting to get permission to record two new productions of *The Country Dressmaker* and *The Magic Glasses* and to broadcast them. He was also hoping to consider other plays at a later date. He asked George to send on a copy of *The Dandy Dolls* so that he could consider a version with music. Fitzmaurice's excuse for not allowing him produce *The Dandy Dolls* was that he only had a printer's copy of the play and refused the twenty-five guineas for a broadcast of *The Country Dressmaker*, and fifteen guineas for *The Magic Glasses*.[282]

When he persuaded George to visit him at his Radio Éireann office, Ó hAodha began a long monologue on the advantages of these radio productions, but all was in vain. Fitzmaurice simply stared out the window during the whole conversation and his eventual reply was, 'What a lovely day to be in Ballybunion'.[283] Despite George's infuriating behaviour, Brian Friel recalls being told by Ó hAodha that George asked him to take the suitcase full of his work to see if he could do something with it. Such was the nature of George's moods, although it is unclear why Ó hAodha did not take the case at this point.[284]

Fitzmaurice's bouts of illness were of such frequency that he often expressed the opinion that he had no further interest in seeing his work produced. He never wanted to, or never could, let go of his earlier feelings of rejection, and his deteriorating mental state seems to have had the effect of exacerbating the problem in his later years. Throughout his life Fitzmaurice was terrified of critics. Eamon Kelly, who played Captain Synan in the 1948 production of *The Moonlighter*, remembered him demanding that no critics be present on its opening night. He wanted no reviews to appear in the press. Fitzmaurice's reclusiveness was becoming more and more measured as he rigidly followed his daily routines. Indeed, his physical health was also deteriorating and by now he was particularly stooped, and he moved about with great difficulty.

By this time, his cousins, Marjorie and Colonel Wilfred Fitzmaurice had begun to visit him regularly whenever they travelled to Dublin from their home in Crosshaven, County Cork. The couple had spent a considerable amount of time in India where the Colonel had served in the Indian Army. Marjorie was an avid member of women's amateur drama groups in Crosshaven and a lifelong advocate of the R.N.L.I.

Whenever the couple called to George it was imperative that he covered everything in his room with newspaper before they were allowed in.[285]

He had long since given up eating in restaurants and now cooked his meals in his room. Apart from the odd bet on a horse, if it had any particular reference to kings in its name, he spent all he could afford on Guinness. He had long since acquired the habit of giving away his second-hand books when he had finished reading them. By now he was so stooped that, as he spoke with his head bowed, his hat covered his face completely. However, when something really interested him, he would look up slowly and display his apple-shaped and rather impish face and those deeply expressive eyes.[286] He often manifested his tendency towards contrariness and once ordered his landlady to allow no Protestant visitors to his room, although he did allow his cousins and Canon Dowse to visit. He still attended occasional music hall shows at the Old Royal Garden with Colonel Wilfred for company, but he never sat down and always walked about at the back. He confessed to Wilfred that this was because of what he termed the 'brainstorms'[287] he experienced from time to time, which had contributed to his not being at the Abbey for many years. By now, he was so afraid of crowds and small spaces that he walked everywhere, despite his difficulty in doing so, rather than take a bus or a train.

Harcourt Street was the ideal location for a man who spent much time sitting in St Stephen's Green, always at the same seat on the *Winter Garden Palace* pub side. He passed the time away by doing the Ximenes Crosswords or reading newspapers. He was very independent and never looked for help, buying his groceries at the corner shop, and always bought the English *Times* newspaper from the stall near his lodgings. Mrs Fennell, who ran the stall, remembered him as a 'very reserved, polite man' who, although he seemed contented, always appeared a lonely 'old Irish gentleman'.[288]

His last publication was in 1957 when *The Enchanted Land* took up a complete issue of the *Dublin Magazine*. This publication had prompted Lord Longford, Director of the Gate Theatre, to write to Fitzmaurice requesting permission to stage the play. Alas, it was to no avail as George failed to reply. It was only after his death that a draft letter was found scribbled on a cover torn from the *Dublin Magazine*. He had written:

> Some good while ago, your Lordship was good enough to send me a note re. a play called *The Enchanted Land* which appeared in the Dublin Magazine. It is regretted that a reply was not sent to your Lordship when the note was received, as it afterwards got mislaid. I daresay your Lordship has forgotten all about it. If not and if you

would still care to put in the play at your theatre I should of course be very glad if you did so. If not, of course, it's all right.[289]

The last line was crossed out. It is obvious that although his wording seems hesitant and nervous, that behind the façade and illness, he still cared. Intent on sending the final draft, he had addressed an envelope to the *Right Hon. Earl of Longford*, although it is unlikely he ever finished such a letter. Sadly, this letter can no longer be accounted for.

In the months after his death, a further letter came to light that he had written to Lord Longford's wife, providing crucial evidence of George's particular state of health during his last years. Written when the playwright was eighty-four years old, it began:

> Excuse my approaching Your Ladyship re a three-act play of mine which appeared in the *Dublin Magazine* for January-March 1957. Shortly afterwards the late Earl of Longford sent me a letter offering to produce the play which is called *The Enchanted Land*. Needless to state if I had been in my normal self I should have jumped at the offer especially in a theatre of the Gate's reputation and also not for years had there been a production of any of my plays.

In the light of our earlier queries regarding his lack of contact with the Gate during the 1920s and 1930s, this letter seems to indicate that Fitzmaurice had indeed been waiting in hope for an invitation from the theatre, as it is unlikely he would have turned down any earlier invitation from 'a theatre of the Gate's reputation'. The letter continues:

> About the same time Radio Éireann asked to be allowed to give a representation of *The Country Dressmaker* on its fiftieth anniversary to which I was also remiss in sending an answer. Afterwards, of course, when I did write accepting the offers it was too late. Sometime afterwards I came to the conclusion to furnish His Lordship with the explanation given above but the lamented demise of your late husband, prevented me doing so. Of course, Your Ladyship may never have read the play, or alternatively if you had done so it might not have been the kind of play you would put on. In that case no harm is done except whatever trouble I may by writing have put Your Ladyship to in explaining what very likely appeared as very bad manners on my part.
>
> I am,
> Your Ladyship's obedient servant,
> George Fitzmaurice'. [290]

Without a shadow of a doubt, his 1961 letter demonstrates the fact that this lost golden opportunity played on his mind over the years.

Critically, it points to an inability on Fitzmaurice's part to accept the consequences of this type of incident, not unlike the rejection of *The Dandy Dolls*. However, the letter gives further insight when Fitzmaurice explains his reasons for not excepting Lord Longford's invitation. He wrote:

> But at the same I was suffering from an attack of acute neurasthenia to which I am subject and renders me, on occasions, a border-line case.[291]

It seems that Fitzmaurice understood, at least to some degree, his own mental ill-health. His psychological condition seems to have deteriorated significantly as he got older. He was always a sharp and intelligent man and his interpretation of his own family background, and his father's manic and obsessive nature, might indicate his belief that he had succumbed to a genetically inherited illness. Although his reclusiveness may have been an element of his personality from the outset, it was aggravated considerably by his participation in the First World War, which left him prone to psychological or nervous disorders.

He was diagnosed with neurasthenia, a 'condition of nervous exhaustion in which, although the patient suffers from no definite disease, he becomes incapable of sustained exertion'.[292] The individual might believe that his or her closest friends think of the sufferer as a failure. This may suggest why Fitzmaurice constantly moved around the city. Today the condition is more readily recognized as a form of neurosis or psychoneurosis,[293] the physical signs of which are 'irritability, fatigue, anxiety and intolerance to noise';[294] symptoms that could very well have been attributed to Fitzmaurice down through the years.

In seeking to understand the writer, we find evidence that the symptoms he appeared to demonstrate might have derived from an obsessive-compulsive disorder, which is an element of high anxiety. His inability to let go of the past; his movement around the city; the covering of his belongings with newspaper before visitors entered;[295] his bets on horses with a reference to kings in their names;[296] sitting at the same seat in St Stephen's Green, etc., all point to the probability of an anxiety-based or obsessive behaviour. In fact, the issues regarding Kilcara Beg and the Stacks may well have become another obsession.

Figure 4: Marjorie Fitzmaurice and the author, 1999.

It may be that Fitzmaurice was manifesting signs of a schizotypal disorder[297] characterized by:

> eccentric behaviour and anomalies of thinking and affect which resemble those seen in schizophrenia, though no definite and characteristic schizophrenic anomalies have occurred at any stage [where] there is no dominant or typical disturbance.[298]

His seeming eccentricity was indicative of his poor rapport with others. His tendency towards social withdrawal, his odd beliefs, his suspiciousness or paranoid ideas, and his stereotyped thinking, are all elements of George's makeup that might be attributed as symptoms of some schizotypal disorder.[299] The disorder was also prone to fluctuations of intensity. The 1961 letter to the Countess of Longford indicates his ability to try and reason what was happening to him. Ironically, his last play, *The Coming of Ewn Andzale*, now seems somewhat autobiographical, in the light of the evidence as outlined here.

Perhaps his obsessions, depressions and eccentricities were also manifested in his sustained use of alcohol over many years. He always stayed on his own at the bar, never bought a round of drinks, and his dramatic themes of obsession readily point to alcohol addiction. He also told Wilfred on one occasion that he could not have gone on without Guinness.[300] However, we must not lose sight of the fact that his reclusiveness might have stemmed from the fact that 'people who are highly imaginative often find it difficult to form relationships with those around them'.[301] Perhaps Fitzmaurice is a case in point, and his imaginative streak did little to help him in the end but tormented him to such an extreme that the only solace he could find was in alcohol.

As his flamboyant father had left the family destitute, his fears were inherent in this joyless paternal inheritance. His father's tendency towards erratic and compulsive behaviour had resulted in the family's im-poverishment. He feared not having enough money to live on and simply could not understand why he had 'lived so long'.[302] During his final months, he used to huddle for warmth near a small gas stove in his bedsit and at one point told Wilfred he had enough money to keep him going for another three years only, despite the hundreds of pounds found in various accounts after his death.[303]

The veil of mystery surrounding the playwright has made students of his life and work concentrate on the image of a lonely old man. However, Colonel Wilfred stressed that George was, by no means, a 'gloomy man',[304] a fact that is sometimes too readily forgotten. Marjorie Fitzmaurice remembered him as being:

proud of his family name, and shy of all those who he considered moved in a higher strata of society, with his brilliant mind he found nothing in common with the others and this drove him more and more into himself.[305]

He did not know how to escape the ghosts of his past, and his genetic inheritance had obviously fuelled his lack of confidence. This imaginative man suffered terribly at times and had no one to share these innermost thoughts with. As he sat over his Guinness, the alcohol that had once invigorated his imaginative spirit and creative mind was now used to deaden the pain of loneliness.

Although George kept in contact with very few people, we do know that he corresponded regularly with Minnie Mulcaire, though none of these letters appear to have survived. The week before his death, Wilfred and Marjorie visited him and thought him more feeble than usual. Their amazement at his unwillingness to do anything about having his work produced manifested itself in an abrupt reply to a comment by Wilfred: 'You take the copyright, see what you can do'.[306] He had already asked the Colonel to take the copyright once before. The Colonel did exactly as George had wished about a year after his death, getting permission from all relatives to do so.[307]

One of the last people to see him on the evening of his death was Mrs Lily Fennell, when they had chatted about the weather. George went in to number 3 Harcourt Street for the very last time and there, on 12 May 1963, he died alone. No one in the building had ever realized that this quiet lodger was an Abbey Theatre playwright.

19 | His Death and the Following Years

A letter from Mícheál Ó hAodha to George Fitzmaurice, which was found by Gardaí in the dead man's room, confirmed the writer's identity. Among his scant belongings were some clothes and two small shelves of books, as well as a brown leather suitcase containing his plays, some in draft form and others that had never been published. Sadly, George did not have a single copy of the 1914 publication of his *Five Plays*, although he did have some of the single issues of those plays that Maunsel had also published. The case also contained receipts for rates on Kilcara Beg, old rent books, and other legal documents regarding the transfer of ownership from Ollie to himself.

Colonel Wilfred was to write later to an American cousin complaining that George 'caused a lot of trouble to everyone, by leaving no will'.[308] On his death, it was also discovered that he had about £800 in various accounts at the Post Office and other banks.[309] This was a very substantial sum of money for the time. Sadly, his later years had been filled with such fear and utter bewilderment at having lived such a long life, that he simply saved to make sure he remained solvent. Wilfred also recorded that on George's death, 'several cousins have put in an appearance' – obviously having heard of his saved money.[310] Wilfred hastened to add that none of these relatives were from his side of the family. These people had never shown the slightest interest in George or his life's work. Hanora Carleton was surprised to hear of a close relative, George, a man whom she had never known. She received the remaining monies once the funeral expenses were met.

The most interesting and perhaps tragic legacy left by the elderly playwright was a note on a torn scrap of paper, stating his readiness to sell the rights pertaining to his plays to 'anyone interested'. This note is now quoted from to such a degree that it has only served to enforce the typical portrait of Fitzmaurice as a lonely, bitter old man, whose disillusionment with the Abbey was lifelong. The note read in full:

> Author is prepared to sell outright all right in 14 plays dealing intimately with life in the Irish countryside. Most have been either produced or published, suitable to which to build musical, television, etc. Pass to anyone interested.[311]

It seems somewhat unfair to have concentrated solely on the negative tone of this directive by Fitzmaurice. The note illustrates that, though disillusioned at the time of writing, Fitzmaurice was forward thinking enough in alluding to the possibility of having his plays produced either as musicals or for television.

His funeral service was attended by those who had helped him in every possible way: Austin Clarke, Bryan MacMahon, Maurice Kennedy, Eamon Kelly, Liam Miller and Thomas MacGreevy, his cousins Marjorie and Wilfred Fitzmaurice and Minnie Mulcaire. Canon Dowse conducted the service at St Peter's Church, Aungier Street, which has since been demolished. The Colonel confirmed that although George did not practise his Protestant faith, he was not an atheist, and during their discussions George had said that 'Christ was a great Jewish reformer'.[312] His personal belongings were divided between his cousins, and Marjorie and Wilfred seem to have taken the books and a few other mementos. Marjorie later donated them to the National Library.[313] It is known that George corresponded with his cousins during the later years of his life, although none of this material can be accounted for. Sadly, even the note he wrote offering his plays for sale has disappeared, as well as the typescripts of plays such as *The Dandy Dolls*.

A year after Fitzmaurice's death, Howard K. Slaughter made his first trip to Ireland in order to complete a doctorate on the life and work of the playwright. To date this work has proved of immense importance and is usually a first point of reference for those studying his plays. Slaughter also produced a number of Fitzmaurice's plays with his students in the United States, beginning in 1964.[314]

Slaughter completed his doctorate in 1966 and his acquaintance with Miller, Clarke, Marjorie and Wilfred helped sustain enough interest in George's work to merit the publications of his plays and short stories by Miller's Dolmen Press. The first of three volumes of Fitzmaurice's plays was published in 1967. In reviewing this volume of *Dramatic Fantasies*, Mervin Wall claimed that it was 'a sad commentary ... that it has not been possible to publish the plays of George Fitzmaurice without a subsidy'.[315] However, despite Wall's observations, the importance of such publications should not be underestimated, for without them, Fitzmaurice's work might possibly have been lost. Two further volumes by Dolmen Press followed in 1969 and 1970: the *Folk Plays* and *Realistic Plays*. Regrettably, there was never any editorial note to explain Slaughter and Clarke's decisions regarding their specific divisions of the plays. For example, though *The Moonlighter* has always been described as a realistic play, it is published by Dolmen as a folk play. Other plays that also illustrate various dramatic devices and themes could merit publication in more than one volume. The collection of short stories, edited by Robert Hogan, followed in 1971.

The publication of the first volume in 1967 coincided with the Abbey's double bill production of *The King of the Barna Men* and *The Magic Glasses*, starring Eamonn Keane and Bill Kearney.[316] In reviewing these productions, Sean Page claimed that both plays were 'so unmistakeably modern that one has to keep reminding oneself they were written approximately half a century ago'.[317] Seamus Kelly, writing in *The Irish Times*:

> marvelled sadly once again that Yeats and his colleagues with all their fondness for Synge, were so blind and deaf to the dancing music of a wayward genius.[318]

He suggested that Samuel Beckett might have known Fitzmaurice's work, and asked if Aeneas Canty in *The King of the Barna Men* might have been 'the progenitor of many a Beckett creature?'[319] It is a possibility that Beckett's close friend and confidante, Thomas MacGreevy, may have introduced him to George's work.

Unfortunately, audiences were denied the possibility of attempting a true understanding of *The Magic Glasses* when producer, Sean Cotter, decided on a completely different ending. Rather than having Jaymony lying dead beneath the rubble of the loft, his jugular cut by the magic glasses, Jaymony is standing in the middle of the rubble alive and well at the close of curtain.

As Listowel staged *The Magic Glasses* in 1969, Hugh Hunt's production of *The Dandy Dolls* that same year attempted to right the wrong done to George in 1913. Sadly, Wilfred Fitzmaurice had died shortly before this production.[320] As the play was met with critical acclaim, Hunt recorded his incredulity at both Yeats and Lady Gregory having rejected the play, and wondered if perhaps the Abbey Directors might had felt 'it was too good'.[321] *The Irish Times* lavished praise on the production. The review describes the play as 'beautifully served by performances by Eamonn Keane (Roger) and Joan O'Hara (Cauth).' While Synge was described as 'the reporter with the poet's ear who listened and observed in Wicklow and the western islands', Fitzmaurice was 'the born poet who absorbed the mode of talk of the

Kerry people and their wild stories with his native air'.[322] Staged as part of a double bill, along with Synge's *The Well of the Saints*, *The Irish Times* reviewed both plays as being about 'grotesque people' and emphasized how they illustrated the 'barbarous cruelty of country people'.[323] This review also raises questions surrounding the earlier rejection of *The Dandy Dolls*. Kelly hinted that, had the play gone on tour to England in 1913, it would also have received similar excellent reviews as *The Pie Dish* had done in 1909, a fear by the Directors that led to the play's rejection in 1913. Though it was some fifty-seven years later, the play was acclaimed by British audiences in August 1970 when, as guests of the British National Theatre, the Abbey performed the play alongside *The Well of the Saints* at the Old Vic. Eric Shorter of the *Daily Telegraph* claimed it was as 'weird and wondrous a double bill as anyone could wish'.[324]

Not only was there growing interest in George's work by the professional theatre, there was also sufficient interest in amateur circles to warrant the 1968 production of *The Moonlighter* by the Listowel Players, who incorrectly assumed this production was the play's premiere.[325] However, this cannot deflect attention from the trojan efforts of the cast and all involved, under the watchful eye of producer John O'Flaherty. Described as 'the combination of lyric fantasy with savage reality',[326] the play was also entered in the Kerry Drama Festival in Killarney and played the night before *The Magic Glasses*, which was produced by Dennis Dennehy. The following year witnessed a prize-winning performance of *One Evening Gleam* in Cork.[327]

Whatever about remembering Fitzmaurice in theatrical circles, it turned out that the task of marking his grave became a long-drawn-out affair. Marjorie had written to Michael O'Connor in September 1969 that Wilfred had intended to use the royalties from *The Dandy Dolls* production to pay for the work.[328] However, a headstone for plot 29414 became the subject of much discussion and contention during the 1970s. A decision had been taken by Marjorie and Liam Miller to take a stone from the ancestral Duagh House, which was by then demolished, and have it inscribed by Michael Biggs and placed on the grave as a headstone. In a letter to Marjorie in December 1971, Liam Miller sent on an assignment declaration form for her signature, as well as two copies of Michael Biggs's drawing for the headstone:

> Please have the form completed and witnessed by a peace commissioner and return it to me with one copy of the drawing signed by you to signify approval.[329]

The wheels were set in motion and, on one occasion when Slaughter was in Ireland, he collected a window sill from Duagh House and brought it to Dublin by car, leaving it at Liam Miller's house.[330]

It seemed a straightforward matter, yet in a further letter of Marjorie's to Miller, she expresses her annoyance at the fact that no work had been done although she had sent back the forms. The end result was that no headstone was erected. Howard Slaughter had expressed his astonishment at the lack of progress during the intervening months and years after the communications took place. It was a sorry state of affairs that the playwright's resting place remained unmarked for thirty-two years until 1995, when the North Kerry Literary Trust and Duagh Historical Society had the work completed.

Whatever anticipation there might have been for an expected frenzy of activity in theatrical circles following the Abbey's success with *The Dandy Dolls*, it was another seven years before his work was seen once more on the Abbey stage. As a third volume of plays was published by Dolmen in 1970 with the available subsidies, articles on his work began to appear from time to time in various academic journals.

Fintan O'Toole believes that the Abbey's revivals of Fitzmaurice's work over the years were short-lived solely because of the theatre's concentration on him as a folk writer, which allowed the play's humour and mischief to become a secondary element of production.[331] Realistically, although productions of his work are welcome, individual and sporadic productions undermine the value and necessity of seeing the one-act plays in relationship to each other. Robert Hogan's declaration that Irish theatre would ignore Fitzmaurice to its detriment fell upon deaf ears.[332] Although Dolmen Press did publish Slaughter's concise biography on George in 1972, the book was never going to be a best seller. Arthur McGuinness published a further biography in 1975 and a third biography by Carole Gelderman followed in 1979, the latter two concentrating more specifically on his plays.

RTE Radio One, or Radio Éireann as it was called at the time, played an important role during the 1970s with two documentaries. Kieran Sheedy's *The Wicked Old Children of George Fitzmaurice* is an invaluable resource, featuring interviews with George's friends and neighbours, including his cousin Minnie Mulcaire. Tim Danaher also produced a second shorter but vital programme: *For Him the Flowers Smile*. These programmes also featured extracts from his plays, while Mícheál Ó hAodha made important radio productions of three plays: *The Dandy Dolls* (1973); *The Magic Glasses* (1976) and *One Evening Gleam* (1976).

The amateur productions continued. The Olivian Players won the All Ireland One-Act Competition in 1974 with *The Dandy Dolls,* while Carysfort College and the Little Theatre Cork both staged *The Enchanted Land* in 1975. The Rathmore Players premiered The *Green Stone* in 1978, reaching the All Ireland One-Act finals held in Naas. Its producer, Val Moynihan, won the overall Sportex Trophy for the most imaginative production at the Festival.[333] Meanwhile, Fitzmaurice made a welcome return to the Abbey stage in 1976 with *The Enchanted Land* and *The Pie Dish*, starring Eamon Kelly:

> His [Fitzmaurice's] language is so full of do be's and does be's, goosoons and ommadauns, that it is too easy to dismiss ... [the] bitter laughing anti-clericalism combined with our darkest traditions of folk tales.[334]

Christopher Fitz-Simon considered this production of *The Enchanted Land* as brilliant and, speaking of Eamon Kelly's performance as Leum Donoghue in *The Pie Dish,* he described it as 'unforgettable'.[335]

The Dolmen Press volumes of his plays allowed many amateur groups access to Fitzmaurice's work. During those early years, Listowel Writers' Week also commemorated the playwright. The 1971 Writers' Week programme included a *Tour to the Fitzmaurice Birthplace* (Bedford), which was led by Michael O'Connor (of Duagh), with a commentary by Liam Miller. That same year the programme also included a discussion of *The George Fitzmaurice Plays* chaired by Mícheál Ó hAodha. This was followed by a production of *The Magic Glasses.* The evening also included a reading of excerpts from *The Dandy Dolls* by Eamon Kelly and his wife Maura O'Sullivan. Two years later, the Writers' Week programme records the Listowel Players' premiere of the play *The Toothache* to mark the tenth anniversary of Fitzmaurice's death. The programme describes the event as a 'Location Drama Tour', which took place in Duagh. The play itself was preceded by a lecture on Fitzmaurice and Eamon Keane's reading from *The Crows of Mephistopheles.*

This interest in Fitzmaurice should have augured well for a series of separate events to mark the centenary of his birth in 1977. It seems, however, that there was a lack of interest in organizing any formal celebrations. Sadly, apart from enclaves of interested people countrywide, Fitzmaurice's name was by now 'only ringing very faint bells in the minds of most casual theatregoers'.[336] On 22 January 1977, Marjorie Fitzmaurice received a letter from Barney O'Reilly explaining how plans for any centenary celebrations would 'regretfully ... not work out ... At this time of the year I have been unable to arouse sufficient enthusiasm among the interested people in Listowel'.[337]

Apart from this seeming lack of interest in an individual commemorative event, Writers' Week did offer some very interesting events to commemorate the Duagh man. The 1977 souvenir programme included written contributions by Mícheál Ó hAodha and Liam Miller[338] and the festival also hosted the George Fitzmaurice Memorial Lecture, given by Professor Robert Hogan. The lecture was then followed by a production of *The Magic Glasses* by Listowel Drama Group. This event took place in Duagh on the opening night of the festival, and was repeated at Teach Siamsa, Finuge, on the Sunday afternoon.

The *Journal of Irish Literature* also marked the centenary of Fitzmaurice's birth with the publication of a newly discovered short story of George's, *Chasing the Ghoul*. However, on a more downbeat note, in his *Limerick Leader* newspaper column, John B. Keane wrote of the Abbey's decision to ignore the centenary: 'There has been no announcement from either the first or second national theatre. Neither has there been any word from the Gate'.[339] However, there was one professional theatre willing to commemorate this centenary: Druid Theatre Company premiered *There are Tragedies and Tragedies* during a summer season of Anglo-Irish Theatre in June of that year. Directed by Garry Hynes, the production was described as 'superbly dramatic and intensely moving'.[340]

1979 brought due recognition for Fitzmaurice when Tim Danaher's efforts resulted in the unveiling of a plaque at Number 3 Harcourt Street, Dublin. Unfortunately, the plaque (long since disappeared), had incorrectly stated that Fitzmaurice lived at Harcourt Street from 1901-1911. It was also inscribed with the famous lines from *The Moonlighter*:

> What signifies it now, what anyone did or didn't, since he is dead?
> But it is for him, and the likes of him, that the flowers smile, and
> always smiled, in the green soil of Ireland.[341]

Radio productions of *The Magic Glasses* and *One Evening Gleam* were repeated in 1983, to mark his twentieth anniversary. Looking through the Listowel Writers' Week programmes from the 1980s, there seems to have been a change in its programme content, and a move in a different direction resulted in Fitzmaurice being left out of the equation, except for a 1989 lecture by Fintan O'Toole, entitled *The Magic Glasses: The Magic Realism of North Kerry Writers*.[342] Fortunately, this lecture also resulted in an article on Fitzmaurice, which was published in *The Listowel Literary Phenomenon,* by its editor, Gabriel Fitzmaurice, a staunch advocate of Fitzmaurice's work and indeed of this biography since its infancy. O'Toole's article, 'The

Magic Glasses of George Fitzmaurice', is undoubtedly one of the best
interpretations of Fitzmaurice's work ever to have been published.
Although it seems the twentieth anniversary of Fitzmaurice's death
was not officially marked in Kerry, Robert Hogan had begun editing
the diaries of Joseph Holloway into five single volumes, having
commenced this work with the help of colleagues in the 1970s. The
fifth volume was completed during the mid 1980s. It was Hogan's
research that brought to light Fitzmaurice's 1913 letter to Lady
Gregory regarding the rejection of *The Dandy Dolls*. It was also Hogan
who discovered and published the three letters by George to the Abbey
Theatre written during the 1930s. Professor Hogan was a man who
thoroughly understood Fitzmaurice's contribution to Irish drama, and
he also displayed that sense of excitement and anticipation one enjoys
during a night at the theatre. Hogan's desire to promote Fitzmaurice's
genius was tireless, and his work resulted in the sourcing of vital
material necessary to any analysis of Fitzmaurice's work. Although the
1980s also resulted in the publication of important articles on his work
in various academic journals, there was little effort to promote
Fitzmaurice's work for the stage.

The flame seems to have been re-ignited following his thirtieth
anniversary in 1993, with the production of the *Rivers of Words*
television documentary series based on the North Kerry writers. Druid
Theatre marked the anniversary in July with two productions. *There
are Tragedies and Tragedies,* was deemed 'a great laugh, with
excellent performances by all'.[343] *The Ointment Blue* also received very
positive reviews and *The Sunday Tribune* newspaper described the
productions as 'a rich celebration of a poorly neglected writer of
exquisite genius'.[344]

The slow and steady regard for Fitzmaurice's work, reawakened
once more by the *Rivers of Words* documentary on the playwright, has
continued. This excellent documentary records vital interviews with
neighbours and retraced Fitzmaurice's steps in North Kerry and
Dublin. It also prompts the viewer to contemplate on just how this
wayward genius might have sunk into anonymity.

The opening of the *Seanchaí* Literary and Cultural Centre in
Listowel in 2000 finally gave people an open opportunity to learn
about Fitzmaurice and indeed about all the North Kerry writers. It is
housed in an old Georgian mansion that was once home to George's
uncle, Ulysses, who had a medical practice there. Each of the North
Kerry writers – John B. Keane, Bryan MacMahon, Maurice Walsh,
Brendan Kennelly and George Fitzmaurice – has been allocated a
room where the landscape, folklore, the local people and the rich
cultural heritage are illustrated as influences on these men's writings.

The George Fitzmaurice Room is designed to give the impression of his bedroom at number 3 Harcourt Street, where he died. As well as the all-important leather suitcase holding his work, dolls are found about the room, lying there just as silently as they exist in the play *The Dandy Dolls*. Ironically, this room overlooks the Square in Listowel and from the window one looks out onto what was once the Church of Ireland, which he and his siblings attended with their father.

With the opening of this Centre, a new initiative was given to devotees of Fitzmaurice's work and The George Fitzmaurice Society was formed. The inaugural meeting of the Society took place in the Stephen's Green Hotel, in June 2001, on the site of number 3 Harcourt Street.[345] On an outside wall a new plaque commemorates the fact that George lived and died there. Eamon Kelly, who was the guest of honour that evening in June, enthralled the membership with his stories of Fitzmaurice, (although he never knew him very well), as well as reading from excerpts from the plays. The George Fitzmaurice Society received its formal Kerry launch in September 2002 with a lecture by Professor Howard Slaughter, attended by a huge audience.

Figure 5: Outside St Stephen's Green Hotel, June 2001. From left: Jimmy Deenihan TD; Ann McAuliffe; Eamon and Maura Kelly (centre); Fiona Brennan (second from right); Greg Collins (first from right). Photographer: Mike O'Sullivan.

RTÉ Radio One broadcast a special Bowman's Saturday programme on 11 May, while the formal commemoration ceremony on Sunday 11 May, organized by The George Fitzmaurice Society, began with an oration at the playwright's graveside, followed by a gathering at the St Stephen's Green hotel.

During 2003, the fortieth anniversary of Fitzmaurice's death was commemorated in great style. In January, the Sliabh Luachra Drama Group, Scartaglin, County Kerry, staged *The Country Dressmaker*. The play was initially staged in Scartaglin for four nights, but public demand resulted in a fifth night. The Group also played for one very special night in Duagh Village. The Lartigue Theatre Group also commemorated the fortieth anniversary by staging *'Twixt the Giltinans and the Carmodys*. Those who had gathered were entertained firstly with an interpretation of *The Magic Glasses*, followed by a talk by Theatre Director, Conall Morrison. Morrison had directed the final year students of the Trinity College School of Drama in a production of four one-act plays, which included *The Dandy Dolls* in March 2002. During his talk, he spoke of his experiences with this production and the fact that he believes Fitzmaurice was a playwright who 'pursued his own route' as someone Yeats simply could not manage.

Although George Fitzmaurice's exclusion from the Abbey may be 'one of the most poignant and shameful' stories of the Theatre's history, Fitzmaurice remains 'one of the great twentieth century playwrights, and ... a figure of international significance'. [346] Though his one-act fantasies are, according to Morrison, 'remarkable by any standards', they are, unfortunately, seen as unworkable in terms of commercial management.

Like Conall Morrison, I remain 'intoxicated by the spirit' that is Fitzmaurice's, and agree firmly with both his and O'Toole's convictions that the work has possibilities for modern interpretation. Fintan O'Toole insists that the way forward for Fitzmaurice's work is its treatment as new works of genius. This has begun with productions of *The Dandy Dolls* by the Trinity School of Drama (2002) and the Abbey Theatre (2004). Both were directed by Morrison. Ironically, the Abbey's 2004 production of *The Dandy Dolls* was part of a triple bill that included Synge's *Riders to the Sea* and *Purgatory* by W.B. Yeats. Long before the successful modern-day Irish playwrights such as Marina Carr, Billy Roche and Vincent Woods began utilizing imagination and realism as well as 'the poetic and theatrical resources of Irish speech in English',[347] Fitzmaurice was doing it. A Fitzmaurice fantasy play is certainly a challenge, but it is one that can, quite realistically, be met by current technology, skilful producers and set designers. Theatre practitioner, lecturer and director, Andy Crook, insists that Fitzmaurice's play, *The Dandy Dolls*, can be read at a similar level to the work and themes of Samuel Beckett, with particular regard to the incredible mix of the human and the mythical that finds one almost in a Freudian world, deep in the recesses of some one person's head.[348]

My hope for the future is that we will see productions of his work on a more regular basis. Perhaps a theatre group might rise to the challenge of producing a season of Fitzmaurice's plays?[349] The challenge of finding new ways to interpret his work will lead to the discovery of a multitude of satisfying ways of dealing with their complexity, brevity, vitality and colour. Interpretations of the sheer physicality of his work most certainly have 'the potential to live on stage now'.[350] Fantasy was once a liberating force for George Fitzmaurice who desperately wanted to share with audiences his vision of theatrical entertainment. He wanted to entertain and delight audiences. His ability to dramatize a melding together of both real and imaginary worlds still results in an energetic vitality. Reviews of the Abbey production of *The Dandy Dolls* suggest that it has identified many new Fitzmaurice fans and illuminated 'a neglected but influential work' in its 'exhilarating choreographed sequences ... and riveting performances'.[351] The Ennis Players won the All Ireland One-Act Drama Finals during 2004 with their production of *The Dandy Dolls*, proving once more that Fitzmaurice's theatre still has the ability to impress astute adjudicators and audiences alike. Having represented Ireland at the World Festival of Amateur Theatre in Monte Carlo in August 2005, the Ennis players have launched Fitzmaurice's long overdue introduction to European and worldwide audiences.[352]

In addition to the many commentaries by critics and academics quoted in the pages of this book, the most enlightening aspect of the quality of George Fitzmaurice's work was made clear to me, not just in the Abbey in 2004, but in a small village hall in County Kerry during the winter of 2003.[353] Despite freezing weather, with more than a hint of snow in the air, an amateur production of a Fitzmaurice play had patrons, who had failed to secure admission because of overcrowding at each of the four scheduled performances, insisting that the director and cast extend the run. Quite simply, not only do the plays work on stage, they are timeless for urban and rural audiences alike and are an extraordinary legacy which will be appreciated for decades, if not centuries, to come. Interpretations of his work need no longer be overshadowed by images of Fitzmaurice's personal demise. Instead, we can begin to envisage Fitzmaurice as the incredible young rogue, eagerly waiting for the latest gossip from those passing through Bateman's Gate to the farm at Kilcara Beg.

On a wet January evening in 2000, I met with Eamon Kelly at the Abbey Theatre. As we sat upstairs chatting, I was enthralled just listening to Eamon speaking about his role as Leum Donoghue in *The Pie Dish*. It was almost as if he had travelled backwards in time visualizing himself on the stage during a performance. Eamon went quiet for a while and looked out into the night. After a short period of time spent in reflection he turned slowly to face me. Looking at me directly with soft, sincere eyes he said very, very gently, 'You know; he was wild in his own way'. And do you know what? I think George would just as quietly agree.

Bibliography

Primary Sources

Fitzmaurice, G., *Five Plays* (Boston: Little Brown, Maunsel, 1914).
---, *The Linnaun Shee. Dublin Magazine.* Vol. 2, No. 3. Oct. 1924.
---, *The Green Stone. Dublin Magazine* (New series). Vol.1, No. 1, Jan – Mar. 1926.
---, *Twixt the Giltinans and the Carmodys. Dublin Magazine.* Vol. 23, No. 3, July – Sept. 1948.
---, *There are Tragedies and Tragedies. Dublin Magazine.* Vol. 23, No. 3, July – Sept. 1948.
----, *One Evening Gleam. Dublin Magazine.* Vol. 24, No. 1, Jan – Mar. 1949.
---, *The Coming of Ewn Andzale. Dublin Magazine.* Vol. 30, No. 3, July – Sept. 1954.
---, *The Terrible Baisht* or *Ireland must have – if not the capital T. at any rate a blue beard. Dublin Magazine.* Vol. 30, No. 4, Oct. – Dec. 1954.
---,*The Enchanted Land. Dublin Magazine.* Vol. 32, No. 1, Jan. – Mar. 1957.
---, *The Plays of George Fitzmaurice.* Vol. 1, *Dramatic Fantasies.* Introduction by Austin Clarke (Dublin: Dolmen Press, 1967).
---, *The Plays of George Fitzmaurice.* Vol. 2, *Folk Plays,* Introduction by Howard K. Slaughter (Dublin: Dolmen Press, 1969).
---, *The Plays of George Fitzmaurice.* Vol. 3, *Realistic Plays.* Introduction by Howard K. Slaughter (Dublin: Dolmen Press, 1970).
Fitzmaurice, G. and John Guinan., *The Wonderful Wedding* (Journal of Irish Literature Vol 7 No. 3, pp.3-36.
---, *The Crows of Mephistopheles and Other Stories,* ed. Robert Hogan (Dublin: Dolmen Press, 1970).

Secondary Sources

Achilles, *Jochen,* 'George Fitzmaurice's Dramatic Fantasies: Wicked Old Children in a Disenchanting Land', *Irish University Review* 15, 2 (1985): 148-63.

---, 'The Glame from That Old Lamp': The Unity of George Fitzmaurice's
    Plays", *Éire-Ireland* (Winter 1985): 106-29.
Boucicault, Dion, *The Dolmen Boucicault*, ed. David Krause (Dublin: Dolmen,
    1964).
Boyd, Ernest, *Ireland's Literary Renaissance* (Dublin: Allen Figgis, 1968).
---, *The Contemporary Drama of Ireland Dublin*: (Dublin: Talbot Press,
    1918).
Broderick, Bernie & Michael O'Donnell, 'George Fitzmaurice', *Macalla Na
    Mainistreach 2001* (Abbeyfeale: Glór na nGael, 2001).
Clarke, Austin, 'The Dramatic Fantasies of George Fitzmaurice', *Dublin
    Magazine* 15 (April-June, 1940): 9-14.
Clarke, Brenna Katz, *The Emergence of the Irish Peasant Play at the Abbey
    Theatre* (Ann Arbor: University of Michigan Press, 1982).
Conbere, John P., 'The Obscurity of George Fitzmaurice' *Eire-Ireland* 6
    (Spring 1971): 17-26.
Cooke, John, ' "Tis Mysterious Surely and Fantastic Strange": Art and Artists
    in Three Plays of George Fitzmaurice', *Irish Renaissance Annual* 1
    (Newark, University of Delaware Press, 1980): 32-55.
Corkery, Daniel, *Synge and Anglo Irish Literature* (Cork: Mercier Press,
    1966).
Coughlin, Matthew Nicholas, 'George Fitzmaurice's *The Magic Glasses*',
    Dublin Magazine 10 (Autumn/Winter, 1973/74): 94-115.
---, 'Farce Transcended: George Fitzmaurice's *The Toothache*': *Éire-Ireland*
    10, 4 (Winter 1975): p.85-100.
Deane, Seamus, *Essays in Modern Irish Literature 1880-1980*. (London:
    Faber and Faber, 1985).
Fallon, Brian, *An Age of Innocence: Irish Culture 1930-1950* (Dublin: Gill and
    MacMillan, 1998).
Ferguson, Robert, *Henrik Ibsen: A New Biography* (London: Richard Cohen
    Books, 1996).
Fitzmaurice, Gabriel, *Kerry on My Mind; of Poets, Pedagogues and Places*
    (County Clare:Salmon Publishing, 1999).
Fitzmaurice, Henry, 'Original Tales', *The Kerry Magazine* Vols. V-IX (May-
    Sept. 1854). Kerry County Library, Tralee: Local Studies Section.
---, Fitz-Simon, Christopher, The Abbey Theatre, Ireland's National Theatre:
    The Last One Hundred Years (London: Thames and Hudson, 2003).
Foster, Roy, *The Oxford History of Ireland*. Reprint (Oxford U.P. 2001).
Furay, Julie & O Hanlon, Redmond, eds, *Critical Moments: Fintan O'Toole on
    Modern Irish Theatre* (Dublin: Carysfort Press, 2003).
Gailey, Alan, *Irish Folk Drama* (Mercier Press, 1969).
Gaughan Anthony, *Listowel and its Vicinity* (Tralee, 1973).
Gelderman, Carole W., 'Austin Clarke and Yeats's Alleged Jealousy of George
    Fitzmaurice', *Éire-Ireland* 8,3 (Summer 1973): 62-70.
---, *George Fitzmaurice* Boston: (Twayne, 1979).
Glassie, Henry, *All Silver No Brass: An Irish Christmas Mumming*
    (University of Pennsylvania Press, 1983).
Greene, David & Stephens, Edward, *John Millington Synge* (New York: The
    MacMillan Co., 1959).

Gregory, Lady Augusta, *Our Irish Theatre* (New York and London: The
  Knickerbocker Press, 1914). Reprinted (Gerrard's Cross: Colin Smythe,
  1972).
Grieson, Introduction to *Ivanhoe* by Sir Walter Scott (London: Collins, 1962).
Halpern, Susan, *The Life and Works of Austin Clarke* (Dolmen Press, 1974).
Harmon, Maurice, 'Cobwebs before the Wind: Aspects of Irish Peasantry in
  Irish Literature 1800-1916', as published in *Views of the Irish Peasantry*,
  by Daniel Casey and Robert E. Rhodes (Connecticut, 1977).
Henderson, Joanne L., 'Checklist of Four Kerry Writers' *Journal of Irish
  Literature* (May 1972): 101-119.
Hennessy, D.C., *The Lays of North Kerry*, North Kerry Literary Trust, reprint
  2001.
Hogan, Robert and Richard Burnham, eds. *The Journal of Irish Literature*,
  Vol. 10, No. 2 (May 1981).
Hogan, Robert, 'The Genius of George Fitzmaurice': After the Irish
  Renaissance: a Critical History of Irish Drama since the Plough and the
  Stars (London: Macmillan, 1968), pp.164-75.
---, ed., *A Dictionary of Irish Literature* (Greenwood Press, 1980).
Hogan R. & Harry T. Moore, eds, Joseph Holloway's Abbey Theatre: A
  Selection From his Unpublished Journal "Impressions of a Dublin
  Theatregoer", Illinois: Southern Illinois University Press, 1967.
Hogan, Robert & James Kilroy eds. *Lost Plays of the Irish Renaissance*
  (California: Proscenium Press, 1970). Distributed in UK by Colin Smythe.
---, The Abbey Theatre: Laying the Foundations: 1902-1904, Vol. 1 (Dublin:
  Dolmen Press, 1978).
---, *The Abbey Theatre: The Years of Synge 1905-1909*, Vol. 2 (Dublin:
  Dolmen Press, 1978).
Hogan, Robert, Richard Burnham & Daniel P.Poteet, eds, *The Abbey Theatre*:
  The Rise of the Realists Vol. 3 (Dublin: Dolmen Press, 1979).
---, Since O'Casey and Other Essays on Irish Drama (Colin Smythe, 1983).
---, & Richard Burnham, eds., *The Abbey Theatre: The Art of the Amateur
  1916-1920*, Vol. IV, Dolmen Press, 1984.
---, The Years of O' Casey 1921-1926: A Critical Documentary, Vol. V, Colin
  Smythe, 1992.
Hunt Hugh, *The Abbey: Ireland's National Theatre* (Dublin: Gill &
  MacMillan, 1979).
Kavanagh, Peter, *The Story of the Abbey Theatre* (New York 1950).
Kelly, Eamon, *The Journeyman* (Dublin: Marino Books, 1998).
Kennedy, Maurice, 'George Fitzmaurice: Sketch for a Portrait', *Irish Writing*
  (June 1951): 38-46.
Levanthal, A.J. review of 'The Dandy Dolls', *Dublin Magazine*, Vol.21, No.1
  Jan-March, 1946, p.49.
---, Review of 'The Magic Glasses', *Dublin Magazine*, Vol. 21, No. 3, July-Sept.
  1946, p.40.
---, Review of 'The Moonlighter', *Dublin Magazine*, Vol.24, No. 1, Jan-March,
  1949, p38.
---, review of ' T he Linnaun Shee', *Dublin Magazine*, Vol.24, No. 3, July-Sept.
  1949, pp.48-49.

Longford, W.U. Desmond, 'The Fitzmaurices of Duagh, Co. Kerry' in *The Irish Genealogist*, 1956.

Lysaght, P., *Notes towards a History of Duagh* (Limerick: Treaty Press Ltd., 1970) Reprinted 2000.

MacMahon, J., 'Padraig Liath O Conchubhair', in the *Shannonside Annual*, 1959.

Malone, Andrew E., *The Irish Drama* London: Constable and Co., 1929.

---, 'The Rise of the Realistic Movement in *The Irish Theatre* ed. Lennox Robinson (New York: Macmillan), pp.89-105.

Martin, Elizabeth A. ed. *Concise Medical Dictionary*, 4ᵗʰ edition. (Oxford University Press, 1994).

Massingberd Montgomery, H., ed., *Burke's Irish Family Records* (Burke's Peerage Ltd., 1976).

Maxwell, D.E.S., A Critical History of Modern Irish Drama 1891-1980 (Cambridge: CU.P., 1984).

---, 'Irish Drama, 1899-1929, the Abbey Theatre': *The Field Day Anthology of Irish Writing*, Vol. 2, general editor, Seamus Deane (Field Day Publications, 1991), p.566.

Mercier, Vivian, *The Irish Comic Tradition* (London: Souvenir Press, 1991).

Miller, Liam, 'Fitzmaurice Country', *Journal of Irish Literature* Vol. 1 No. 2, (May 1972): 77-89.

---, 'George Fitzmaurice: A Bibliographical Note', *Irish Writing* no. 15 (June 1951): p.47-48.

---, 'Fitzmaurice in Print', Listowel Writers' Week Programme, 1977, p.14-15.

Morash, Christopher, *A History of Irish Theatre 1601-2000*, Cambridge U. P., 2002.

McGuinness, Arthur E., *George Fitzmaurice* Lewisburg, PA: Bucknell University Press, 1975.

Murray, Christopher, ed. Brian Friel Essays, Diaries, Interviews: 1964—1999 (London: Faber 1999).

Nicholls, Ken, 'The Fitzmaurices of Kerry', *Journal of the Kerry Archaeological and Historical Society*, No. 3 1970.

Ó hAodha, Mícheál, 'Fitzmaurice and the Pie-Dish' *Journal of Irish Literature*, (May 1972): 90-94.

---, *Theatre in Ireland* (Oxford: Basil Blackwell, 1974).

---, Introduction to *The Dandy Dolls*; Abbey Theatre Programme: performances from Monday 8 Sept. 1969.

O Malley, Conor, *A Poet's Theatre*, (Elo Press Ltd, 1988).

Ó Súillebháin, Sean, 'The Oral Tradition': *A View of the Irish Language*, ed. Brian Ó Cuív (Dublin: Stationery Office, 1969), pp.47-56.

O'Sullivan, Seumas, ed., *Dublin Magazine*: 1945; 1948; 1949: Reviews by A.J. Levanthal.

O'Toole, Fintan, 'The Magic Glasses of George Fitzmaurice': in *The Listowel Literary Phenomenon: North Kerry Writers: A Critical Introduction*, ed. Gabriel Fitzmaurice (Indreabhán, Conamara, Éire : Cló Iar-Chonnachta, 1994), p.13-25.

Ó Tuama, Sean, Repossessions: Selected Essays on Irish Literary Heritage (Cork University Press, 1999).

Owens, Cóilín D. & Joan N. Radner, *Irish Drama: 1900 – 1980* (Washington D.C.: Catholic University of America Press, 1990).
Pilkington, Lionel, 'Theatre History and the beginnings of the Irish National Theatre Project': *Theatre Stuff: Critical Essays on Contemporary Irish Theatre*, ed. Eamonn Jordan (Carysfort Press, 2000), pp.27-33
Power, Patrick C., *A Literary History of Ireland* (Mercier, 1969).
Riley, J. D., 'The Plays of George Fitzmaurice' *Dublin Magazine* 31 (Jan-March, 1955): pp.5-19.
Robinson, Lenox, *Ireland's Abbey Theatre: A History 1899-1951* (New York: Kennikat Press, 1951). Reprinted 1968.
Saddlemyer, Ann, ed., Theatre Business: the correspondence of the first Abbey Theatre directors, William Butler Yeats, Lady Gregory, and J.M. Synge(Gerrards Cross: Smythe, 1982).
Sanger, Wolfgang R., 'Caught between Tradition and Experiment: George Fitzmaurice's *The Moonlighter*', in *Studies in Anglo-Irish Literature*, (volume number unrecorded), ed. Heinz Kosok.
Schrank Bernie & William Demestes, eds., *Irish Playwrights 1880-1995I* (Connecticut: Greenwood Press 1997).
Sihra, Melissa, Writing in Blood': Programme foreword to *Ariel* by Marina Carr, staged at the Abbey Theatre, 2 Oct.– 9 Nov. 2002.
Slaughter, Howard K., *George Fitzmaurice and his Enchanted Land* (Dublin: Dolmen Press, 1972).
---, 'Fitzmaurice and the Abbey' in *Educational Theatre Journal* 22 (May 1970): 146-54.
Thomson, William A.R., *Black's Medical Dictionary, 32nd edition* (London: Adam and Charles Black, 1979).
Unterecker, John, 'Countrymen, Peasant and Servant in the Poetry of WB Yeats', in *Views of the Irish Peasantry 1800-1916*, eds Daniel J. Casey and Robert E. Rhodes (Connecticut: Archon Books 1977).
Wade Allan, ed., *The Letters of W. B. Yeats* (London: Rupert Hart-Davis, 1954).
Watt, Stephen, Joyce, O'Casey and the Irish Popular Theatre (1991).
Welch, Robert, The Abbey Theatre 1899-1999: Form and Pressure (Oxford: U. P., 1999).
---, ed., *The Oxford Companion to Irish Literature* Oxford (The Clarendon Press: 1996).

Unpublished Sources

Brennan, Fiona, George Fitzmaurice, Playwright: His Early Life and Influences, (UCC, 2002).
Browne, Kathleen, A Dictionary of Kerry Writers; Local Studies Section, Kerry County Library, Tralee, Co. Kerry.
Deenihan, Jimmy, Archival Material including undated newspaper clippings and recorded video material.
Eriksen, Gordon Gullman, The Wonderful and the Probable in the Plays of George Fitzmaurice (University of Colorado: 1973).

(Ph.D. dissertation thesis)
Gelderman, Carole W., *In Defense of George Fitzmaurice* (Northwestern University: 1972).
Irish Folklore Commission: Schools manuscripts Collection, Vol. 406/407, on microfilm, Killarney Local Library, Co. Kerry.
Keane, Dan. Unpublished notes regarding North Kerry folklore and placenames. (PhD. dissertation thesis).
Leahy Mark, 'To Prop Up Myths: Objects in the Plays of George Fitzmaurice'. Lecture given to the American Conference for Irish Studies, University of Maryland, College Park, October 2003.
Leslie, Canon John, 'Biographical Index of the Church of Ireland Clergy', Church of Ireland Library, Braemor Park, Dublin.
O'Connor, Brian, Undated description of Fitzmaurice; letters; and Abbey programmes from the personal papers of the late Mr Michael O'Connor, Springmount, Duagh, Co. Kerry.
Russell Ann, 'The Dramatic Fantasies of George Fitzmaurice: Allegories of Frustration (MA: UCD, 2001).
Slaughter, Howard K., 'A Biographical Study of Irish Dramatist George Fitzmaurice together with critical editions of his folk and realistic plays' (University of Pittsburgh, Pittsburgh, 1966).
Slowey, Desmond, 'Haunted Kitchens: The Two Worlds of George Fitzmaurice's Symbolist Quartet' (MA: St. Patrick's College, Drumcondra, 2001).
Valuation Records Vols. I, II, III for Bedford Listowel & Duagh, Listowel: Valuation Records Office, Irish Life Building, Lwr. Abbey St., Dublin.

Newspapers, Magazines & Reviews.

'An Irishman's Diary' *The Irish Times*, 28 January 1977.
Billington, Michael, Review of 'The Dandy Dolls' , London, Wed. 5 Aug. 1970.
Dublin Magazine Reviews: The Dandy Dolls (1945); The Moonlighter (1948); The Linnaun Shee (1949); One Evening Gleam (1952).
Fallon, Gabriel, Review of 'The King of the Barna Men', and 'The Magic Glasses', *The Evening Press*, 18 Sept. 1967.
Kelly, Seamus, 'Two Fitzmaurice Plays at the Peacock', *The Irish Times*, 16 Sept. 1967.
Kennedy, Mary, 'Fitzmaurice plays at the Peacock'. *Irish Times* 6 August 1976.
Keane, John B., A Pathetic Note Near Death Bed: Anyone Interested?' *Limerick Leader*, 19 March, 1977.
Kelly, Seamus, 'Play about Grotesque People', *The Irish Times*, 9 Sept. 1969.
Obituary, *Irish Times*, 12 May, 1963.
Ó hAodha, Mícheál, 'Fitzmaurice and the Pie-Dish' *The Irish Times*, 13May 1972.
'An Irishman's Diary' *The Irish Times*, 28 Jan. 1973.
---, 'The Quest for George Fitzmaurice: 1877-1963', unspecified and undated newspaper clipping from the archive of Jimmy Deenihan, T.D. Lixnaw, Co. Kerry.

---, 'The Casting out of George Fitzmaurice?' unspecified and undated
newspaper clipping from the archive of Jimmy Deenihan, T.D. Lixnaw, Co.
Kerry.
'Plaque to George Fitzmaurice', *The Kerryman*, 18 May 1979.
Sheedy, Kieran, "The Wicked Old Children of George Fitzmaurice', *RTE
Guide*, 23June 1972.
'The Abbey Theatre: Two New Plays', *The Daily Express*, 25 April 1913.
The Cork Examiner, 7 November 1900, Cork City Library.
'The Country Dressmaker', *The Irish Times*, 10 Jan. 1913, *The Irish Times*, 6
Oct. 1942 and 24 May 1949.
The Irish Press, May 22, 1963. ??
'The Magic Glasses & The Country Dressmaker', *The Times*, London, 25 June
1913.
The Daily Maroon (Chicago) short column that mentions *The Country
Dressmaker* during Abbey Tour; 14 March 1914: *Fine Arts Scrapbook*
978RN1073 March 1914 to Sept. 1918.
Wall, Mervyn, 'Resurrected Irish Playwright', *The Irish Times*, 8 July, 1967.

Correspondence and Interviews

Ben Barnes, Correspondence, June 2000.
John Bowman, Radio One. Correspondence, April 2003.
John Bridges, Associate Dean, The Theatre School, De Paul University, USA.
E-mail Sept 2002.
Mary Rose Callaghan. Correspondence, May 2000.
Patricia Casey. Correspondence, Oct. 2001 & Telephone interview Oct. 2002.
Greg Collins. Correspondence, November 2001.
Andy Crook. Interview, April 2005.
Jimmy Deenihan, TD. Various conversations and meetings.
Gabriel Fitzmaurice. Various conversations.
Marjorie Fitzmaurice. Conversations, June 1999 & 2000.
Christopher Fitz-Simon. In conversation, June 2004.
Dan Flynn, Duagh. Interview, January 2003.
Brian Friel. Personal correspondence, April 2004.
John Guinan, Co. Offaly. Telephone Conversation, Nov. 2001 (re. John
Guinan, playwright).
Danny Hannon, various conversations.
Maurice Harmon. E-mail Nov 2002.
Dan Joe and Eileen Hartnett, Duagh. Interview, Sept 2001.
Kieran Hoare, Hardiman Library, NUIG. E-mails re. Lyric Theatre Archive.
Gary Hynes, & Yvonne Corscadden. Correspondence, Druid Theatre Co.
Various dates.
Una Kealy, Conversations Sept. 2001& and other dates.
Dan Keane, Interview. Sept. 2001 & February, 2005.
Mary Keane, In conversation, February, 2003.
Paddy Keane, Duagh. In conversation, Nov. 2002.
Eamon Kelly, Correspondence, November 1999 and interview, January 2000.

Nora Kelley, Correspondence, August 2001 and e-mail August 2002.
Declan Kiberd, Correspondence, April 2004.
Tom Kilroy. Correspondence, 2004.
Sr Laboure, Mercy Convent, Tralee. Interviews and conversations, Nov. 2002 and Jan. 2003.
Owen MacMahon, in conversation, June 2004.
Ann McAuliffe, Duagh, various conversations.
Margaret McElligott, Creggane, Duagh Interview, Nov. 2002.
Patrick McKeon, correspondence, Oct. 2001.
Chris Morash, NUI Maynooth, interview, Nov. 2002.
Conall Morrison, interview, July 2002.
Paddy Murphy, Bedford, Listowel, interview, Nov. 2001.
Robert Nicholson, Dublin Writers Museum, Dublin, correspondence, Nov. 1998.
Barbara Ní Fhloinn Irish Folklore Commission UCD, telephone Conversation, Oct. 2001.
Bridie O'Connor, Finuge, Lixnaw, interview, Nov. 2002.
Barney O'Reilly, correspondence, July 1999.
Stuart Ó Seanóir, Assistant Librarian, Manuscripts Dept., TCD, August 2001, correspondence regarding the Thomas MacGreevy Papers.
Maura O'Sullivan, Abbey Actress, in conversation Sept. 2004.
Fintan O'Toole, Dublin, interview, July 2003.
Tadhg Pey, Co. Offaly, correspondence, 2001. (re. John Guinan, playwright).
Sr Loreto Relihan, Presentation Sister, Caherciveen and formerly of Bedford House, Listowel, telephone interview, Nov. 2001.
Tom Relihan, Bedford, Listowel. Various conversations.
Dr Susan Schreibman, UCD, correspondence, Feb. 1999.
Howard Slaughter, personal correspondence, June 2001 & various e-mails; interviews. Sept. 2001.
Dr Sharon Snow Head of rare Books and Manuscripts, Z. Smith Library, Wake Forest University, various e-mails re Dolmen Press collection, May 2003.

Manuscript, Archive and Internet Sources

Abbey Theatre Archives; early programmes and photographs regarding George Fitzmaurice's plays.
Births and Deaths Register; General Register Office, off Pearse St., Dublin: for register of Fitzmaurice siblings' births and deaths.
Chicago Historical Society: *Fine Arts Scrapbook* 9F38RNk93, re *The Country Dressmaker* in the USA in 1914. (with the help of Mr Leslie Martin Research Specialist Chicago Historical Society, Chicago).
Cork City Library, Grand Parade, Cork: Local Studies Section for newspapers.
National Archives, Bishop's St., Dublin: Search for relevant details regarding the Fitzmaurices of Duagh.
National Library of Ireland, Dublin, Manuscripts Room: George Fitzmaurice Papers, MS33,564 and MS28,919.
http://www.druidtheatre.com/archives; regarding the 1993 productions of *There Are Tragedies and Tragedies* and *The Ointment Blue*.

http://www.olivian players.com/ArchivesNaybar.htm.
http://www.wolfsonian.fiu.edu.
Kerry County Library Local Studies Section: for first edition of *Five Plays*, the
  1921 single edition of *The Country Dressmaker* and other archival material
  on North Kerry and George Fitzmaurice.
Killarney Library; Local Studies Section: Irish Folklore Commission
  notebooks on microfilm: for Duagh Volumes 406 & 407.
Lyric Theatre Archives: NUI Galway: correspondence with Mr Kieran Hoare
  regarding any available material regarding George Fitzmaurice.
Brian O'Connor, Springmount, Duagh: Archival material belonging to his later
  father, Mr Michael O'Connor, including letters and programmes regarding
  George Fitzmaurice.
Offaly County Library, Birr, Co. Offaly: Correspondence regarding available
  material on John Guinan: Ms. Mary Butler, Executive Librarian.
Poetry Ireland Archives: The Austin Clarke Library.
Seanchaí Literary and Cultural Centre, Listowel, Co. Kerry: Archive of
  Listowel Writers' Week Programmes, with thanks to Cara Trant, Manager.
The National Archives, Kew, Richmond, Surrey, UK
The Times, online source available at the National Library of Ireland, Dublin:
  Regarding the London performances of *The Magic Glasses* and *The
  Country Dressmaker* in 1913.
Trinity College, Dublin: Manuscripts Reading Room: a search of available
  manuscript sources of Thomas MacGreevy for any relevant information
  regarding George Fitzmaurice; TCD MSS 7985-8190: with kind permission
  from Ms. Margaret Farrington and Mr Nicholas Ryan, joint copyright
  holders.
Radio Centre: Radio One archival recordings of *The Wicked Old Children of
  George Fitzmaurice* and *For Him the Flowers Smile*, produced by Tim
  Danaher, with thanks to Ian Lee.
Valuation Records Office, Irish Life Building, Lower Abbey St., Dublin: All
  volumes regarding Bedford and Duagh, Listowel Co. Kerry.

Broadcasts & Lectures

Bowman's Saturday: Broadcast 10 May 2003 to mark the fortieth anniversary
  of George Fitzmaurice's death. With special thanks to John Bowman.
Declan Kiberd: lecture on J.M. Synge's *In the Shadow of the Glen* Radio One
  Autumn 1999.
Brennan, Fiona, *George Fitzmaurice and the Literary Revival; a Lecture*:
  presented at the Tarbert Education Centre, July 2003.
'Living Voices; Irish Life and Lore Series: George Fitzmaurice, *Radio Kerry*:
  Howard Slaughter and Fiona Brennan in conversation with Maurice
  O'Keeffe; first broadcast March 2003 & subsequently produced as part of a
  C.D. collection, Oct. 2003.
Morrison, Conall: 'A talk on the Trinity School of Drama production of *The
  Dandy Dolls*', May 11th 2003.

Rivers of Words: Television Documentary produced by the North Kerry Literary Trust in association with RTE, 1994: Executive producers Jimmy Deenihan T.D. & Joe Murphy.

The Dandy Dolls: produced by Tim Danagher for Radio Telefís Éireann featuring Eamon Keane, Neasa Ní Annracháinn, Eamon Kelly, Brendáin O'Dúill and Thomas Studley.

The Wicked Old Children of George Fitzmaurice: Radio Telefís Éireann. Radio programme first broadcast on 25 June 1972 and produced by Kieran Sheedy.

For Him the Flowers Smile: Radio Telefís Éireann: Radio broadcast produced by Tim Danagher 1973.

Endnotes

[1] The family's ancestral home was Duagh House, (also known as Springmount) and was situated across from the graveyard. It was allowed to fall into a dilapidated state and demolished during the 1960s. Today, the land is owned by Brian O'Connor, whose late father, Michael, was involved in the local amateur drama scene in Listowel. Michael was an advocate of Fitzmaurice's work and Brian still has some of his father's memorabilia that includes letters and Abbey Theatre programmes from the 1960s.

[2] Canon John Leslie, *Biographical Index of the Church of Ireland*, p.75 & p.225.

[3] He already saw one of his brothers, Ulysses (a doctor), living in a Georgian residence. Ulysses once resided at 24 The Square, Listowel, now home to *Seanchaí* Kerry Literary and Cultural Centre.

[4] Both the Valuation Records for Listowel, Vol. I 1859-1876, and Samuel Lewis's *Topographical Dictionary of Ireland*, 1837, substantiate this.

[5] Sr Loreto Relihan, Presentation Sister, Caherciveen, Co.Kerry, formerly of Bedford, Listowel: telephone interview, Nov. 2002.

[6] From the unpublished notes of Dan Keane, Poet and Writer, Moyvane, Co. Kerry: interview Sept.2002.

[7] Montgomery Massingberd, ed., *Burke's Irish Family Records*, p.436.

[8] See MS 33564/16, NLI, Dublin: a letter written by Marjorie Fitzmaurice to Fitzmaurice biographer, Carole Gelderman, during the 1970s, records the Bateman's ownership of Bedford House. Marjorie was a distant cousin of George's family, who was married to Colonel Wilfred Fitzmaurice, a second cousin of the Fitzmaurices.

[9] In conversation with Ann McAuliffe, Duagh, Sept. 2002, whose husband, the late Dan McAuliffe, was a relative of Winifred O'Connor's.

[10] This corrects the assumption that Winifred was originally from Kilcara Beg: interview with Sr Loreto Relihan, Nov. 2002.

[11] MS 33564/16 NLI, Dublin.

[12] Information on the years of the Fitzmaurice daughters' births is available at the General Register Office, Dublin. For information on the sons' births,

see *Burke's Irish Family Records*, p.436.

13 Fr Anthony Gaughan, *Listowel and its Vicinity*, p.248.

14 Arthur McGuinness, *George Fitzmaurice* p.19.

15 The change of ownership within the Valuation Records was made i n 1893. Staff at the Valuation Records Office reliably informed me that it took staff a couple of years to make the written changes to the records after the actual change in ownership took place. (Fiona Brennan, 'George Fitzmaurice: His Early Life and Influence's, unpublished dissertation, UCC, 2002, p.20).

16 Interview Nov. 2002: Bridie is a daughter of the late Catherine Morrissey who was a dressmaker and shop owner in Creggane.

17 Marjorie Fitzmaurice interviewed in the *River of Words* documentary.

18 Maurice Harmon, *Cobwebs before the Wind*, p.278.

19 When recalling the Fitzmaurices, locals never refer to any of the siblings by their first names only, but refer to them by their titles *Mister* or *Miss*, as they had always done.

20 Sean Ó Súillebháin, 'The Oral Tradition', p.47: *A View of the Irish Language*, ed. Brian Ó Cuív, p.47-56.

21 piseóga: superstitions.

22 *Listowel and its Vicinity*, p.256

23 ibid.

24 Eamon Kelly, *The Journeyman*, p.97.

25 Gabriel Fitzmaurice, *Kerry on My Mind: Of Poets, Pedagogues and Places*, p.6

26 ibid.

27 Paddy Lysaght, *A History of Duagh*, p.41.

28 See *The Plays of George Fitzmaurice: Folk Plays, Vol. II;* Introduction by Austin Clarke, p.xvi.

29 Bridie O'Connor recounted a warning she received in the confessional regarding the fact that she should not even visit a Protestant family: interview Nov. 2002.

30 Paddy Keane, Duagh, in conversation regarding local lore surrounding George, Nov. 2002.

31 See Paddy Lysaght's *The History of Duagh*. Locals tell of this cave that is on the Fitzmaurice's farm.

32 Grierson's introduction to *Ivanhoe*, Sir Walter Scott, p.11- 14.

33 Just as George would later enjoy reading European history, Scott was an avid reader of both Scottish and medieval European histories.

34 D.C. Hennessy reported on the 1869 Tenants' Rights demonstration in Listowel that Parson Fitzmaurice spoke at. See *Listowel and its Vicinity*, p.153.

35 D.C. Hennessy, *The Lays of North Kerry* p.22-23.

36 Introduction by Robert Hogan to *The Crows of Mephistopheles*, p.10.

37 Cited in Carole Gelderman's *George Fitzmaurice*, p.32.

38 Professor Hogan was a lifelong advocate and admirer of Fitzmaurice's work. Following the publication of this volume of short stories, he discovered another of George's stories, entitled *Chasing the Ghoul* (1905) and

published it in the *Journal of Irish Literature* Sept. 1977, to celebrate the centenary of the playwright's birth.

39 George was believed to have been seeing a lady by the name of Joan Stack, around this time. This is, however, refuted by Sr Labouré, Mercy Sister, St John's, Tralee, formerly of Kilcara, Duagh: interview Nov. 2002 and in conversation Jan. 2003.

40 See 'Cupid and Cornelius' in *The Crows of Mephistopheles*, p.109.

41 Robert Hogan and Richard Burnham, eds., *The Journal of Irish Literature*, Vol. VII No.3, 1977; p.57-63.

42 *Cobwebs before the Wind*, p.130.

43 'The People of the Glens' was serialized in *The Shanachie*, Summer 1907. Ironically, the excerpt as quoted is from the same issue that featured the story *The Crows of Mephistopheles*.

44 Sean Ó Tuama, *Repossessions: Selected Essays on Irish Literary Heritage*, p.224.

45 Bryan MacMahon told a story he told of a rabbit trapper who had once ' ... heard a voice comin' from under the ground. It was telling of kings and queens, of moonlighters, quack doctors, of pookas and chariots ridin' across the sky.' He thought he was bewitched, until he saw ' ... George struttin' up and down the field and he manufacturin' drama'. See Arthur McGuinness, *George Fitzmaurice*, p.26.

46 According to *Guy's Munster Directory*, (Cork City Library, Local Studies Section), there was no branch of the Hibernian Bank in Cork at this time. It is uncertain if George and Mossie worked in the same bank in Cork with Mossie transferring to the Hibernian Bank later.

47 Stephen Watt, *Joyce, O'Casey and the Irish Popular Theatre*, p.5.

48 ibid., p.6.

49 ibid., p.17.

50 ibid., p.23.

51 See Christopher Morash, *A History of Irish Theatre: 1601-2000*.

52 This was Hyde's address to the National Literary Society that argued for the preservation and revival of the Irish language and culture.

53 A collection of the series of poems published in the *Nation* in 1890 and continued in the *Weekly Freeman* 1892-3.

54 Chris Morash, *A History of Irish Theatre*, p.116.

55 ibid., p.116.

56 ibid., p.117.

57 Cited in *A History of Irish Theatre: 1601-2000*, p.119.

58 Holloway's diaries prove to be an invaluable source regarding Fitzmaurice's life in Dublin.

59 Lady Gregory, *Our Irish Theatre*, p.61.

60 Yeats's association with the Fay brothers proved an important element of this decision. See Hugh Hunt *The Abbey: Ireland's National Theatre*, p.35.

61 ibid., p.32.

62 Conor O'Malley, *A Poet's Theatre*, p.17.

63 Robert Welch, *The Abbey Theatre 1899-1999: Form and Pressure*, pp.25-6.

168Wild in His Own Way

[64] Lionel Pilkington, 'Theatre History and the Beginnings of the Irish National Theatre Project': Eamonn Jordan ed., *Theatre Stuff: Critical Essays on Contemporary Irish Theatre*, p. 29.

[65] Hugh Hunt, *The Abbey: Ireland's National Theatre*, p.63.

[66] His short story, *A Prayer for St Anthony*, was published in *The Shanachie*, (Autumn 1907), just a few months after George's *The Crows of Mephistopheles* was published in the same journal.

[67] *John Millington Synge*, Greene and Stephens, p.212. NOTE: This play may have been an earlier version of *The Plough Lifters* that was staged in Mar. 1916. (See *Joseph Holloway's Abbey Theatre: Impressions of a Playgoer* ed. Hogan, p.276).

[68] Cited in *The Abbey Theatre: The Years of Synge*, Hogan et al, p.247.

[69] ibid., p.240.

[70] ibid., p.246.

[71] *A Biographical Study of Irish Dramatist George Fitzmaurice together with critical editions of his folk and realistic plays* Howard K. Slaughter. Unpublished thesis, p.26-7. (This will be cited in following chapters as; Slaughter, Unpublished Thesis).

[72] *Since O'Casey and Other Essays on Irish Drama*, Robert Hogan, p.30.

[73] In the manuscripts in the National Library of Ireland, Dublin, are two old drafts of this play (NLI, Dublin, MS 33564). The final draft is titled *The Ointment Blue* and was premiered by Druid Theatre Co. in 1977, to commemorate the centenary of Fitzmaurice's birth.

[74] *The Plays of George Fitzmaurice: Realistic Plays*, Vol. 3, Introduction by Howard Slaughter, pp.3-14.

[75] Matthew Nicholas Coughlin, 'George Fitzmaurice's Magic Glasses': *Dublin Magazine* 10. Autumn/Winter 1973-74: p.85 & p.87.

[76] *The Plays of George Fitzmaurice: Folk Plays*, Vol. 2, Introduction by Howard Slaughter, pp.3-40.

[77] The play was also published separately as part of the *Lost Play Series*, by Proscenium Press, 1978.

[78] Robert Hogan, *The Journal of Irish Literature* Vol. 7. No. 3, 1978, p.4.

[79] *The Abbey Theatre :The Years of Synge*, p.247.

[80] *The Journal of Irish Literature* Vol. 7. No. 3, p.4.

[81] John Guinan and George Fitzmaurice, *The Wonderful Wedding*, as published in the *Journal of Irish Literature* Vol. 7. No. 3, pp.3-36.

[82] Ann Saddlemyer, ed., *Theatre Business: The Correspondence of the First Abbey Theatre Directors*, p.253, note 2.

[83] Holloway recorded this entry on 22 March 1907, which verifies that the Abbey had already accepted Fitzmaurice's play at that point in time. Cited in *The Abbey Theatre :The Years of Synge*, p.90.

[84] Cited in *George Fitzmaurice and His Enchanted Land*, p.19.

[85] Carole Gelderman, *George Fitzmaurice*, pp.119-121.

[86] Holloway cited in *The Abbey Theatre: The Years of Synge*, p.95

[87] See *The Country Dressmaker* in the *Five Plays* edition published by Maunsel & Roberts (1914), p.37.

[88] 'Chaney teapot' is the china teapot or what was more commonly known as

the 'good' teapot.

89 It is important to correct Maxwell's assertion that this change was a 'precursor' to the dark writing of the dramatic fantasies, when in fact Fitzmaurice made this change more than ten years AFTER *The Dandy Dolls* and *The Magic Glasses* had been written: D.E.S. Maxwell, *Irish Drama, 1899-1929, the Abbey Theatre:* General Editor, Seamus Deane, *The Field Day Anthology of Irish Writing*, Vol. 2I, Field Day Publications, 1991, p.566.

90 Slaughter, Unpublished Thesis, p.51.

91 Carole Gelderman, *George Fitzmaurice*, p.83.

92 *The Abbey Theatre: The Years of Synge*, p.178.

93 Ernest Boyd, *Ireland's Literary Renaissance*, p.358.

94 Cited in *George Fitzmaurice and His Enchanted Land*, p.19.

95 ibid., p.25.

96 Cited in *The Abbey Theatre: Form and Pressure*, p.47.

97 Andrew Malone, *The Irish Drama*, p.91.

98 See William Boyle's letter to Holloway: *The Years of Synge* p.210.

99 Cited in *The Abbey Theatre: Form and Pressure*, p.47.

100 Among the plays he attended was Lady Gregory's *Dervorgilla*. George believed it would have been 'excessively tedious' were it not for Sara Allgood in the title role. See *The Abbey Theatre: The Years of Synge*, p.227.

101 Cited in *George Fitzmaurice and His Enchanted Land*, p.26.

102 Holloway recorded how George was modest in receiving the applause from an appreciative audience on the opening night of *The Country Dressmaker*.

103 J.D. Riley, 'The Plays of George Fitzmaurice', *Dublin Magazine* 31, Jan.-Mar. 1955, p.8.

104 *The Abbey Theatre: The Years of Synge*, p.247.

105 ibid., p.128

106 *George Fitzmaurice and His Enchanted Land*, p. 21.

107 ibid., p.22.

108 ibid., p. 33.

109 George was not the only one to experience the negative reactions of audiences. Such reactions caused playwright Winifred Letts to never write for the Abbey again: see Maurice Kennedy's 'Sketch for a Portrait', p.40.

110 *The Abbey Theatre: The Years of Synge*, p. 284-5.

111 Cited in *George Fitzmaurice and His Enchanted Land* p.24.

112 Slaughter, Unpublished Thesis, p.56.

113 This may indeed be a reference to the reality the Fitzmaurice family endured as it was TB that killed George's five sisters.

114 See *The Magic Glasses* p.11.

115 Cork playwrights, such as Lennox Robinson and T.C. Murray, were noted for their playwriting which departed from the 'ancient idealism' of the ILT's original manifesto: See Chris Morash *A History of Irish Theatre*, p.151.

116 It is not surprising that George liked *The Clancy Name* for its satirical

qualities and its brutal portrayal of the Irish. It tells the story of a mother would rather see her son dead than see him confess his crime to the police. It was simply a question of the importance of the family name being protected, at any cost. See *The Abbey Theatre: The Years of Synge*, p.227.

117 See *George Fitzmaurice and His Enchanted Land*, p. 20.

118 According to Robert Hogan, this was submitted to the Abbey in 1909. The play was accepted for presentation but never produced.

119 See *The Plays of George Fitzmaurice: Dramatic Fantasies, Vol. I*. Introduction by Austin Clarke, p.1-17.

120 The farmhouse at Kilcara Beg also had a loft where George probably spent time during his teenage years.

121 'peeler': policeman.

122 NOTE: It is probably a typing error that Fitzmaurice failed to correct, but after he names the peeler sons Roger and Frynk, (Fitzmaurice's spelling), he later refers to Roger as Robin: See *The Magic Glasses* p.5.

123 Irish Folklore Commission: Schools manuscripts Collection, Vols. 406/407, on microfilm, Killarney Local Library, Co. Kerry.

124 Maurice Kennedy mentions the similarity in the theme and the plot of *The Magic Glasses* in a Japanese play *The Madman on the Roof* by Kan Kikuchi, leading to the possibility that Kikuchi took his idea from Fitzmaurice'a play: see Maurice Kennedy's 'Sketch for a Portrait', p.40.

125 *The Plays of George Fitzmaurice: Dramatic Fantasies Vol. I* p.19-38.

126 Mícheál Ó hAodha's introduction to *The Dandy Dolls*; Abbey Theatre Programme: performances from Monday, 8 Sept. 1969.

127 Fintan O'Toole, 'The Magic Glasses of George Fitzmaurice': Gabriel Fitzmaurice, ed., *The Listowel Literary Phenomenon*, p.23.

128 *The Abbey Theatre: The Years of Synge*, p.307.

129 Melissa Sihra, Lecturer in Drama, Trinity College Dublin: 'Writing in Blood': Programme foreword to *Ariel* by Marina Carr, staged at the Abbey Theatre, 2 Oct. – 9 Nov. 2002.

130 See *The Pie Dish* p.56.

131 The farm and house was purchased in 1907, under the Wyndham Land Act; see the Valuation Records for Duagh, Listowel, Vol. II.

132 Hogan et al, *The Abbey Theatre: The Rise of the Realists*, p.211.

133 Slaughter, Unpublished Thesis, p.27: Slaughter incorrectly records that Fitzmaurice made this statement in Jan. 1914 whereas *The Country Dressmaker* actually played in Jan. 1913 and Oct. 1914.

134 Staged in Mar. 1913, one reviewer recorded its weak characterization, but that 'we could hardly expect perfection in a young playwright in his first play'. The 'picturesque diction' was praised, as it was believed to have been modelled on Synge's. See *The Abbey Theatre: The Rise of the Realists*, pp.248-9.

135 *The Abbey Theatre: The Rise of the Realists*, p.251.

136 English reviews were very positive. *The Times* newspaper recorded both plays as being 'remarkably good': See 'Irish Players at the Court' in *The Times* Monday 30 June 1913. The fact that *The Country Dressmaker* played in London that year has gone unrecognized until now.

137 *The Abbey Theatre: The Rise of the Realists* p.251: Robert Hogan was the first to discover this letter's existence.

138 *The Daily Maroon* recorded this performance: see Chicago Arts Society: Fine Arts Scrapbook 9F38RNk93. *The Times* (London), 19 Jan. 1914, also records *The Country Dressmaker*'s inclusion in the Abbey Theatre's American tour.

139 Slaughter, Unpublished Thesis, p.27.

140 *George Fitzmaurice and His Enchanted Land*, p.27.

141 Maunsel and Roberts also published a single hardbacked issue of *The Country Dressmaker* that same year.

142 Two thousand sheets of the entire volume were printed by Maunsel. Of these, one thousand had the title page for the whole volume; and five cancel titles, one for each play, were printed in editions of a thousand. This meant it was possible for Maunsel to make up one thousand bound volumes and one thousand copies of each of the plays. Sheets of the complete volume were used in 1917 with a cancel title to produce the American volume. *The Country Dressmaker* sold as a separate edition by 1921 and was reprinted by Maunsel. On the dissolution of Maunsel in 1926, the remaining sheets of the five plays were taken over by Talbot Press, who offered copies of *Five Plays* in their catalogue for three and sixpence. See 'Fitzmaurice in Print' by Liam Miller, Listowel Writers' Week Programme, 1977, p.15.

143 *The Abbey Theatre: The Rise of the Realists*, pp.359-60.

144 *The Abbey Theatre: The Rise of the Realists*, pp.106.

145 Christopher Fitz-Simon, *The Abbey Theatre: Ireland's National Theatre; the First 100 Years*, p.43.

146 Roy Foster, *The Oxford History of Ireland*, p.203.

147 *A History of Irish Theatre; 1601-2000*, p160

148 *George Fitzmaurice and His Enchanted Land*, p.27.

149 The Duagh Historical Society has carefully restored Winifred Fitzmaurice and her children's graves. A new plaque naming all the family was unveiled during a commemorative ceremony in 2003, to mark the fortieth anniversary of George's death.

150 Hogan et al, *The Years of O' Casey 1921-1926: A Critical Documentary*, p.143.

151 Slaughter, Unpublished Thesis, p.39.

152 ibid., p.29.

153 Holloway records an argument, involving George, during 1914, regarding religious bigotry in Ireland, George's argument being, that ' ... if Home Rule ever comes to Ireland ... all the Protestants are worried'. See Slaughter, Unpublished Thesis, p.27.

154 *The Years of O' Casey 1921-1926*, p.69.

155 Carole Gelderman surmises that this was the first play he wrote on his return.

156 Again, speculation sees J.D. Riley suggesting this was the first play he wrote on his return.

157 *The Years of O'Casey 1921-1926*, pp.142-3.

158 *George Fitzmaurice and His Enchanted Land*, p.32.
159 Arthur McGuinness, *George Fitzmaurice*, p.60.
160 *The Years of O' Casey 1921-1926*, p.138.
161 *The Plays of George Fitzmaurice*, Vol.3, *Realistic Plays* pp.77-100.
162 J.D. Riley, 'The Plays of George Fitzmaurice', p.14.
163 Maurice Kennedy, 'Sketch for a Portrait', p.42.
164 Cited in *George Fitzmaurice and His Enchanted Land*, p.28.
165 *The Years of O' Casey 1921-1926*, p.140.
166 ibid., p143.
167 The only other record of his attendance at a theatre after 1923, is at a rehearsal of *The Dandy Dolls* by the Lyric Theatre Co. in the Peacock Theatre.
168 *The Years of O' Casey 1921-1926*, pp.80-81.
169 ibid., p.128.
170 *George Fitzmaurice and His Enchanted Land*, p.32.
171 At this point it is interesting to note George's handwritten directive found after his death regarding the sale of the rights of his plays that he deemed suitable for TV, stage, or radio.
172 Robert Welch, *The Abbey Theatre: Form and Pressure*, p.95.
173 ibid., p.96.
174 Interview with Fintan O' Toole.
175 A reply to this request was found in draft form in George's room after his death.
176 Indeed, Micheál Mac Liammóir was well aware of George's writing.
177 Interview with Fintan O'Toole.
178 http://www.wolfsonian.fiu.edu.
179 MacGreevy was one of the few who attended Fitzmaurice's funeral in 1963.
180 *The Plays of George Fitzmaurice Vol. I Dramatic Fantasies*, p.77-121.
181 Robert Hogan, ed., *A Dictionary of Irish Literature*, p.442.
182 Unfortunately, this play also illustrates George's laziness regarding plot construction, which was not helped by his lack of participation in theatre life.
183 *The Plays of George Fitzmaurice, Vol. I, Dramatic Fantasies*, p.39-55.
184 Unpublished Thesis, Slaughter, p.147.
185 *Dublin Magazine*, Vol. XXIV, No. 3, July-Sept. 1949, p.48.
186 'Sketch for a Portrait', p.44.
187 Slaughter, Unpublished Thesis, p.147.
188 Carole Gelderman, *George Fitzmaurice*, p.101-102.
189 Riley, 'The Plays of George Fitzmaurice', p.15.
190 'Sketch for a Portrait', p.44.
191 *The Plays of George Fitzmaurice, Vol..I. Dramatic Fantasies*, p.57-75.
192 a 'glosha' is a little stream.
193 *The Plays of George Fitzmaurice, Vol. I Dramatic Fantasies*, p.122-156.
194 *The Plays of George Fitzmaurice, Vol. II, Folk Plays*, p.57-78.
195 Slaughter Unpublished Thesis, p.86.
196 *The Plays of George Fitzmaurice, Vol. III, Realistic Plays*, p.101-141.
197 Slaughter, Unpublished Thesis, p.222.

[198] The *Dublin Magazine* ceased production after O'Sullivan's death
[199] MS33564/3 NLI, Dublin: There are two draft copies of this play in the archives. The first is a handwritten draft and the second again handwritten with the date 17/5/46 on the cover.
[200] *The Plays of George Fitzmaurice Vol. II, Folk Plays*, p.79-92.
[201] See Chapter 19.
[202] The action is taking place six weeks after they first heard the unfortunate news regarding the bank.
[203] Peter Kavanagh, *The Story of the Abbey Theatre*, p.147.
[204] *A History of Irish Theatre: 1601-2000*, p.185.
[205] *A Poet's Theatre*, p.17.
[206] These letters were published in the *Journal of Irish Literature* Vol. 10, No. 2, May 1981, p.125-127. The originals are now held in the National Library Dublin; MS 28919.
[207] Slaughter, Unpublished Thesis, p.35.
[208] Sr Labouré Sheehy's family lived very near the Fitzmaurice's farm. As a child, she was a regular visitor to the farm.
[209] Interview with Margaret McElligott, (née Relihan), Creggane, Duagh, Sept. 2002.
[210] *The Wicked Old Children of George Fitzmaurice*, producer Kieran Sheedy, Radio Éireann, 1972.
[211] On her deathbed, Georgina admitted that she would have become a Catholic if her mother had ever asked her: Interview Sr Labouré.
[212] Interview with Dan Flynn, Kilcara, Duagh, Nov. 2003.
[213] *George Fitzmaurice and his Enchanted Land*, p.11.
[214] ibid., p.11.
[215] Interview with Dan Flynn.
[216] Interview with Sr Labouré. NOTE: Is it plausible to consider that Miss Una may have had to spend some time in hospital in St Finan's Mental Hospital, Killarney? Given George's later psychological makeup; their father's personality; the family's reservedness; the obsessive nature of the sisters' trips back to Bedford; as well as the evidence that Winifred's sister-in-law used to spend long periods in the asylum, could this be the case? Might the Fitzmaurices have allowed everyone believe she used to visit Ollie instead of dealing with another family 'scandal'?
[217] Interview with Dan Flynn.
[218] As above.
[219] *Macalla na Mainistreach 2001*: Abbeyfeale Journal, p.45: see article on George Fitzmaurice by Bernie Keane. NOTE: The Creagh Hartnett's were friends or acquaintances of the Fitzmaurice's. In fact Jackie Creagh Hartnett has been identified as one of the individuals standing in the same photograph that is the only photo now surviving in which George appears.
[220] Bridie O Connor, Finuge, Lixnaw: Interview Nov. 2002.
[221] Interview with Sr Labouré.
[222] Interview with Dan Flynn.
[223] *Macalla na Mainistreach*, p.45.
[224] Interview with Sr Labouré Sheehy.

225 Interview with Bridie O'Connor.
226 *Macalla na Mainistreach*, p.45.
227 Marjorie Fitzmaurice recalled these trips to London when I met and spoke with her in 1999, but this information, unfortunately, could not be substantiated.
228 Interview with Mr and Mrs Dan Joe and Eileen Galvin, Duagh, Sept. 2002.
229 Interview with Dan Flynn.
230 *The Irish Times*, 6 Oct. 1942.
231 *A Poet's Theatre*, pp.17-18.
232 Bernie Schrank and William W. Demestes, eds., *Irish Playwrights 1880-1995*, p.58.
233 Carole Gelderman, *George Fitzmaurice*, p.137.
234 Susan Halpern, *Austin Clarke: His Life and Works*, p.153.
235 Slaughter, Unpublished Thesis, p.34.
236 *George Fitzmaurice and His Enchanted Land*, p.33.
237 ibid., p.32.
238 *Dublin Magazine*, Vol. XXI, No. 3, Jan.-Mar. 1946, p.45.
239 ibid., p.45.
240 'Sketch for a Portrait', p.41.
241 *George Fitzmaurice and His Enchanted Land*, p.34.
242 Slaughter, Unpublished Thesis, p.36.
243 *The Plays of George Fitzmaurice*, Vol. 2, *Folk Plays*, introduction, xii.
244 *The Plays of George Fitzmaurice*, Vol. 2, *Folk Plays*, pp.93-150.
245 Wolfgang R. Sanger, 'Caught between Tradition and Experiment: George Fitzmaurice's *The Moonlighter*': Heinz Kosok, ed., *Studies in Anglo-Irish Literature*.(Volume/date of publication unrecorded.)
246 Personal correspondence with Howard Slaughter, June 2001.
247 Riley, 'The Plays of George Fitzmaurice', p.147.
248 In 1947 the Abbey considered producing the play, but the project lapsed: see Maurice Kennedy 'Sketch for a Portrait', p.41.
249 *The Moonlighter* p.150.
250 *Dublin Magazine*, Vol. XXIV, No. 1, Jan.-Mar. 1949, p.38.
251 ibid., p.38.
252 Cited in *George Fitzmaurice and His Enchanted Land*, p.33.
253 ibid., p.33.
254 MS 33564/11(1), NLI, Dublin. He left his personal estate to George.
255 *The Irish Times* 24 May 1949.
256 ibid.
257 Cited in *George Fitzmaurice and His Enchanted Land*, p.39.
258 ibid., p.39: this is discussed in chapter 19.
259 *The Irish Times* 24 May 1949.
260 ibid.
261 *George Fitzmaurice and His Enchanted Land*, p.39.
262 An Eamon Kelly story may substantiate this possibility. George, on seeing an advertisement for an amateur production of *The Country Dressmaker* at the Dagg Hall, made his way there, where he informed those involved that he had written this play. The group

had failed to secure permission for this production and therefore he refused to allow the production to go ahead. Eventually, a meeting was convened with the playwright and the leading lady's tears were enough to make Fitzmaurice relent and withdraw his objections. The play went ahead, once the group agreed that there would be no critics present at the performance.

263 Hugh Hunt, *The Abbey: Ireland's National Theatre*, p.174.
264 Slaughter, Unpublished Thesis, p.125.
265 Riley, 'The Plays of George Fitzmaurice', p.17.
266 Slaughter, Unpublished Thesis, p.126.
267 *The Plays of George Fitzmaurice: Vol. III, Realistic Plays*, pp.59-76.
268 Slaughter, Unpublished Thesis, pp.101-102.
269 Arthur McGuinness, *George Fitzmaurice*, p.82.
270 *The Plays of George Fitzmaurice, Vol. III Realistic Plays*, pp.143-164.
271 Slaughter dates it as having been written in 1950, which is about the time that Fitzmaurice moved to Rathmines.
272 Arthur McGuinness, *George Fitzmaurice*, p.75.
273 Arthur McGuinness is one of the only people who have ever given this some thought, particularly with regard to *The Coming of Ewn Andzale*.
274 Marjorie Fitzmaurice, *Rivers of Words* documentary.
275 A man by the name of John Walsh who had made this offer to George: in conversation with Mary Keane, Listowel; Feb. 2003.
276 George liked this pub because its name suggested a music hall.
277 Slaughter, Unpublished Thesis, p.38.
278 Bryan MacMahon interviewed in the *Rivers of Words* documentary.
279 Owen MacMahon, Bryan's son, recounted this story of his father's love of George's work, and genuine affection for the man, at Listowel Writers' Week 2004. Bryan had been anxious that George attend the Abbey with him that night, because he was so determined to see Fitzmaurice get the recognition he deserved.
280 *George Fitzmaurice and His Enchanted Land*, p.39.
281 Mícheál Ó hAodha interviewed in the *Rivers of Words* documentary.
282 MS 33564 NLI, Dublin.
283 Mícheál Ó hAodha interviewed in the *Rivers of Words* documentary.
284 Brian Friel, playwright, recalls Ó Aodha telling him this story: personal correspondence with Mr Friel, April 2004.
285 Marjorie Fitzmaurice interviewed in the *Rivers of Words*. documentary
286 Harry Kernoff, artist, captured this impishness in a portrait of George, sometime before George left his Stamer St accommodation. The original sketch is of a lonely man while the final colour portrait illustrates that individual impishness.
287 *George Fitzmaurice and His Enchanted Land*, p.36.
288 ibid., p.43.
289 ibid., p.39.
290 *George Fitzmaurice and His Enchanted Land*, p.40.
291 ibid., p.40.
292 William A.R. Thomson, Adam & Charles Black, eds, *Black's Medical*

Dictionary, p.628.
293 ibid., p.628.
294 Elizabeth A. Martin, MA, ed., Concise Medical Dictionary, pp.442-3.
295 Marjorie Fitzmaurice interviewed in Rivers of Words.
296 The Wicked Children of George Fitzmaurice, RTE Radio One programme, produced by Kieran Sheedy, 1972.
297 Patricia Casey, Professor of Psychiatry, Mater Hospital, Dublin, telephone conversation, Oct. 2003.
298 http://www.mentalhealth.com/icd/p22-pe03.html.
299 ibid.
300 Slaughter, Unpublished Thesis, p.39.
301 Correspondence with Dr Patricia Casey, Professor of Psychiatry, Mater Hospital, Dublin, Oct. 2001.
302 George Fitzmaurice and His Enchanted Land, p.41.
303 MS 33564/11(4) NLI, Dublin: the Colonel explains this in a letter shortly after George's death.
304 MS 33564 NLI, Dublin: letter by the Colonel to Thomas MacGreevy.
305 MS 33564/16(9), letter of Marjorie's to Carole Gelderman, 24/6/'71.
306 George Fitzmaurice and His Enchanted Land, p.41.
307 In a letter to Harry Fitzmaurice in Oregon, the Colonel explains how Thomas MacGreevy had also suggested that the Colonel become literary executor: See MS33564/16, National Library, Dublin. He became Literary Executor on July 29th 1964: See MS 33564/11(4).
308 MS 33564/11(4), NLI, Dublin.
309 ibid.
310 ibid.
311 George Fitzmaurice and His Enchanted Land, pp.40-41.
312 NLI, Dublin MS 33564/11(5).
313 Marjorie made this donation in 1998. The National Library of Ireland donated Fitzmaurice's glasses and hat, as well as the leather suitcase, to Seanchaí Literary and Cultural Centre, Listowel, in 2002.
314 Slaughter produced The Enchanted Land, July 1964 and One Evening Gleam, Nov. 1964.
315 Mervin Wall writing in the Irish Press, 8 July 1967: MS 33564, NLI.
316 Staged at the Peacock Theatre, Sept. 1967.
317 'Fitzmaurice's Crazy World' by Sean Page (Sept. 1967); see MS 33564, NLI, for newspaper clippings.
318 Seumas Kelly writing in The Irish Times Sept. 1967: see MS 33564 for newspaper clippings.
319 ibid.
320 The Colonel had been unwell for some time and had been in hospital for three weeks. He had been looking forward to seeing this Abbey production with Marjorie. She did attend The Dandy Dolls: letter to Michael O'Connor, Springmount, Duagh, dated Sept. 10th 1969, courtesy of Brian O'Connor.
321 Hugh Hunt cited in George Fitzmaurice and His Enchanted Land, p.45.
322 The Irish Times 9 Sept. 1969.

323 ibid.
324 Hugh Hunt, *The Abbey Theatre*, p.217.
325 Colonel Wilfred pointed this out to the group in a letter: MS 33564/15, NLI, Dublin.
326 *Kerryman* newspaper; 9 Mar. 1968.
327 Letter from Wilfred Fitzmaurice to Michael O'Connor, Springmount, Duagh, dated 10 March 1969: he mentions *One Evening Gleam* won a prize at a festival: from Michael O'Connor's papers, courtesy of his son Brian O'Connor.
328 Marjorie Fitzmaurice writing to Michael O'Connor, letter dated 10 Sept. 1969. It was her suggestion that s stone be taken from Duagh House and she asked Michael for his help: letter courtesy of Brian O'Connor, Springmount.
329 MS 33564/15: these drawings have not survived.
330 In conversation with Howard Slaughter, Sept. 2002, during his visit to Ireland.
331 Interview with Fintan O'Toole, Dublin, July 2003.
332 See Robert Hogan's article, 'The Genius of George Fitzmaurice' in *After the Irish Renaissance: A Critical History of Irish Drama Since The Plough and the Stars*, pp.164-175.
333 Cited in the *Now and Then* newspaper 9 August 1983: photocopy from the archive of John Stephen O'Sullivan, Rathmore, Co. Kerry.
334 *The Irish Times* 6 Aug. 1976.
335 Rather than playing the part as expected, an angry old man, Eamon Kelly played Leum Donoghue as a very sad man: in conversation with Christopher Fitz-Simon at Listowel Writers' Week, June 2004.
336 ibid.
337 Barney O'Reilly in a letter to Marjorie Fitzmaurice, dated 22 Jan. 1977; MS 33564, NLI Dublin.
338 Listowel Writers' Week Programme, 1977, pp.14-15.
339 Mar. 1977 *Limerick Leader*: Keane had a regular column in this newspaper at the time.
340 Quoted in the Druid Archive - http://www.druidtheatre.com/productions.
341 See the *Kerryman* newspaper; 18 May 1979.
342 Listowel Writers' Week Programme, 1989.
343 Quoted in Druid Theatre archives: http://www.druidtheatre.com/productions.
344 ibid.
345 No. 3 where Fitzmaurice lived is now a small conference room in the hotel.
346 'The Magic Glasses of George Fitzmaurice', p.14.
347 *The Abbey Theatre: Form and Pressure*, Robert Welch, p.250.
348 In conversation with Andy Crook, April 2005, who choreographed the 2002 Trinity School of Drama production, *The Dandy Dolls*.
349 Fintan O'Toole sees the production of a Fitzmaurice season as vital in order to allow audiences to see these plays in relationship to one another.
350 Interview with Fintan O'Toole, July 2003.
351 Helen Meany's review of *The Dandy Dolls* in *The Guardian*, Mon. 4 Oct.

2004.

352 The Ennis Players also won awards for Best Director, Geraldine Greene,
and Best Young Performer, Mary Neylon, who played the part of the Child.
The Dandy Dolls was staged at the Princess Grace Theatre, Monaco, for
two nights in Aug. 2005, during this non-competitive festival of world
theatre.

353 *The Country Dressmaker* staged by the Sliabh Luachra Drama Group, in
Scartaglin, and Duagh, Co. Kerry, during Jan. & Feb. 2003.

Index

The Press aims to produce high quality publications which, though written and/or edited by academics, will be made accessible to a general readership. The organisation would also like to provide a forum for critical thinking in the Arts in Ireland, again keeping the needs and interests of the general public in view.

The company publishes contemporary Irish writing for and about the theatre.

Editorial and publishing inquiries to:

CARYSFORT PRESS Ltd

58 Woodfield, Scholarstown Road, Rathfarnham, Dublin 16, Republic of Ireland

T (353 1) 493 7383   F (353 1) 406 9815
e: info@carysfortpress.com
www.carysfortpress.com

Carysfort Press was formed in the summer of 1998. It receives annual funding from the Arts Council.

The directors believe that drama is playing an ever-increasing role in today's society and that enjoyment of the theatre, both professional and amateur, currently plays a central part in Irish culture.

NEW TITLES

MUSICS OF BELONGING:
THE POETRY OF MICHEAL O'SIADHAIL
EDITED BY MARC CABALL AND DAVID F. FORD

An overall account is given of O'Siadhail's life, his work and the reception of his poetry so far. There are close readings of some poems, analyses of his artistry in matching diverse content with both classical and innovative forms, and studies of recurrent themes such as love, death, language, music, and the shifts of modern life.

Paperback €25
ISBN 978-1-904505-22-8

Casebound €50
ISBN: 978-1-904505-21-1

EDNA O'BRIEN
'NEW CRITICAL PERSPECTIVES'
EDITED BY KATHRYN LAING
SINÉAD MOONEY AND MAUREEN O'CONNOR

The essays collected here illustrate some of the range, complexity, and interest of Edna O'Brien as a fiction writer and dramatist...They will contribute to a broader appreciation of her work and to an evolution of new critical approaches, as well as igniting more interest in the many unexplored areas of her considerable oeuvre.

ISBN 1-904505-20-1
€20

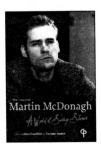

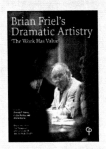

THE THEATRE OF MARTIN MCDONAGH 'A WORLD OF SAVAGE STORIES'

EDITED BY LILIAN CHAMBERS AND
EAMONN JORDAN

The book is a vital response to the many
challenges set by McDonagh for those involved in
the production and reception of his work. Critics
and commentators from around the world offer a
diverse range of often provocative approaches.
What is not surprising is the focus and
commitment of the engagement, given the
controversial and stimulating nature of the work.

ISBN 1-904505-19-8
€30

BRIAN FRIEL'S DRAMATIC ARTISTRY 'THE WORK HAS VALUE'

EDITED BY DONALD E. MORSE, CSILLA
BERTHA, AND MÁRIA KURDI

Brian Friel's Dramatic Artistry presents a
refreshingly broad range of voices: new work
from some of the leading English-speaking
authorities on Friel, and fascinating essays from
scholars in Germany, Italy, Portugal, and Hungary.
This book will deepen our knowledge and
enjoyment of Friel's work.

ISBN 1-904505-17-1
€25

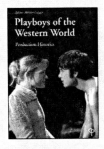

GEORGE FITZMAURICE: 'WILD IN HIS OWN WAY'

BIOGRAPHY OF AN ABBEY PLAYWRIGHT
BY FIONA BRENNAN
WITH A FOREWORD BY FINTAN O'TOOLE

Fiona Brennan's...introduction to his
considerable output allows us a much greater
appreciation and understanding of Fitzmaurice,
the one remaining under-celebrated genius of
twentieth-century Irish drama.
Conall Morrison

ISBN 1-904505-16-3
€20

PLAYBOYS OF THE WESTERN WORLD

PRODUCTION HISTORIES
EDITED BY ADRIAN FRAZIER

'Playboys of the Western World is a model of
contemporary performance studies.'

'The book is remarkably well-focused: half is a
series of production histories of Playboy
performances through the twentieth century in
the UK, Northern Ireland, the USA, and Ireland.
The remainder focuses on one contemporary
performance, that of Druid Theatre, as directed by
Garry Hynes. The various contemporary social
issues that are addressed in relation to Synge's
play and this performance of it give the volume
an additional interest: it shows how the arts
matter.' *Kevin Barry*

ISBN 1-904505-06-6
€20

EAST OF EDEN

NEW ROMANIAN PLAYS
EDITED BY ANDREI MARINESCU

Four of the most promising Romanian playwrights, young and very young, are in this collection, each one with a specific way of seeing the Romanian reality, each one with a style of communicating an articulated artistic vision of the society we are living in.
Ion Caramitru, General Director Romanian National Theatre Bucharest

ISBN 1-904505-15-5
€10

IRISH THEATRE ON TOUR

EDITED BY NICHOLAS GRENE AND CHRIS MORASH

'Touring has been at the strategic heart of Druid's artistic policy since the early eighties. Everyone has the right to see professional theatre in their own communities. Irish theatre on tour is a crucial part of Irish theatre as a whole'. *Garry Hynes*

ISBN 1-904505-13-9
€20

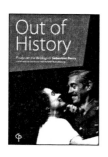

OUT OF HISTORY
'ESSAYS ON THE WRITINGS OF SEBASTIAN BARRY'

EDITED WITH AN INTRODUCTION BY CHRISTINA HUNT MAHONY

The essays address Barry's engagement with the contemporary cultural debate in Ireland and also with issues that inform postcolonial criticial theory. The range and selection of contributors has ensured a high level of critical expression and an insightful assessment of Barry and his works.

ISBN 1-904505-18-X
€20

THE POWER OF LAUGHTER

EDITED BY ERIC WEITZ

The collection draws on a wide range of perspectives and voices including critics, playwrights, directors and performers. The result is a series of fascinating and provocative debates about the myriad functions of comedy in contemporary Irish theatre. *Anna McMullan*

As Stan Laurel said, it takes only an onion to cry. Peel it and weep. Comedy is harder. These essays listen to the power of laughter. They hear the tough heart of Irish theatre – hard and wicked and funny. *Frank McGuinness*

ISBN 1-904505-05-8
€20

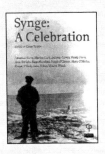

POEMS 2000–2005
BY HUGH MAXTON

Poems 2000-2005 is a transitional collection written while the author – also known to be W. J. Mc Cormack, literary historian – was in the process of moving back from London to settle in rural Ireland.

ISBN 1-904505-12-0
€10

SYNGE: A CELEBRATION
EDITED BY COLM TÓIBÍN

Sebastian Barry , Marina Carr, Anthony Cronin, Roddy Doyle, Anne Enright, Hugo Hamilton, Joseph O'Connor, Mary O'Malley, Fintan O'Toole, Colm Toibin, Vincent Woods.

ISBN 1-904505-14-7
€15 Paperback

CRITICAL MOMENTS
FINTAN O'TOOLE ON MODERN IRISH THEATRE
EDITED BY JULIA FURAY & REDMOND O'HANLON

This new book on the work of Fintan O'Toole, the internationally acclaimed theatre critic and cultural commentator, offers percussive analyses and assessments of the major plays and playwrights in the canon of modern Irish theatre. Fearless and provocative in his judgements, O'Toole is essential reading for anyone interested in criticism or in the current state of Irish theatre.

ISBN 1-904505-03-1
€20

HAMLET
THE SHAKESPEAREAN DIRECTOR
BY MIKE WILCOCK

"This study of the Shakespearean director as viewed through various interpretations of HAMLET is a welcome addition to our understanding of how essential it is for a director to have a clear vision of a great play. It is an important study from which all of us who love Shakespeare and who understand the importance of continuing contemporary exploration may gain new insights."

From the Foreword, by Joe Dowling,Artistic Director, The Guthrie Theater, Minneapolis, MN

ISBN 1-904505-00-7
€20

GEORG BÜCHNER: WOYZECK
A NEW TRANSLATION BY DAN FARRELLY

The most up-to-date German scholarship of
Thomas Michael Mayer and Burghard
Dedner has finally made it possible to establish
an authentic sequence of scenes. The wide-
spread view that this play is a prime example of
loose, open theatre is no longer sustainable.
Directors and teachers are challenged to "read
it again".

ISBN 1-904505-02-3
€10

THE THEATRE OF FRANK MCGUINNESS
STAGES OF MUTABILITY
EDITED BY HELEN LOJEK

The first edited collection of essays about
internationally renowned Irish playwright Frank
McGuinness focuses on both performance and
text. Interpreters come to diverse conclusions,
creating a vigorous dialogue that enriches
understanding and reflects a strong consensus
about the value of McGuinness's complex work.

ISBN 1-904505-01-5
€20

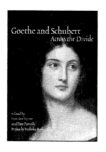

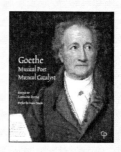

GOETHE AND SCHUBERT
ACROSS THE DIVIDE
EDITED BY LORRAINE BYRNE & DAN FARRELLY

Proceedings of the International Conference,
'Goethe and Schubert in Perspective and
Performance', Trinity College Dublin, 2003. This
volume includes essays by leading scholars –
Barkhoff, Boyle, Byrne, Canisius, Dürr, Fischer, Hill,
Kramer, Lamport, Lund, Meikle, Newbould, Norman
McKay, White, Whitton, Wright, Youens – on Goethe's
musicality and his relationship to Schubert;
Schubert's contribution to sacred music and the
Lied and his setting of Goethe's Singspiel, Claudine.
A companion volume of this Singspiel (with piano
reduction and English translation) is also available.

ISBN 1-904505-04-X
Goethe and Schubert: Across the Divide. €25

ISBN 0-9544290-0-1
Goethe and Schubert: 'Claudine von Villa Bella'. €14

GOETHE: MUSICAL POET, MUSICAL CATALYST
EDITED BY LORRAINE BYRNE

'Goethe was interested in, and acutely aware of, the
place of music in human experience generally - and of
its particular role in modern culture. Moreover, his own
literary work - especially the poetry and Faust -
inspired some of the major composers of the
European tradition to produce some of their finest
works.' *Martin Swales*

ISBN 1-904505-10-4
€30

THEATRE TALK

VOICES OF IRISH THEATRE PRACTITIONERS
EDITED BY LILIAN CHAMBERS &
GER FITZGIBBON

"This book is the right approach - asking practitioners what they feel."
Sebastian Barry, Playwright

"... an invaluable and informative collection of interviews with those who make and shape the landscape of Irish Theatre."
Ben Barnes, Artistic Director of the Abbey Theatre

ISBN 0-9534-2576-2
€20

THE THEATRE OF MARINA CARR

"BEFORE RULES WAS MADE" - EDITED BY
ANNA MCMULLAN & CATHY LEENEY

As the first published collection of articles on the theatre of Marina Carr, this volume explores the world of Carr's theatrical imagination, the place of her plays in contemporary theatre in Ireland and abroad and the significance of her highly individual voice.

ISBN 0-9534-2577-0
€20

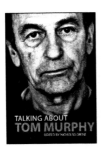

TALKING ABOUT TOM MURPHY

EDITED BY NICHOLAS GRENE

Talking About Tom Murphy is shaped around the six plays in the landmark Abbey Theatre Murphy Season of 2001, assembling some of the best-known commentators on his work: Fintan O'Toole, Chris Morash, Lionel Pilkington, Alexandra Poulain, Shaun Richards, Nicholas Grene and Declan Kiberd.

ISBN 0-9534-2579-7
€15

THE DRUNKARD

TOM MURPHY

'The Drunkard is a wonderfully eloquent play. Murphy's ear is finely attuned to the glories and absurdities of melodramatic exclamation, and even while he is wringing out its ludicrous overstatement, he is also making it sing.'
The Irish Times

ISBN 1-904505-09-0
€10

SACRED PLAY
SOUL JOURNEYS IN CONTEMPORARY
IRISH THEATRE BY ANNE F. O'REILLY

'Theatre as a space or container for sacred play allows audiences to glimpse mystery and to experience transformation. This book charts how Irish playwrights negotiate the labyrinth of the Irish soul and shows how their plays contribute to a poetics of Irish culture that enables a new imagining. Playwrights discussed are: McGuinness, Murphy, Friel, Le Marquand Hartigan, Burke Brogan, Harding, Meehan, Carr, Parker, Devlin, and Barry.'

ISBN 1-904505-07-4
€25

THE IRISH HARP BOOK
BY SHEILA LARCHET CUTHBERT

This is a facsimile of the edition originally published by Mercier Press in 1993. There is a new preface by Sheila Larchet Cuthbert, and the biographical material has been updated. It is a collection of studies and exercises for the use of teachers and pupils of the Irish harp.

ISBN 1-904505-08-2
€35

THREE CONGREGATIONAL MASSES
BY SEÓIRSE BODLEY,
EDITED BY LORRAINE BYRNE

'From the simpler congregational settings in the Mass of Peace and the Mass of Joy to the richer textures of the Mass of Glory, they are immediately attractive and accessible, and with a distinctively Irish melodic quality.' Barra Boydell

ISBN 1-904505-11-2
€15

THEATRE OF SOUND
RADIO AND THE DRAMATIC IMAGINATION
BY DERMOT RATTIGAN

An innovative study of the challenges that radio drama poses to the creative imagination of the writer, the production team, and the listener.

"A remarkably fine study of radio drama – everywhere informed by the writer's professional experience of such drama in the making...A new theoretical and analytical approach – informative, illuminating and at all times readable." Richard Allen Cave

ISBN 0-9534-2575-4
€20

SEEN AND HEARD (REPRINT)

SIX NEW PLAYS BY IRISH WOMEN
EDITED WITH AN INTRODUCTION
BY CATHY LEENEY

A rich and funny, moving and theatrically exciting collection of plays by Mary Elizabeth Burke-Kennedy, Síofra Campbell, Emma Donoghue, Anne Le Marquand Hartigan, Michelle Read and Dolores Walshe.

ISBN 0-9534-2573-8
€20

UNDER THE CURSE

GOETHE'S "IPHIGENIE AUF TAURIS",
IN A NEW VERSION BY DAN FARRELLY

The Greek myth of Iphigenie grappling with the curse on the house of Atreus is brought vividly to life. This version is currently being used in Johannesburg to explore problems of ancestry, religion, and Black African women's spirituality.

ISBN 0-9534-2572-X
€10

IN SEARCH OF THE SOUTH AFRICAN IPHIGENIE

BY ERIKA VON WIETERSHEIM
AND DAN FARRELLY

Discussions of Goethe's "Iphigenie auf Tauris" (Under the Curse) as relevant to women's issues in modern South Africa: women in family and public life; the force of women's spirituality; experience of personal relationships; attitudes to parents and ancestors; involvement with religion.

ISBN 0-9534-2578-9
€10

THE STARVING AND OCTOBER SONG

TWO CONTEMPORARY IRISH PLAYS
BY ANDREW HINDS

The Starving, set during and after the siege of Derry in 1689, is a moving and engrossing drama of the emotional journey of two men.

October Song, a superbly written family drama set in real time in pre-ceasefire Derry.

ISBN 0-9534-2574-6
€10

THEATRE STUFF (REPRINT)

CRITICAL ESSAYS ON
CONTEMPORARY IRISH THEATRE
EDITED BY EAMONN JORDAN

Best selling essays on the successes and
debates of contemporary Irish theatre at home
and abroad.

Contributors include: Thomas Kilroy, Declan
Hughes, Anna McMullan, Declan Kiberd, Deirdre
Mulrooney, Fintan O'Toole, Christopher Murray,
Caoimhe McAvinchey and Terry Eagleton.

ISBN 0-9534-2571-1
€20

URFAUST

A NEW VERSION OF GOETHE'S
EARLY "FAUST" IN BRECHTIAN MODE
BY DAN FARRELLY

This version is based on Brecht's irreverent and
daring re-interpretation of the German classic.

"Urfaust is a kind of well-spring for German
theatre… The love-story is the most daring and
the most profound in German dramatic
literature." *Brecht*

ISBN 0-9534257-0-3
€10

HOW TO ORDER
TRADE ORDERS DIRECTLY TO

CMD
Columba Mercier Distribution,
55A Spruce Avenue,
Stillorgan Industrial Park,
Blackrock,
Co. Dublin

T: (353 1) 294 2560
F: (353 1) 294 2564
E: cmd@columba.ie

or contact
SALES@BROOKSIDE.IE

*FOR SALES IN NORTH AMERICA
AND CANADA*

Dufour Editions Inc.,
124 Byers Road,
PO Box 7,
Chester Springs, PA 19425,
USA

T: 1-610-458-5005
F: 1-610-458-7103

ST. PATRICK'S
COLLEGE
LIBRARY